COMPUTER PROGRAM DESIGN

Elizabeth A. Dickson

Northern Virginia Community College

Irwin
McGraw-Hill

Boston, Massachusetts   Burr Ridge, Illinois   Dubuque, Iowa
Madison, Wisconsin   New York, New York   San Francisco, California   St. Louis, Missouri

Irwin/McGraw-Hill

A Division of The **McGraw·Hill** Companies

Irwin Book Team

Publisher: *Tom Casson*
Sponsoring editor: *Garret Glanz*
Project editor: *Karen J. Nelson*
Production supervisor: *Laurie Kersch*
Manager, Prepress Purchasing: *Kim Meriwether David*
Cover designer: *Laurie J. Entringer*
Printer: *Malloy Lithographing, Inc.*

Library of Congress Cataloging-in-Publication Data

Dickson, Elizabeth A.
    Computer program design / Elizabeth A. Dickson.
      p.   cm.
    Includes index.
    ISBN 0–697–26836–5
    1. Electronic digital computers—Programming. I. Title.
  QA76.6.D5196 1996
  005.1′2—dc20   95–50835

Printed in the United States of America

2 3 4 5 6 7 8 9 0 ML 3 2 1 0 9 8 7

Preface

Computer Program Design is a flexible, student-oriented introduction to design. It can be used as a stand-alone text for a program design course taught as a prerequisite to programming courses or as a supplemental text in a programming course. The book is a programming language independent, pseudocode-based introduction to design concepts and practices. While the example designs and exercises are typical of a business programming environment, the underlying foundation is appropriate for all beginning programming students.

The first six chapters should be presented in order since they provide a cumulative foundation for the remainder of the book. Chapter 5 can be skipped or inserted later if the instructor (and the students) are willing to ignore the references to headings in later designs and exercises. Chapter 7 reinforces the structured design concepts that have been given in the preceding chapters and could be presented at any time after the first six chapters although there are some examples and exercises in later chapters that will utilize interactive designs. Chapter 8 introduces the design students to arrays as soon as they have the necessary background to understand them. Arrays are presented earlier than in many design texts so that students will have as much opportunity as possible to see the use of arrays in a variety of other programs. Arrays are then used within either example or exercise designs in the input edit and control break chapters. Chapter 14, which introduces two dimension arrays, is separated from the array introduction so that students will have acquired a firmer mastery of arrays before venturing further on the topic.

After chapter 8, the chapters can be presented in almost any order. If the book is used as a supplement text in a programming course, some chapters will probably need to be omitted to fit into the term length. The instructor can keep those chapters that best fit with the programming text being used. All the chapters should fit into a three or four credit semester course in program design. If the program design course is fewer credits or if the term is shorter than a semester, the instructor will need to be more selective.

Example designs are shown with some variations in style through the book and in some cases alternative solutions are shown for the same design problem. Although there is always the risk that these variations will introduce more confusion than elucidation, they have been included to emphasize that many solutions and styles can be equally correct.

A separate instructor's supplement provides chapter notes and sample tests. Your comments, criticisms, ideas, or random thoughts are always welcome. You can email me at nvdicke@nv.cc.va.us or write to me at Northern Virginia Community College, Loudoun Campus, 1000 Harry Byrd Hwy, Sterling, VA 20164.

A note to students:

Designing programs is tough work! That's neither a warning nor a threat, just an acknowledgment that you are going to work hard. But the skills you will gain are well worth the hard work. Designing programs is a skill, not an art. But it is a skill that some will learn more easily and quickly than others. No one will learn the skill without doing it. Like playing a piano, swimming, or wood carving, designing is a learn-by-doing skill. It took you months to learn to walk, so don't expect to learn to design programs in a week or so. But you now walk without even thinking about it, eventually you will design with ease also.

If you eventually get a job as a program designer or programmer, your employer will, no doubt, give you very specific style requirements for both your designs and your programs. For now, think of your instructor as your employer. Your instructor may give you style requirements that differ somewhat from the style of designs in this book. For the most part, style issues are not a question of what is right or wrong, but of what style the supervisor or instructor prefers.

For any design requirement, there will be many correct solutions. Some solutions may be more efficient, more easily maintained, or more sophisticated, but they may all "work." Appendix C has solutions to the even numbered exercises at the end of each chapter. Your solution will probably not be exactly like the solution in the book. That doesn't mean you are wrong. Your solution may be better. (If it is, be a friend and send me a copy.)

Enjoy your designing experience. Programming may give more immediate reward (it's hard to beat seeing output print out), but program design gives better long term benefits.

Acknowledgments
This book was originally written at the urging of my students in program design classes, and their continued support has been invaluable. They have freely critiqued each draft, suggested additions (and some deletions), and always made sure I remembered that the book was for students. In many cases when I had a "bright new idea" they voted on whether it should be included. Most of the time, their vote ruled. Any errors that remain are, of course, my own, but my students should get the credit for shaping any parts of value. My thanks to each and everyone of them. My deepest thanks go to my parents, who believed in me even before I did and who truly taught me almost everything I needed to know *before* kindergarten.

Table of Contents

Chapter 1
Introduction to Program Design

Objectives

After completing this chapter, you should be able to:

1. Describe the program development cycle.
2. Describe the place of formal and informal program design within the development cycle.
3. Explain why it is important to complete the program design steps before the actual program coding.
4. List the primary questions you should ask yourself when starting a program design.
5. Identify the major tasks of a design solution, given the design problem.
6. Identify the subtasks of a design solution, given the design problem.

INTRODUCTION

Most of us like to *do* things more than we like *planning* the doing. We would rather take a vacation than read travel books about a vacation. That tendency leads to all kinds of complications. If you try planting a new hedge without first spacing the plants, you will inevitably end up with extra plants and no room to plant them or no plants and lots of room to plant them. There are many examples and plenty of cartoons based on the results of poor planning. Picture in your mind the popular photo of two sets of railroad tracks approaching the center from each side and not quite lining up.

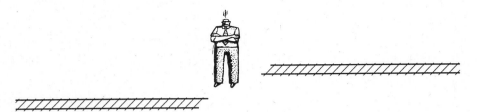

The urge to jump in and do something appears almost irresistible around computers. New users of application programs avoid manuals like the plague, preferring to work it out "hands on." Computer programmers are famous for fiddling with a program until it will work instead of planning out a workable solution to begin with. The problem with that approach is that it takes longer, usually leads to round-about solutions, and probably leaves undiscovered logic errors in the program. It is programming by reacting to crisis (crisis being defined here as a discovered "bug" or error in the program), instead of planning in advance to avoid the crisis. If you were going to build a house, even a doghouse, you wouldn't just start nailing boards together. You would work out what you wanted the completed house to look like and plan the steps needed to accomplish the goal. Lack of planning results in problems like a doghouse that is built in the basement and is too big to fit through the door to the backyard, a hot tub added to a deck that hasn't been reinforced to hold the extra weight, or a fireplace added without a chimney. In a computer program, we can have similar, disastrous results like a program to select award recipients that selects the wrong people because it tests the criteria incorrectly or a program to calculate payroll for the entire company that only calculates it for the first employee in the list.

This book is about avoiding crises by doing the planning. You will study how to plan out program solutions to problems. Since the book is really about the planning, you will never actually implement the solutions. We will never write (code) the programs and run them on the computer. Coding and executing a program is one way to test to see if a program will work, but it's a pretty inefficient way. You wouldn't think much of an architect who designed a building, but couldn't tell you if the building would stand up without actually building it. We need to be able to test our program logic without having to "build" the program. This book will cover designing the logic solutions to a variety of programming problems and testing those solutions to be sure they will work.

PROGRAM DEVELOPMENT CYCLE

Every program goes through the same development process. You may use different terms or descriptions, but you will still follow these steps.

Program Development Cycle

Review the specifications
Informal Design
    List major tasks
    List subtasks, sub-subtasks, and so on
Formal Design
    Create formal design from task lists
    Desk check design
Code and compile the program
Test and, if necessary, debug the program
Use and, as necessary, maintain the program

Let's look at each of these steps in detail.

REVIEW THE SPECIFICATIONS—Some need has been presented to you that has initiated the

What Is a Program?

A *program* is a set of instructions written so the computer can follow them. If we want a computer to calculate what the pay should be for each employee this week, we would need to give the computer two different types of information.

First we tell it all the steps that must be completed to calculate the payroll. This might include calculating a gross pay figure, calculating multiple deductions, and subtracting the deductions from the gross pay figure. In addition the computer needs to know if it should repeat all the defined steps for a second employee, and, assuming it should, when it should stop repeating the steps. All these steps are included in the program.

The second type of information we must give the computer are the values it should use in the calculations. To calculate the gross pay, the computer needs to know the hourly pay rate and the number of hours worked. To write the paycheck, the computer needs to know the name and Social Security number of the employee. This information forms the input data.

program creation. Programs always grow out of a need for some form of information, which is another way of saying that we need some form of output from the computer. The specifications may be very specific and define exactly what the output should look like, which columns certain data should go in, what should be double spaced, and so on. Or the "specs" may be a very casual, oral request ("Hey, could you give me a list of students eligible for the Dean's List?") without any formatting requirements. When you review the specs, ask yourself (1) do you understand what is required? (2) do you have sufficient instructions to carry it out? (do you know the eligibility requirements for the Dean's List?), and (3) do you have the necessary input available to generate the desired output?

INFORMAL DESIGN—Don't expect to be able to just sit down and write the design. You need to experiment with a variety of possible solutions and then decide on a general approach, before you formalize those ideas in a design. The informal design step lets you make changes in your plan before you invest too much time in one approach. There are two steps in the informal design that need to be completed frequently in a repeated cycle.

- List the Major Tasks—What are the three to seven major tasks that need to be taken to satisfy the specs? Most people have trouble getting "major" enough. Don't get caught listing the detail tasks, you're not ready for them yet. If you are designing a program to create a list of students eligible for the Dean's List, your major tasks might be (1) read a record, (2) check the record against the Dean's List criteria, and (3) write the record if the criteria are met. You would repeat the tasks for each student in the file. Don't worry here about where you're going to write it, how you're going to read it, or what the criteria actually are.

- List the Subtasks—Now go back to each major task, one at a time, and list the subtasks for each major task. The advantage with this approach is that you only need to concentrate on one major task at a time. Now is the time to dig down into some of the specifics. For each major task, you may have up to six or seven subtasks, and each subtask may have additional sub-subtasks under it. You are creating an outline of WHAT needs to be done in our program.

Once you have completed the major task and subtasks lists, you should figuratively step back a bit, reread the specifications, and make sure you have met all the requirements in the specs. Now is the simplest time to make modifications to your lists of WHAT. You can easily reorder your subtasks, change the break-down into major tasks, and so on. You are not committed to the first attempt, and frequently the first attempt will not be the best solution. Play with your lists a bit until you are satisfied that you have included everything in a "logical" approach. Keep in mind that there is no single, right answer.

FORMAL DESIGN—The formal design takes your lists and puts them into a recognized format that others could easily read and use. Before an architect does the formal plans, time is spent with sketches and rough ideas. Only when those have evolved into a coherent concept will the architect invest the time into a formal building plan. The rough sketches probably wouldn't be enough for a builder or another architect to know what is planned. The blueprints, or formal design, utilize a standard form for communicating the plan. You're taking the same approach. Your informal design (task lists) are the best time to "play around" with possible solutions. When you convert them into a formal design, you are investing your time into putting the solution into a complete design that others could easily follow. The task lists defined WHAT needed to be done, the formal design adds HOW it will be done.

- Create formal Design From Task Lists—Just as the blueprint is a standard communication tool for architects and builders, the formal design is a communication tool for program designers and coders. We need a design format that will be understandable by other designers (because we frequently design programs in teams with each team member working on a part of the whole program) and by coders (because they will actually translate it into code). In addition, eventually your formal design will become a part of the program's documentation package that will stay with the program as long as it is in use. There are many possible design tools, but this book will concentrate on two of them: flowcharts and pseudocode. Both are somewhat standard means for communicating the design steps. Each has its advantages (and its disadvantages). In the next chapter, we will look at flowcharting as a design tool, and the chapter following it introduces pseudocode.

- Desk Check the Design—Just as the architect doesn't want to have to build the house to see if it meets the specifications, you don't want to have to code your program to check it. Desk checking is the way to check the logic of your design. You will work through the design, step by step, implementing each step as the computer would, "reading" the test data, doing any calculations, and "writing" output. Desk checking will tell you if there are any logic errors (assuming you have created good test data) before you invest the time in coding. What if you have errors? Go back to the task lists, make the necessary changes, implement those changes in the formal design, and try the desk checking again. The Informal Design and Formal Design are really a cycle that you perform *until* your desk checking tells you the logic is perfect. The first example of desk checking is in Chapter 2 with the first formal design. We will desk check some of the designs throughout the book, but you should get in the habit of desk checking *all* of your designs.

CODE AND COMPILE THE PROGRAM—Once you know that you have a good design, coding the program is simply translating each design statement into the proper syntax for the desired programming language. All the hard work has already been done; in literary terms, you've just written the Great American Novel. Coding it is merely translating it from English to French. Frankly, you can hire a coder or a translator to do it; your skills are better used designing the next great program or writing the next great novel. Although it won't be necessary in the study of this book, you should know that a coded program is still not in a form that the computer can understand. Programming languages like Pascal, C, or COBOL are not computer languages. They must be "compiled" or translated into the machine's language. Fortunately for us, this translation process is done by a compiler, another program. The compiler first checks the code to be sure it is written in correct syntax (i.e., follows the rules of that programming language) and will write out error messages if problems are found. Please remember that a syntax error is like a grammar error. If your subject and verb don't agree, you have to make a correction, but you don't have to rewrite the novel. The compiler will find syntax errors, but it will not find logic errors. You must find them.

TEST AND DEBUG THE PROGRAM—Once the program is compiled, it can be executed on the computer. Before you hand it over to the person who initially requested it, you need to execute it with some test data to be sure it works as intended. We know that it will work, because you carefully desk checked it with the test data prior to coding. However, it's still a good idea to check it again. All those other programmers who didn't plan ahead frequently spend most of their program development time trying to get the "bugs" (logic errors) out of their programs.

What Is a Compiler?

A compiler translates your coded program into the machine language that the computer can understand. If you write a program in Pascal, for example, you would use a Pascal compiler that could generate the appropriate machine language for the computer on which you plan to execute your program. A compiler actually has two forms of output: syntax error messages indicating the syntax rules of the program language were not followed or, if the syntax was correct, object code, the machine language translation of your program.

If you need to make a change to your program after it has been compiled, you change your original program code (called source code) which you must then compile again to create the new object code. If your program is not changed, you can continue to use your object code over and over to execute the program without having to recompile it.

USE AND MAINTAIN THE PROGRAM—Even after a program is certified bug free and put into use, it will still need to be "maintained." Sometimes maintenance means that new errors have been found, but frequently it simply means that changes are necessary because of changes in the company, the form of the input, the form of the desired output, and so on. Every time the federal government changes the income tax code, all payroll programs must be revised to reflect the new requirements. Program maintenance will always be a part of the programmer's life. It's also a good reason why it is so important to include your formal design in the program documentation package.

All programs follow this program development cycle. This book will concentrate on the informal and formal design steps. These steps in the cycle give you an order in which to work, but it is still difficult sometimes to get started and organize your thinking. Some people start by listing as many tasks as they can think of and then try to organize the list. Another approach is to start developing a list of the questions you should ask yourself when you begin a design. After you have studied the specifications and are ready to start your list of major tasks and subtasks, try asking yourself these questions:

> What output do you need to generate?
> What input do you have/need? What form will it be in?
> Will the program have a list of tasks that needs to be done repeatedly (e.g., for each
>> employee, each sale, etc.)? If the program does repeat a set of tasks, we say the
>> program contains a *loop*.
> If it has a loop:
>> What will be done in the loop?
>> What controls the loop? (How do we know it is time to stop looping?)
>> What needs to be done before the loop?
>> What needs to be done after the loop?
> If it does not have a loop:
>> What are the major tasks of the program?

The answers to these questions will give you the major task list. Then you only need to fill in the details in the form of subtasks, sub-subtasks, and so on.

LISTING MAJOR TASKS

Let's implement the major task list part of this program development cycle. Assume you have been given the following program specifications:

Given a file of all the VHS video tapes now on sale (in order by number of sales for December, 1994, highest to lowest) create a report, with headings, of the top 10 sellers.

What's your input: The file of tapes (which you know is in order by sales).
What's your output: A heading, then the first ten tapes from the file.
Do you have a loop: Yes, because you need to do the process 10 times.
What controls the loop: A counter that will go from 1 to 10 (or from 0 to 9).
What happens in the loop: Read a tape name and write it to the output.
What happens before the loop: Write a heading.
What happens after the loop: Nothing.

Now we can probably come up with a list of tasks:

> Write headings
> Read tape
> Write tape

Another way to write this would be to show the loop with a line bracketing the tasks to be repeated and writing to the left of the bracket how we know when it is time to stop repeating the tasks (the loop control):

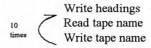

10 times
> Write headings
> Read tape name
> Write tape name

We've added a bit more information to the first task list. Now we can see that "Write headings" will be done once, but "Read tape name" and "Write tape name" will be done repeatedly, in a loop in other words. And we can see that the loop will be repeated 10 times, that is, those two tasks will be done 10 times.

This looks pretty good for a list of major tasks, but when we study our task list, we may realize that an important detail is missing. How do we know when we have read and written the 10 tapes? We need a counter to help us keep track of how many times we have repeated the loop. This is just like counting how many times you have jogged around the track. If you are running on a quarter mile track and want to jog 2½ miles, you know you need to do the loop 10 times. So you probably count to yourself as you run. Each time you pass your starting point, you mentally add 1 to your counter. When your counter gets to 10, you stop running. We use the same kind of counter here. One of the tasks in the loop will be to add to the counter, and we can check to see if the loop should be repeated by asking if the counter is less than or equal to 10. If you're jogging, you automatically start counting at 1, but we have to tell the computer to start at 1, so before the loop tasks begin, we set the count to 1. When we add these steps to our task list, we get this:

> Write headings
> Set up counter
> Read tape
> Write tape
> > (subtask: Add to counter)

Or in the other version:

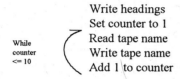

Write headings
Set counter to 1
Read tape name
Write tape name
Add 1 to counter

While
counter
<= 10

Try another one. Assume you have the following specifications:

Create a payroll report listing the name, gross pay, deductions, and net pay for all employees in the payroll file. Each employee entry in the file contains name, hours worked, hourly rate, and deduction rate.

You answer the following questions (my answers are on the next page):

> What is the input?
> What is the output?
> Is there a loop?
> What are the major tasks in the loop?
> What subtasks are under each task (if any)?
> What controls the loop?
> What must be done before the loop?
> What must be done after the loop?

Now try to do your own task list, first just as a list of tasks and then as an ordered list with the loop indicated.

Here are my answers to the questions:

What is the input: Name, hours, pay rate, and deduction rate for each employee
What is the output: Name, gross pay, deductions, net pay for each employee
Is there a loop: Yes
What are the major tasks in the loop: Read record
Calculate values
Write output line

What subtasks are under each task (if any): Under Calculate values:
Calculate gross pay
Calculate deductions
Calculate net pay
What controls the loop: Whether there are more data in the file to be processed
What must be done before the loop: Nothing
What must be done after the loop: Nothing

Our task list then comes out something like this:

Read record
Calculate values
Write output

Calculate values subtasks
Gross pay = hours times pay rate
Deductions = gross pay times deduction rate
Net pay = gross pay minus deductions

Or written the other way:

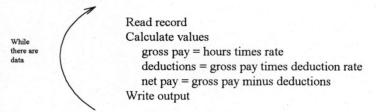

While
there are
data

Read record
Calculate values
    gross pay = hours times rate
    deductions = gross pay times deduction rate
    net pay = gross pay minus deductions
Write output

We have been asking questions to see if the loop tasks should be repeated (Are there more data? Is the counter up to 10?), but we can also ask questions in other places in our tasks. If we changed the specifications for the last example so that we are to calculate and list the payroll only for the employees who worked under 30 hours, we need to ask a question as one of the tasks in the loop: Has this employee worked less than 30 hours? If the answer is yes, we then continue to calculate the payroll values and write the output. If the answer is no, we don't need to calculate the values or write the record. Our revised task lists might then look like this:

> Read record
> Is hours less than 30?
>> yes: Calculate values
>>> Write output
>
>> no: Do nothing
>
> <u>Calculate values subtasks</u>
> Gross pay = hours times pay rate
> Deductions = gross pay times deduction rate
> Net pay = gross pay minus deductions

Or written the other way:

> While
> there are
> data
>
> Read record
> Is hours less than 30
>> yes: Calculate values
>>> gross pay = hours times rate
>>> deductions = gross pay times deduction rate
>>> net pay = gross pay minus deductions
>>
>> Write output
>> no: Do nothing

EXERCISES

Write the task lists for each of the following problems.

1. Given a file containing the name and age of each person enrolled in your class, write out the average age.

2. Given a file containing the name and year of birth of each person enrolled in your class, write out the average age as of the end of 1995.

3. Given a file containing a record for each part kept in inventory (name, quantity, per unit cost), write out the name of all parts with a per unit cost greater than $100.

4. Given a file containing the name, major, and GPA of all students enrolled at your school, write out the average GPA for the COMPUTER majors.

5. Given a file containing the name, major, and GPA of all students enrolled at your school, write out the names of all the ACCOUNTING majors and at the end of the list write out a count of the ACCOUNTING majors.

6. Given a file containing the name, address, balance due, and a "Daily" or "Sunday" identifier for everyone on your neighbor's paper route, write out the name and balance due of all people who receive only the Sunday paper.

Chapter 2

Flowcharts and Design Structures

Objectives

After completing this chapter, you should be able to:

1. Recognize and define the major flowcharting symbols.
2. Identify the appropriate flowcharting symbol for a design statement.
3. Define the three basic design structures.
4. Combine flowcharting symbols into the basic structures.
5. Identify the basic structures given a complete flowchart.
6. Identify "nested" structures in a flowchart.
7. Define and differentiate between the two major loop types.
8. Describe when each loop type is appropriate.
9. Create a complete flowchart using appropriate symbols and structures.
10. Differentiate between an internal process and an external process.

INTRODUCTION

Flowcharting is the first formal design tool that we will use. It is a symbol-oriented design system that identifies the type of statement by the shape of the symbol containing the statement. If a picture is really worth a thousand words, flowcharts should save us a lot of time writing. The computer industry has agreed on the symbols to be used and that agreement is an ANSI (American National Standards Institute) standard. If you buy a flowcharting template (you don't need to rush out and get one for this text), it should say that it conforms to the ANSI standard.

Once we have created our list of tasks and subtasks, our informal design, we can convert those tasks to symbols in the flowchart. Generally, the lowest level of our subtasks (sub-sub-sub-subtasks?) will each become one symbol in the flowchart. These symbols are connected by flow lines that show the flow of *control* through the program.

The primary flowcharting symbols are:

FLOW LINES—These are the left to right or top to bottom lines connecting the symbols. These lines show the flow of control through the program. Some designers prefer to include an arrowhead on all flow lines. Since the general direction of the flow is either down or to the right, some designers include an arrowhead only when the flow is an exception, that is, when it flows up or to the left. Your instructor may have a preference for your work. Most symbols in a flowchart will have one flow line entering the symbol and one flow line exiting. There are a few exceptions to this rule that are described below.

TERMINAL SYMBOL—This oval always begins (with START written inside) and ends (with STOP written inside) the flowchart. As you will soon see, it can also be used to indicate the beginning and end of a subsection within the flowchart, known as a module. The terminal symbol will have only one flow line since a Start will have an exit flow line but no entering flow line and a Stop will have an entering flow line, but no exit.

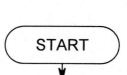

INPUT/OUTPUT SYMBOL—This parallelogram is used for both input (READs) and output (WRITEs) so you must be sure to label the particular use. You should also get in the habit of being specific about what is being read or written. For example, don't say READ Record, say READ Name, Address. Input (read) means the program is receiving data from an "external source," something connected to the computer but not part of the main processing/memory core. The input could come from a keyboard, a disk drive, a tape file, and so on. The received values are stored in memory. Output (write) indicates the program is sending data from memory to an external device like a printer, a monitor screen, or a disk drive.

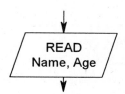

PROCESS SYMBOL—This rectangle is used primarily for calculations and initialization of memory locations. An initialization process means to assign a starting value to a location in memory, like count = 0. A calculation means to perform some calculation and assign the result of the calculation to a location in memory. The calculation could be as simple as ADD 1 to count, or very complex.

PREPARATION SYMBOL—This symbol is used for any initialization done, usually at the beginning of a program. Anything done in a preparation symbol could be shown in a process box.

DECISION SYMBOL—The diamond either asks a Yes/No question OR makes a True/False statement. There will always be two exits from a decision symbol, one labeled Yes or True and the other labeled No or False. Be sure you include your labels. *This is the only symbol that can have two exits*.

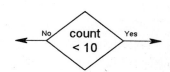

CONNECTOR—This symbol can be used any time multiple flow lines are being joined, although some people prefer to just connect the lines rather than include the connector symbol. As you will see below, it can be very useful to indicate the end of a "structure" where lines join. Another use of the connector is to avoid long flow lines by writing a letter or number within the circle where the branch would begin, omitting the flow line, and including the same letter or number within the connector where the flow line would otherwise end. You can use the connector in the same fashion to indicate a flow from one page to another.

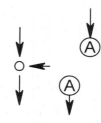

You can see that writing space in a flowchart symbol is often limited. "Year-to-Date Gross Pay" or "Name of Program Design Student" would be difficult value desciptions to fit in a symbol. "Name," "Age," and "Count" are short enough descriptions to fit in the symbol. You will probably be tempted to use very short descriptions of the values referred to. A certain amount of abbreviation is acceptable, but be sure that your design is still meaningful to other possible readers.

BASIC DESIGN STRUCTURES

With these basic symbols you can design any program you might need. Obviously, we will be combining them to design solutions to more complicated problems. In fact, the ways in which you combine them have a lot to do with the clarity and acceptability of your designs. There are three generally accepted design STRUCTURES: Sequence, Selection, and Loop. You should limit your designs to these structures. As you will see in Chapter 7, by limiting your design to the accepted structures you will make the design more easily and more universally understood. Every structure has a single entrance flow line and a single exit flow line. Let's look briefly at how you combine the symbols to form these structures.

The **SEQUENCE STRUCTURE** is the simplest because it is nothing more than a series of statements performed one after another. It is a sequence because the flow lines always continue in the same direction every time the structure is executed. A sequence could include many instructions, but each would be done in turn, in the same order. To the right is a sequence. Identify each step in the structure.

The **SELECTION STRUCTURE** uses the decision symbol to ask a question. The structure as a whole includes the decision plus the operations done in response to the decision. There will be two exits from the decision box, but both of these branches are still a part of the selection structure. And both branches must rejoin a single flow line to exit the structure. Notice the use of the connector to emphasize the end of the selection and the single exit from the structure. With the sequence structure, we said the same steps in the same order would be done each time the structure is executed. With the selection structure, different steps may be executed depending on the result of the decision test.

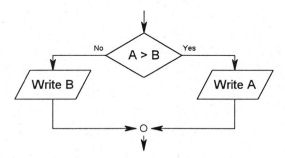

If the selection only has an operation on the true side (or less commonly, only on the false side), it is called a one-sided selection. With the one-sided structure, the "null" or empty side still must have its exit from the decision box, but there are no operations along the flow line.

The **LOOP STRUCTURE** also uses the decision symbol since there must always be a way to get out of the loop. The loop structure in general will have a decision, one or more additional symbols indicating the steps to be done within the loop, and *a flow line that sends control back to the beginning of the loop.* There are two main loop types: the WHILE loop and the UNTIL loop. The basic loop is the WHILE or DO WHILE loop. What follows is a WHILE loop that will continue while count is less than 10.

WHILE loops are Leading Decision Loops, meaning that the decision symbol always is the first statement of the loop. If the test is *true*, control follows the flow line that goes into the loop. If the test is *false*, control follows the flow line to the first statement after the loop. In other words, we stay in the loop *WHILE the decision is true*.

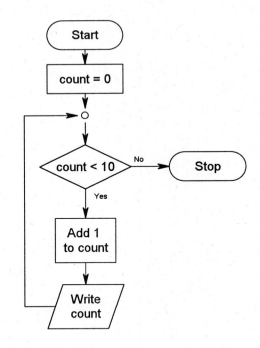

In this example, count = 0 will be executed once, before the first loop test. The decision test count < 10 is the beginning of the loop. Think of this test as the gatekeeper for the loop, determining whether the flow line into the loop or the flow line to the Stop will be followed. After the two statements in the loop (ADD 1 to count and WRITE count) are executed, control goes back to the decision test. Since the loop adds 1 to count, eventually count will be equal to 10 which, of course, is not less than 10, so the decision test will be false and control goes to the Stop.

UNTIL loops are Trailing Decision Loops, meaning the decision is always the last statement of the loop. The body of the loop will be executed once before control even gets to the loop test. In the Until Loop, if the test is false, control follows the flow line back to repeat the loop. If the test is true, control follows the branch from the decision box that exits the loop structure. We continue to repeat the loop *UNTIL the decision is true*.

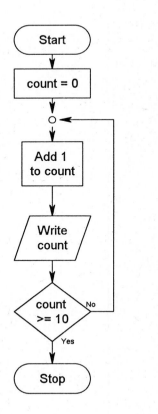

This example looks very similar to the WHILE loop: there are the same two symbols before the loop and the same statements/symbols within the body of the loop. The differences are the location of the loop test and the test itself. For the two loops given, the output will be identical: the numbers 1 through 10.

There is a very important difference between the two loops, however, that may not be immediately obvious. Look at the sample loops once again. We initialized our counter to 0 before our WHILE loop and repeated the loop WHILE the counter was less than 10. What happens if we initialize the counter to 10 before the WHILE loop? Since the very next statement is the decision testing the value of counter and the result of the test is false (counter is *not* < 10), control follows the false branch to the Stop. The program never enters the body of the loop. With the leading decision test, it is possible to avoid the loop completely. Let's walk through (desk check) the WHILE loop shown on the left below.

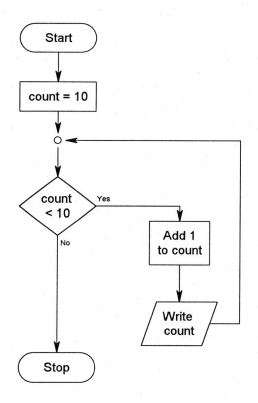

This design does not have any input, so we only need to keep track of the values stored in memory and the output. As you can see, we set up a section to keep track of both and then step through the design, one statement at a time.

Stmt: Start
Memory:
Output:
[Nothing in memory or in output at beginning.]

_____

Stmt: count = 10
Memory: count
                    10
Output:

_____

Stmt: Test if count < 10
Memory: count
                    10
Output:
[Result is false.]

_____

Stmt: Stop
Memory: count
                    10
Output:
[Program exits without entering loop.]

Now try the same kind of walk through with the UNTIL loop, shown below.

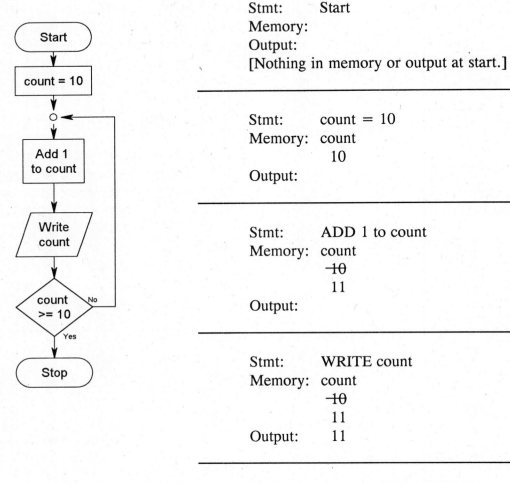

Stmt: Start
Memory:
Output:
[Nothing in memory or output at start.]

Stmt: count = 10
Memory: count
            10
Output:

Stmt: ADD 1 to count
Memory: count
          ~~10~~
          11
Output:

Stmt: WRITE count
Memory: count
          ~~10~~
          11
Output: 11

Stmt: Test if count $>= 10$
Memory: count
          ~~10~~
          11
Output: 11
[Test is True—Program is exited.]

We again initialize the counter to 10, but we don't test its value until after we have entered the loop, incremented the counter, and written the counter. Only at the end of the loop do we test to see if we should do the loop *again*. With an UNTIL loop we will always do the loop at least once since there is no test prior to the first iteration.

Which is the better loop? There really isn't a better one, but there is a safer one. The WHILE loop will always work, since we always begin with a test. The UNTIL loop may not work, since in some conditions we would want to avoid the loop completely. If you know that you will want to do the loop at least once, the UNTIL loop will work. If you don't absolutely know that, use the WHILE loop. It is worth noting that some programming languages include loop structures that don't fit exactly into these two loop types. COBOL, for example, offers an "UNTIL" loop that is not a trailing decision loop, so the condition is tested before the first iteration of the loop. When you start to implement your designs in code, be sure you understand how the chosen programming language interprets the looping commands.

One of the things that makes life (or at least program design) interesting is that you can combine these structures. Anything can go inside a loop, even another loop or a selection. And anything can go inside a selection. You can probably easily picture a sequence within a selection structure; it would be just a series of operations to be performed in one of the branches. Can you also picture a loop structure within a selection OR a selection within a sequence within a loop? Try to identify the structures in flowcharts contained in this book or in other books. Be sure to look for "nested" structures, where one structure is contained within another.

There are still a few more flowcharting symbols that you need to know.

INTERNAL PROCESS—This variation of the Process Symbol indicates a call to a module that is within the same program. As we will see very soon, sub-modules are frequently used to break a design down into bite-size chunks. This Internal Process symbol is our means of "invoking" those sub-modules. A "call" to an internal process transfers control to that process (module) without using flow lines to connect the two parts. The call automatically indicates a branch to the other part (module) of the flowchart with an automatic branch back when the other module is completed. An internal process helps us keep our design (and our resulting program) organized. We can group tasks that are related into one module, so they can be easily checked and modified.

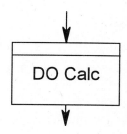

EXTERNAL PROCESS—Another variation of the Process Symbol, this symbol indicates a call to a module that is *not* included within the current program. An external module would be something like a "utility" made available by the operating system or the compiler or some other program. As with the internal process call, the external process call indicates an automatic branch and return, but this time the branch is to a set of instructions outside the program.

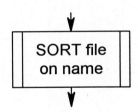

ANNOTATION SYMBOL—The annotation allows you to add comments to your design without cluttering the flowchart itself. The comment is "connected" to the relevant box or area with a dashed line (so it isn't confused with a flow line).

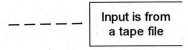

Now for a few examples. Go back to the payroll example from the previous chapter. We worked out the major tasks and subtasks. Our final task list is repeated here.

        Read record
        Calculate values
        Write output

        <u>Calculate values subtasks</u>
        Gross pay = hours times pay rate
        Deductions = gross pay times deduction rate
        Net pay = gross pay minus deductions

Now let's put them into a flowchart. The chart that follows includes a WHILE loop with a sequence inside the loop.

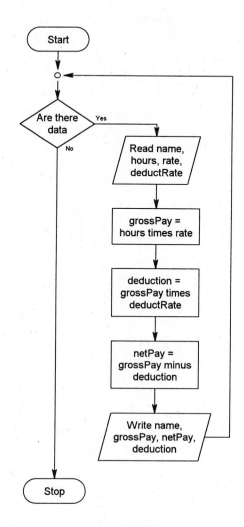

We could include exactly the same steps but move the calculations into a module. The idea is to take the details and "force" them into a lower level in the design. We use the internal process symbol to "call" the module when it is needed. The call transfers control to the module. Notice that the Internal Process symbol says **DO Calculation**, and the module begins with a terminal symbol labeling the module as **Calculation**. The call from the internal process symbol says "look for a module with a beginning terminal symbol with the same label." The RETURN at the end of the module transfers control back to the statement that follows the call.

This type of design is consistent with our list of major tasks and subtasks. We indicated (in Chapter 1) major tasks of Read record, Calculate values, and Write output. These are the three steps in the loop in our main module. The subtasks under Calculate values are included as steps in the Calculation module.

Each time through the loop a record is read, control goes to the Calculation module, the three calculations are done, control returns to the main module, and the name along with the three calculated values are written. We can look at the main module to get an overview of what the design does. If we need the specifics of how the pay is calculated, we can look in the calculation module.

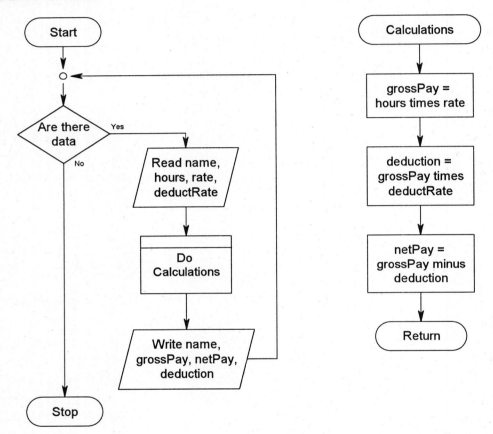

You may be wondering how the computer will treat the loop control test "Are there data." The test probably makes sense to you (if there are data left to be processed, go into the loop and process; if we have finished all the data or there weren't any data to begin with, don't go into the loop), but does it make sense to the computer? The answer is "yes," although in different programming languages the question will take different forms. Our design is assuming that we are going through the data file "sequentially," starting with the first record and processing the data, one record at a time, until we have finished the last record in the file. You need to have two concepts in mind. The first is that the computer keeps track of what has been read from the file and what remains. It may help you to think of the computer as having a "bookmark" that it can place in the file to mark where it stopped reading and therefore where it should begin with the next read. When we prepare the input file for use, the bookmark is placed before the first record. When the first record has been read, the bookmark is moved so that it is before the second record. Eventually, the last record is read and the bookmark is moved so that it is after the last record but before the end of the file. And that brings us to the second concept. When the file is created, the computer (we're using the term computer rather loosely here to include the hardware and software) automatically adds an end-of-file indicator at the very end of the file. The end-of-file indicator is set by the operating system and will be the same for all computer systems using that operating system. When the computer reads the file as input, it looks for the end-of-file indicator to know when the file has been completely read. When we ask "Are there data," we are asking the computer if the bookmark is before a data record or before the end-of-file indicator.

Let's try another example. Suppose we wanted to survey a sample of the students in a class by calling every fifth student. We need a program to read completely through a file and write out every fifth record from the file, so we would write out the fifth, tenth, fifteenth, and so forth. Our list of tasks appears very simple:

> Read a record
> If it's a "fifth record": Write it

But how are we going to know if it is a "fifth record"? We could keep adding to a counter, and if the counter is 5 or 10 or 15 or 20 or 25 and so on, write out the record. But what would our test be? "Counter = 5 OR Counter = 10 OR Counter = 15 OR . . . ." That could get pretty long if we expect to have several hundred records. There must be a better way.

Once we count up to 5, why not start counting over again at 1? We don't really care how many records there are, just if this is the fifth record since we last wrote a record. We still need the counter, but our decision is much simpler: Counter = 5. If the statement is true, we'll write the record and set the counter back to 1. If the statement is false, we'll just add 1 to the counter. Here's our new list of tasks:

> Counter = 1   <u>Test and Write</u>
> Read a record   If counter equals 5
> Test and Write   Yes: Write record
>   Set counter to 1
>   No: Add 1 to counter

Don't confuse this use of a counter with the counter we used in an earlier program. Previously we used a counter to keep track of how many times we had done our loop, so we initialized the counter *before* the loop, added one to it *in* the loop, and tested it to determine if we should enter the loop. Now our counter is not controlling the loop, it's determining only if we should write a line. And we reset the counter to 1 every time we get to 5 (and write the line). Really we are reusing the counter over and over again to count to 5. The flowchart that implements the task list is below.

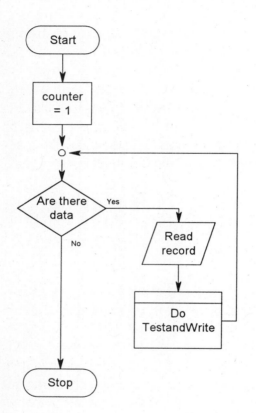

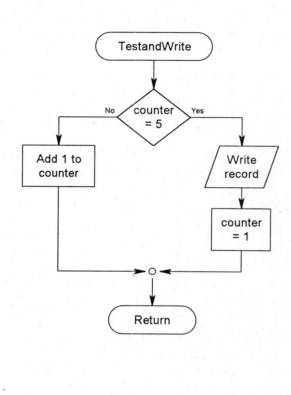

EXERCISES

1. Identify all of the basic design structures (sequence, loop, and selection) included in the design on the previous page.

2. Draw examples of the following nested structures in flowchart format. Don't worry about putting words in the symbols.
   A. A selection within a WHILE loop.
   B. A selection within an UNTIL loop.
   C. A WHILE loop within a selection.
   D. A WHILE loop within a WHILE loop.
   E. A selection within a selection.

3. List the major tasks and then create a flowchart design solution for the following problem. You have a list of the name and grade point average (GPA) for all the students graduating at the end of this semester. You want to create a report of the names of all students who should be included on the dean's list. To be eligible for the dean's list, a student must have a GPA of at least 3.5.

4. Using the same file (name and GPA for all graduates), list the major tasks and provide a flowchart solution to create a report giving the name and GPA for all graduates and, at the end of the report, the average GPA for all graduates.

5. List the major tasks and then create a flowchart design solution for the following problem. You want a study sheet that includes the square and cube of the numbers 1 through 20. There is no input for this design. Use an UNTIL loop.

6. List the major tasks and then create a flowchart design solution for the following problem. You have a file containing the lengths and widths for multiple rooms. You want to calculate the number of gallons of paint needed to paint the walls in each room. Assume eight foot ceilings and do not worry about subtracting out for doors and windows. Assume that one gallon of paint will cover 500 square feet. Write out the length, width, and number of gallons. If five or more gallons will be needed for one room, also write out the message, "Look for quantity discounts."

variable name first

5)
```
count = 0
REPEAT
     ADD 1 to count
     sq = count * count
     cube = count * sq.
     WRITE count, sq., cube
UNTIL count >= 20
```

Chapter 3
Pseudocode

Objectives

After completing this chapter, you should be able to:

1. Understand and apply the rules of pseudocode.
2. Convert a flowchart to pseudocode.
3. Convert pseudocode to a flowchart.
4. Describe the advantages and disadvantages of pseudocode.
5. Describe the advantages and disadvantages of flowcharting.
6. Design complete, one-sided, and nested IFs in flowcharts and pseudocode.
7. Design WHILE and UNTIL loops in pseudocode.
8. Design programs in pseudocode that include multiple modules.
9. Convert a design done in one large module to a design using multiple modules.

INTRODUCTION

Flowcharts are only one of the possible formal design tools. They were one of the earliest forms used and are still very popular with many people because they give a visual image of the design. Unfortunately, the flowcharting symbols were established before the concepts of structured programming (which we will look at in greater depth in a few chapters). As a result, flowcharts aren't able to handle some of the concepts that we now assume will be present in a design. Pseudocode is another formal design tool, but it was developed along with structured programming. Pseudocode works very well with the rules of structured design and programming. But it isn't visual—it's narrative. Because pseudocode is more easily used for "structured design," it will be our primary design tool in this text.

INTRODUCTION TO PSEUDOCODE

Unlike flowcharts which have very clear and agreed upon rules, pseudocode is more individualistic. We will use the following rules:

RULES FOR PSEUDOCODE

Write only one statement per line
Capitalize initial keyword
Indent to show hierarchy
End multiline structures
Keep statements language independent

Let's look at each of these rules separately.

Write only one statement per line
By the time we get to our formal design, pseudocode in this case, we have already done our lists of major tasks, subtasks, and so on. Now our job is to convert that rough list into a formal design that can be used as the basis for coding. We have broken each task down into the smallest level of subtask or sub-subtask necessary to be sure that we have defined what

needed to be done. We now convert each of those detail elements into one line in our pseudocode. Each pseudocode line will represent one "action" in our design or, as we will see later, will mark the boundaries of an action.

Let's try a variation of our payroll design from the last chapter. We'll assume our input includes name, the hours worked, and the hourly rate and that we are to write out the gross pay as well as the gross pay minus a deduction of $15 for dues and uniforms. Our list of tasks might look something like:

Read name, hourly rate, hours worked
Calculate gross pay and net pay
Write name, gross pay, net pay

Our pseudocode will just fill in the details a bit:

```
READ name, hourly rate, hours worked
Gross pay = hourly rate times hours worked
Net pay = Gross pay minus 15
WRITE name, Gross pay, Net pay
```

Notice that each statement is a single action and is written on a separate line.

Capitalize initial keywords

Look again at the pseudocode that we just completed. READ and WRITE are written in all capitals. They are "initial keywords" because they begin the statement and they are command words that give special meaning to the operation. In the statement, Net pay = Gross pay minus 15, we don't put any word in all capitals because we don't have a keyword. Net pay begins the statement, but it is not a command word. In pseudocode, we will use a limited set of keywords, primarily READ, WRITE, IF, WHILE, and UNTIL. You will find it easy to recognize these keywords.

Indent to show hierarchy

In the pseudocode above, we don't have any indentation; all statements are lined up with an even left margin. As long as we have only sequence structures, we won't have indentation because we don't have any questions of hierarchy. Each statement is independent of the others. But if we have a loop or a selection, we must indicate which statements fall within the loop or which statements fall within the selection. Indentation is one of the ways we use to show the "boundaries" of these structures.

Assume that in our previous pseudocode, there is an additional deduction for workers with over 40 hours. Our pseudocode changes to this:

```
READ name, hourly rate, hours worked
Gross pay = hourly rate times hours worked
Net pay = Gross pay minus 15
IF hours worked is greater than 40
    Net pay = Net pay minus 10
ENDIF
WRITE name, Gross pay, Net pay
```

We have included a selection by using the keyword IF followed by the "condition" to be tested. IF the condition is true, we will subtract an additional $10 from Net pay. The calculation statement is indented because it is dependent on the IF statement. We have used indentation to show which statements are within the IF. (We will come back to IFs later in this chapter to show what all the IF forms are like in pseudocode.)

End multi-line structures

In our IF structure above, we also included the line ENDIF. We're being a bit redundant here since we have already said we use the indentation to indicate what statements go within the IF structure, but the advantages of increased clarity are worth the repetition. Including the ENDIF (or ENDwhatever) makes sure the reader recognizes that we've finished with that structure and are now going on to a new statement. It also helps make sure that *you* know where the loop or selection is completed. The ENDIF should be aligned (same left margin) with the IF it is ending. When we get to nested IFs (very soon), it will be particularly important to keep our IFs and ENDIFs all present and accounted for.

Keep statements language independent

This "rule" doesn't mean that you can do your pseudocode in French, Russian, Chinese, or whatever language you may know. It refers to programming languages. You should not let your pseudocode turn into the code that you will eventually write in. In this book, since we will not take our designs into code, we will be free of the temptation to gravitate toward code-like pseudocode. But what if you are taking a class in Pascal, COBOL, C, or some other language, then can your design become language *dependent?* It may be tempting to let your design grow more and more like the code you will eventually write. Resist the temptation! When you are doing your design, all your "little grey cells" should be focused on the design and your logic. When you code the program, your attention should be on writing correct syntax (because you know the logic is perfect). If you let yourself slip into designing and writing code in one step, you have two problems. First, you have only given half your attention to developing the best design you can. Second, when (not if) you find that you have a logic error, you need to make not just a simple change to your design, but to redo your code.

Some programming languages have special capabilities (commands) that are not available in other languages. Generally, you should design your program so that it is free of those special requirements. That way you can easily transport your design from one language to another. However, if you KNOW that you will be writing in a specific language and will NEVER want to convert the program to another language, you might as well design the program so that it takes advantage of the capabilities.

Advantages and Disadvantages

Pseudocode isn't perfect. We need to be aware of potential pitfalls so that we don't get caught later.

Disadvantages:
- It isn't visual: we don't get a picture of the design.
- There is no universal standard on the style or format, so one company's pseudocode might look very different from another's.

Advantages:
- It can be done easily on a word processor, and therefore
- It is easily modified.
- It implements structured design elements well.

We have already looked at flowcharting, but let's summarize the advantages and disadvantages here for comparison.

Disadvantages:
- It is difficult to modify: a simple change may mean redoing the entire flowchart.
- To do it on a computer, you need a special flowchart package.
- Structured design elements are not implemented.

Advantages:
- It is standardized: all agree on acceptable symbols.
- It is visual (but the advantage has limits as we shall see).

As we know, there is no standardization of the form to use in pseudocode. We will add to our "rules" by developing a format for our design structures. Your instructor may add additional rules for your pseudocode. If you are working as a program designer, your company will certainly have style standards that you must follow.

HOW WE STORE AND ACCESS DATA

Let's go back to our brief pseudocode segment and review what each statement indicates about storing and accessing our data. When we say READ name, hours worked, hourly rate, we are saying that we want the computer to go out to some external input device (a keyboard, a disk, etc.) and retrieve three values. These values will be stored in the computer's memory. Each memory location has an address, and we could use that memory address as the way we refer to the value when giving instructions to the computer. We could say, READ a character value and store it at address 56934. Then, read a numeric value, store it at address 61253, read a second numeric value, and store it at address 67952. Then we could tell the computer to multiply the values at addresses 61253 and 67952 and store the result of that multiplication at address 71234. But as you can see, it would get very cumbersome very soon (and also lead to some major problems in more complex programs). We could also refer to a friend's house by the exact address and say as we walk out the door "I'll be at 5198 Bentana Way, Reston, Virginia 22090, USA, if anyone needs me." Usually, though, we use a more familiar name for the address and we say, "I'll be over at Sarah's if anyone needs me."

The computer refers to the memory locations by address, but our programming languages allow us to identify a name for the memory locations. The value that is stored in memory is called a variable (because the value can vary), and the name we use to refer to it is the variable name. So when we say READ hours worked, we are really saying, "READ a value and store it in a memory address that I will refer to as hours worked." We have to be consistent with our variable names so that there is no confusion when it is time to convert the design to program code. Don't use a variable name of HoursWorked one place, then shorten it to HrsWrkd another place, and simply Hours a third place. Most programming languages have rules about how variable names can be formed. In our pseudocode, we will not limit the number of characters (as some languages do), but we will not allow the name to include a space. Some languages see a capital letter as the same character as a lowercase letter, so the variable name HOURS would refer to the same variable as hours. Other languages distinguish between capitals and lowercase. Consistency is a good habit to develop when working with computers, so (beginning with our next design) we will use lowercase and capitals consistently. We will begin variable names with a lowercase letter, but capitalize the first letter of additional "words" in the same name, as in hoursWorked.

The next line, Gross pay = hours worked times hourly rate, is a different kind of statement: an assignment. This statement is saying, "Multiply the hours worked by the hourly rate and put the result of the multiplication in a memory address that I will call Gross pay." This statement uses three memory addresses. The statement uses the variables hours worked and hourly rate but does not change their values. The result of the multiplication is "assigned" to the variable Gross pay. It is best to read this statement as "Gross pay is assigned the result of hours worked times hourly rate." We don't have a handy symbol on the keyboard to represent assigned other than the equal sign—so we use the equal sign but think of it as "assigned," not as "equal." **Assignments always go from the right side of the = sign to the left side.** Some designers prefer to use the keyword SET for assignment, in which case the statement would be SET Gross pay to hours worked times hourly rate.

The pseudocode ends with the statement WRITE Name, Gross pay, Net pay, which says "Get the values stored under the variables name, Gross pay, and Net pay and send them to the output device."

CALCULATION SYMBOLS

We used text to describe the operations in the calculations, but you are probably used to using mathematical symbols for the operations. We all recognize the + sign as addition, but you may expect to see ÷ for division and an x for multiplication. Since the ÷ symbol isn't on the keyboard and the x could be easily confused with the letter x used as a variable, we usually use other symbols. These symbols are standard across programming languages and you should get used to seeing (and using) them.

ARITHMETIC SYMBOLS FOR CALCULATIONS

/	Division	+	Addition
*	Multiplication	–	Subtraction
^ or **	Exponentiation		

DESIGN STRUCTURES IN PSEUDOCODE

The **SEQUENCE** structure we have already seen. Since a sequence is really just an ordered list of statements, we implement it in pseudocode by giving an ordered list of pseudocode statements.

The **SELECTION** structure we have seen in its abbreviated form. A complete (two-sided in flowchart terms) IF would look like:

```
IF hoursWorked is greater than 40
    regularPay = hourlyRate times 40
    overtimeHours = hoursWorked minus 40
    overtimePay = overtimeHours * hourlyRate * 2
    grossPay = regularPay plus overtimePay
ELSE
    grossPay = hoursWorked times hourlyRate
ENDIF
```

We have three lines that line up without indentation: the IF which begins the structure, introduces the condition, and also marks the beginning of the "true" section; the ELSE which marks the end of the "true" section and the beginning of the "false" section; and finally the ENDIF which marks the end of the "false" section and of the selection structure as a whole. The indented lines between the IF and the ELSE form the "true" section—the statements to be performed if the condition is true. The indented lines between the ELSE and the ENDIF form the "false" section—the statements to be performed if the condition is false. We will never do *both* the true and false sections since the condition could not be both true and false at the same time.

We (or the computer) perform the selection or IF structure by first testing the IF condition. If the condition is true, we continue with the statements that follow until we see the ELSE. As soon as we get to the ELSE, we know that we have completed the true section, so we skip the following lines until we get to the ENDIF. We continue "processing" with the line that follows the ENDIF.

If the condition is false, we skip all the statements until we see the ELSE, and then we begin to perform the statements, performing all statements between the ELSE and the ENDIF. When we see the ENDIF, we continue with the line that follows the ENDIF.

In flowcharting, we branched to the right or left after testing the condition and continued along that branch until we hit the connector circle indicating the selection structure was over. In pseudocode, we do the same sort of thing, but this time we "branch" to the top half or the bottom half of the structure.

In flowcharting, we had one-sided selection structures when we only had statements to perform if the condition was true. We can have the same kind of operation in pseudocode; for a selection with only a true "side," we just leave off the ELSE portion.

```
IF hoursWorked is greater than 40
    netPay = netPay minus 10
ENDIF
```

If the condition is false, we scan down looking for the ELSE, but see the ENDIF first, so we know that there is nothing to be done if the condition is false. We continue with the statement that follows the ENDIF.

Usually, we would not have a one-sided selection when the only statements would be in the false section. Most languages require that we have something in the true section. The usual solution is to rewrite the condition so that values that previously would have given a false result will now give a true result. It sounds worse than it is. Assume that we want to write num3 if it is *not* greater than num4. We could write this selection so that we write num3 when the condition num3 greater than num4 is false, as follows.

```
IF num3 greater than num4

ELSE
    WRITE num3
ENDIF
```

But then we have this awkward gap in the true section with nothing to put there. A better way would be to rewrite the condition. What's the reverse of greater than? Less than or equal to! To say the condition num3 greater than num4 is false means than num3 must be less than num4 or equal to num4. So we can rewrite our IF structure as:

```
IF num3 less than or equal to num4
    WRITE num3
ENDIF
```

Our new structure does the same thing and is much easier to understand.

Just as we used symbols to show arithmetic operations, we frequently use symbols to show relational operations in selection statements (in loop conditions too). Usually when we're writing the condition for a selection statement, we're testing the relation between two variables or values: Is one value less than the other? Is one value greater than or equal to the other? In the previous examples, we used words to describe the relationship, but usually we use the following symbols to indicate these relations.

RELATIONAL CONDITION SYMBOLS

<	Less than	< =	Less than or equal to
>	Greater than	> =	Greater than or equal to
=	Equal to	< >	Not equal to

Whenever we compare two values there are only three possible relationships: the first equals the second, the first is less than the second, or the first is greater than the second. Sometimes it is helpful to be able to describe the relationship by what it is not. For example, if the first number is equal to the second, then it is not less than the second and it is not greater than the second. We can summarize these relationships in a table of opposites:

< is the opposite of > =
> is the opposite of < =
= is the opposite of < >

We know that we can put any statement within a selection structure. That means that we can include another selection structure—called a NESTED IF because the second IF is "nested" within the first or outer IF. Nested IFs are not particularly difficult as long as we pay attention to where the IFs end. A nested IF must be completely contained within either the true section or the false section of the outer IF. Always look for the ENDIF when you are working with nested IFs. For example:

```
IF enrolled = 'yes'
    IF credits > 12
        WRITE 'Full-time student'
    ENDIF
ELSE
    WRITE 'Not currently enrolled'
ENDIF
```

With this IF we have a second IF completely contained in the true section of the outer IF. If the student is currently enrolled for classes, we go into the true section of the IF. In the true section, we encounter a second IF testing the number of credits the student has registered for. IF the student has registered for more than 12 credits, we write the message that the student is a 'Full-time student.' IF the student has enrolled but has 12 credits or fewer, what do we do? Nothing! There is no false (ELSE) section to the inner IF. If the credits condition is false, we usually fall to the statement after the inner ENDIF, but what follows the inner ENDIF here is the ELSE for the outer IF. Since we know we have completed both the inner IF and the true portion of the outer IF, we fall through to the statement following the complete IF structure. When do we write 'Not currently enrolled'? When the first, outer IF is false. What would this look like in a flowchart?

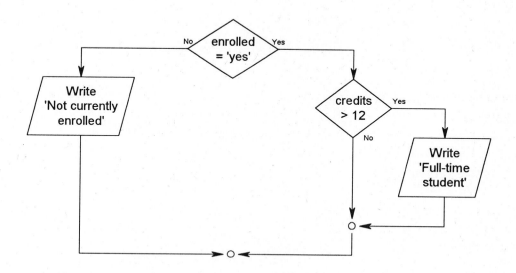

Try another one.

no quots not text but numeric.

```
IF month = 'February'
    IF day = 12
        WRITE 'Lincolns Birthday'
    ELSE
        IF day = 22
            WRITE 'Washingtons Birthday'
        ENDIF
    ENDIF
ELSE
    IF month = 'July'
        WRITE 'Summer at last'
    ENDIF
ENDIF
```

This one's a bit more complicated. Our outer IF is the test for month = 'February.' Inside that IF we have a nested IF in the true section (day = 12) and another nested IF in the false section (month = 'July'). To make matters even worse, we have a third nested IF (day = 22) inside the false section of the first nested IF. Let's try it with some data.

Assume we have a date of March 8. Here's what happens:
   month = 'February'? False (go to false section)
   month = 'July'? False (there is no false section—fall out of IF)

Assume we have a date of March 12. What happens?
   month = 'February'? False
   month = 'July'? False   (Notice we never get to the day = 12 test because that is part
    of the true section for Month = February)

Assume we have a date of February 22. What happens?
   month = 'February'? True (Go into the true section)
   day = 12? False (Go into the false section of the nested IF)
   day = 22? True (Write the Washingtons Birthday message)

The flowchart for this nested IF is below.

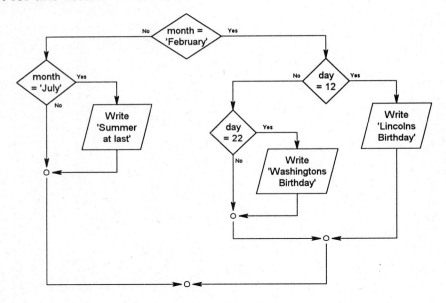

The **LOOP** structure shows pseudocode's greatest advantages over flowcharting. Since a flowchart WHILE loop begins with a decision symbol, it is easy to misread the loop as a selection structure. Unless you carefully follow the flow lines, you cannot distinguish a flowchart loop from a selection. In pseudocode, we use the keyword WHILE to introduce a while loop (seems logical) and the ENDWHILE to mark the end of the loop. The WHILE statement also includes the condition that is used to test whether the loop should be entered. All statements that are within the loop will be indented.

```
count = 0
WHILE count < 10
    READ name
    WRITE name
    ADD 1 to count
ENDWHILE
WRITE 'The End'
```

We have three statements within the WHILE loop. Our loop is controlled by the value of the count variable. As long as count has a value that is less that 10, we will go into the loop. When we test the loop condition and count is greater than or equal to 10, we will not enter the loop. Where do we go?—to the statement that follows the ENDWHILE.

The first time we see the WHILE statement, count is 0, which is certainly less than 10, so we enter the loop. We read a name, write a name, and add 1 to count (count is now 1). Our next statement is ENDWHILE which tells us to return to the WHILE statement to recheck the condition. (ENDWHILE always returns us to the WHILE.) The WHILE statement tests the loop condition (again). If the condition is true, we repeat the loop. If it is false, we exit the loop and continue processing at the first statement after the ENDWHILE.

It is very common (but certainly not required) to put the steps in a loop in a separate module. Our design would then look like the one below.

```
Mainline
count = 0
WHILE count < 10
    DO Process
ENDWHILE
WRITE 'The End'

Process
READ name
WRITE name
ADD 1 to count
```

Notice that we've added a "name" to the first module. Mainline is a common name because the first module acts as a command center, controlling module for the entire program. We can look at the mainline module and get an overview of the program. (We do something in a loop while count goes from 0 to 10 and then we write The End.) The details are pushed down into the lower level module Process. We pass control to the module by using the keyword DO, meaning "Go do the module called Process and when you finish that module, return to the statement that follows."

We will continue to keep our designs so that we have a Mainline module that "controls" the program but doesn't do any detail work. Flowcharts have terminal symbols at each end of a module. Pseudocode usually starts each module with a name but does nothing to indicate the end of a module. We can recognize that one module has ended because we're at the beginning (name) of the next module or because we're at the end of the design.

Let's convert this loop into an UNTIL loop. Everything stays pretty much the same, but remember that our UNTIL loop tests the condition at the END of the loop, and we exit the loop when the condition is true. So we need to change the way we phrase the condition.

```
Mainline
Count = 0
REPEAT
    READ name
    WRITE name
    ADD 1 to count
UNTIL count > = 10
WRITE 'The End'
```

The WHILE loop "boundaries" were given by the WHILE and ENDWHILE keywords and the loop controlling condition was included after the WHILE keyword. With an UNTIL loop we are using the keyword REPEAT to mark the beginning of the loop body and UNTIL to mark the end of the loop body. The loop controlling condition follows the UNTIL to emphasize that this is a trailing decision loop structure.

A FEW EXAMPLES

Those are our major structures (sequence, selection, and loop). How can we put them all together to create our designs?

1. We want to design a program to handle the weekly payroll. Our input is from a file that includes the name, pay rate, hours worked, and deduction rate for each employee. We want to process the entire file, calculating the gross pay and net pay for each employee, and writing out the name, deductions, net pay, and gross pay for each employee. Just for fun, let's also try to find the total gross pay of everyone on the payroll. To get the total, we need a variable (memory address) in which we can keep a running total, we need to make sure that address stores a 0 before we start, and we then need to add each gross pay to that running total.

Our task list would look something like:

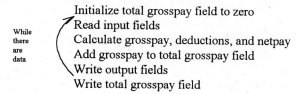

Initialize total grosspay field to zero
Read input fields
Calculate grosspay, deductions, and netpay
Add grosspay to total grosspay field
Write output fields
Write total grosspay field

While there are data

Our finished design looks like:

<u>Mainline</u>
totalPay = 0
WHILE there are data
    DO Process
ENDWHILE
WRITE totalPay

<u>Process</u>
READ name, payRate, hoursWorked, deductionRate
grossPay = payRate * hoursWorked
deductions = grossPay * deductionRate
netPay = grossPay - deductions
ADD grossPay to totalPay
WRITE name, deductions, netPay, grossPay

You should try to convert this design into a flowchart. Do one module at a time, and convert the statements one at a time. Generally, one statement in pseudocode will equal one symbol in a flowchart. My solution is shown here, but try yours first before you look.

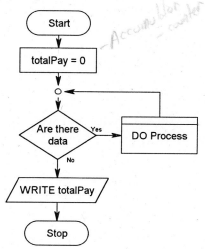

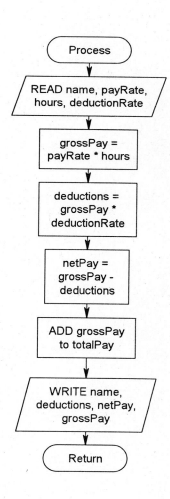

2. We want to design a program that can be used to calculate the overall score at a diving competition. There are 10 judges so we will read in 10 scores. The overall score is the average of the scores not including the highest and lowest scores. Our program should then write out the overall score. Ask yourself the planning questions and try to create your list of major tasks and subtasks. Don't peek at mine until you try it yourself.

We have a loop which is controlled by a counter. To calculate an average score we need both the total of the scores and the count. Each time through the loop we will read one score and add it to an accumulator to total the scores. We don't want to add the highest score or the lowest score to our total, but we don't know if a score will end up to be the highest or lowest until we have read all 10 of the scores. So we need to add all the scores to the total. When we have identified the highest and lowest scores, we can subtract them back out.

Tasks:

Initialize accumulator and comparison variables
Read score
Add score to accumulator
While there are data
Add 1 to score counter
Check for high and low score
Subtract out high and low scores
Calculate average score
Write average score

Let's look at it in a pseudocode design

<u>Mainline</u>
DO StartUP
WHILE scoreCount < 10
    DO ProcessDive
ENDWHILE
DO Finish

<u>StartUP</u>
scoreCount = 0
scoreTotal = 0
highScore = -1
lowScore = 11

44

ProcessDive
READ score
ADD 1 to scoreCount
ADD score to scoreTotal
IF score > highScore
    highScore = score
ENDIF
IF Score < lowScore
    lowScore = score
ENDIF

Finish
SUBTRACT highScore from scoreTotal
SUBTRACT lowScore from scoreTotal
average = scoreTotal / 8
WRITE 'Final Score = ', average

Try desk checking the design by making up some data and walking through the design. Again, you should try to convert this design into a flowchart as an exercise. (My solution is below and on the next page.)

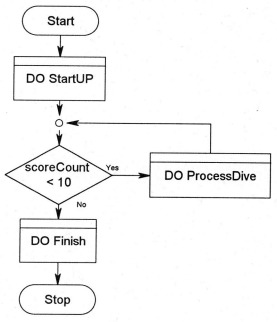

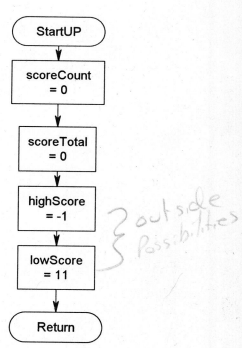

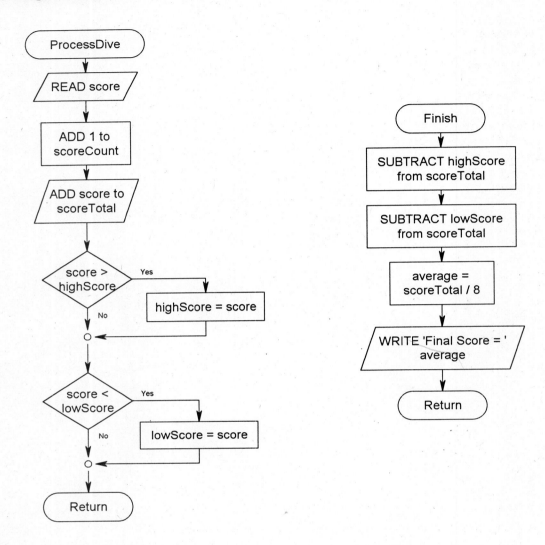

Try desk checking the design by making up some data and walking through the design.

EXERCISES

Do the first three in flowchart form and then convert them to pseudocode. Do the last three in pseudocode and convert them to flowchart form.

1. Read the first 50 records from a file containing the name and batting average of all players in the league. Write out the name and average of every player with an average of .200 or greater.

2. Read a file containing the name and batting average for every player in the league. Write out the highest average in the file. Notice that your output is only one number: the highest average.

3. Read a file containing the high temperature of each day in December. Write out the average high temperature for the month. You can assume the input file includes only the 31 temperatures for December.   *READ temp*

4. Read a file containing the name, classcode, and GPA of each student in a class. A classcode of 1 means Freshman, and a classcode of 2 means Sophomore. Write out the name, class *name* (freshman or sophomore), and GPA for each input record.

use Primary Read

5. Design a program to create a graduation list given an input file of graduates including name and GPA for each graduate. Any graduate with a GPA above 3.5, but below 3.8 should have "Honor Roll" written next to his/her name. Any graduate with a GPA that is greater than or equal to 3.8 should have "Dean's List" written next to his/her name. *solution on pg. 40*

6. Read a file containing the name, major, and GPA of all students enrolled in your school. Your output should be a complete listing of the names of all students. Those students who have a GPA of less than 1.0 should have the phrase "Unsatisfactory Progress" printed next to their name.

Before loop

2)   highAvg = -1
WHILE data
READ name, avg
IF avg > highAvg
highAvg = avg
ENDIF
ENDWHILE
WRITE high Avg.

5) READ
IF GPA > 3.5
IF GPA < 3.8
WRITE
ELSE
WRITE name

47

Chapter 4
Modules, Flags, and Priming Reads

Objectives

After completing this chapter, you should be able to:

1. Explain why we break our designs into modules.
2. Suggest appropriate modules given a sample problem.
3. Suggest appropriate module breaks given a design all in one module.
4. Explain the "rules" for linking modules.
5. Define a flag or switch.
6. Describe why we use flags and switches.
7. Design a program showing an example of flag usage.
8. Explain what a sentinel value is.
9. Design a program using a loop controlled by a sentinel value.
10. Design a program using a priming read.
11. Describe how a flag might be used with a priming-read loop.

MODULARITY

We have already seen the use of modules in our designs. Several of our designs have called a loop module as the only statement in our Mainline WHILE loop. And several have called a module to do a series of calculations within a loop. Those examples demonstrate several of the reasons for breaking our designs up into smaller modules.

In the "good old days" a program would very likely be designed in one long (hundreds, possibly thousands of lines) module. As you can imagine, there were some problems with that style of design. The module quickly became unwieldy to work with. Whenever a change was made to any part of it, the designer had to consider the impact on the rest of the design since there was no way to isolate any part of it from the rest. If several people were working together on the program, it was difficult to merge their contributions into the single module. And modifying the design/program later seemed next to impossible!

The solution that was derived was to split programs up into modules where each module handled a given function or task. We've already looked at beginning our designs by listing the main tasks. We just need to continue that approach by breaking our design into task-related modules. Frequently (but not always) one main task equals one module.

What are the advantages?
1. The design is much more "readable" and "maintainable."
2. Teamwork is much easier because team members can divide the design by modules.
3. Designs can be "built" by including completed modules from other designs.
4. A segment of code that is repeated at different points in a program can be separated into a module and simply "called" each time it is needed.

One key is in deciding how the modules should be defined. The easy answer is that each major task becomes a separate module (or module system including a module with sub-modules), but usually life isn't quite that simple. In fact, there is no easy answer, and there isn't a single answer. Our goal should be to define our modules so that all the statements within one module are very closely connected or related and so that modules are loosely connected. Usually we think of connecting the statements within a module by function. All the statements within a module are related to the same function or task, and, from a different perspective, all the statements related to that function are in the same module. That is, we don't scatter statements related to a single task over several modules.

If we were designing a program to create a report, we might have very specific instructions about how the report should look, for example, a one-inch margin at the top of the page, multi-line headings on each page, a page number printed in the top right corner, and so on. All of the statements that implement these page formatting instructions would be closely related to the same function, and we would probably put them together in the same module. If someone later needed to modify the design and program to change the page format, he or she could go directly to the single module that held all the related statements.

Sometimes, we connect the statements because they all occur at the same time within a design. It is common to have a module called prior to the loop to do all the one-time-only tasks needed to get the program going. Sometimes called HouseKeeping or StartUp, this module would include beginning tasks such as opening files and initializing counters. These tasks are not related to a single function, but are all performed once prior to the loop.

There are very few hard and fast rules for you to go by. Some suggest that a module shouldn't be more than 50 lines, but that number just comes from the number of lines that will fit neatly on a page. It is true that it is easier if the entire module is on one page, but it isn't a rule without exceptions.

There could reasonably be modules with only two or three lines in them. Generally, I would not recommend modules with just a few lines unless (1) the module performs a task that is so well-defined and unique that it makes sense to separate it (like a READ module as we will see below) or (2) you expect to have additional lines in future modifications that would go into the module.

The "connection" between modules will usually be the variables or values that are passed from one module to another. If we have a module that calculates needed variables, we are probably assuming that those calculated values will be available to other modules. Different programming languages will control what values are passed from one module to another and how they are passed in different ways. We certainly don't want our design to get caught in the syntax intricacies of a particular language. But we do want to be aware that there is a flow of data among modules.

A module may *receive* a value from another module. A module may also *return* a value that has been input or modified. In some cases, a value will be both received and returned by a module. Some variables will be neither received nor returned; they are used only within the one module. Look at the Process and Calculation modules that follow.

<u>Process</u>
READ name, hours, rate
DO Calculation
WRITE name, pay, deduction, netPay
ADD pay to payTotal
ADD deduction to deductionTotal

<u>Calculation</u>
pay = hours * rate
IF pay > 800
    deductionRate = .2
ELSE
    deductionRate = .15
ENDIF
deduction = pay * deductionRate
netPay = pay - deduction

The Calculation module uses six variables: hours, rate, pay, deductionRate, deduction, and netPay. Where do the values come from? Hours and rate are input variables that are read in the Process module. Since the Calculation module uses these values that are read in the other module, we could say that the Calculation module *receives* hours and rate from the Process module. Using these two received values, Calculation calculates the pay variable, and based on the value of pay, it also assigns a value to deductionRate. And finally it calculates the deduction and netPay variables. Most of these variables are calculated so they can be written out in the output report, but they don't get written in the Calculation module. Calculation *returns* pay, deduction, and netPay to the Process module so they can be written out there.

In programming languages, this communication between modules is an important concern. Many languages require the programmer to specify which variables are passed to the called module whenever a module is called. We won't indicate the passing of variables in our pseudocode, but you should be aware that when you begin programming, you will probably need to identify which variables are received by a module and which variables are returned to the calling module.

FLAGS AND SWITCHES

A flag is a variable that we "control" so that we can remember that a certain condition has occurred. Frequently in designing and implementing a program, we need to know at one point in the program if a specified condition has been met or an action has occurred earlier in the program. We use a flag to "remember" that our condition has occurred. We simply establish a variable (a location in memory), and we establish possible values that will have meaning for us. Let's look at a non-programming example first.

In my household, and probably in yours too, it sometimes happens that the dishwasher is run through but the dishes are not put away immediately. And on occasion, someone, not realizing that the dishes are clean, adds dirty dishes to the load. Once I even put away the dirty dishes! My solution is a magnetic circle that is stuck on the outside of the dishwasher and can be flipped so the appropriate side is showing.

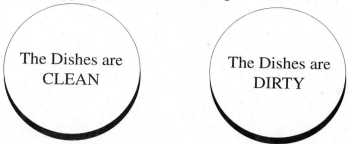

The condition that needs to be "remembered" here is that the dishwasher has been run through but the dishes have not been put away. So when the dishwasher is started, the "flag" is turned to "The Dishes are CLEAN," and when the clean dishes are later put away, the "flag" is switched to "The Dishes are DIRTY." And when somebody wants to put some dishes in the dishwasher, he or she can check the value of the flag to know if the dishes are clean or dirty. Of course, there's a catch to it. The flag is only as good as the faithfulness of the flag-setter. The dishwasher will not automatically reach out and change my flag. I have to remember to change it. We have the same potential problem with flags in our designs.

Let's look now at a program design. Assume that we are designing a program to read and write a list of names from an input file. As we read through the list, we are to check for the name "Sylvester." If we find a Sylvester in the input file, we are to write the message "Sylvester is included in the list" *at the end* of the complete listing. Now how can we do that? The first part is pretty easy. We would have a design that looks like this:

```
Mainline
WHILE there are data
    READ name
    WRITE name
ENDWHILE
```

But, of course, that design ignores the need to check for the name Sylvester. We could add an IF test inside the loop like this:

```
Mainline
WHILE there are data
    READ name
    WRITE name
    IF name = 'Sylvester'
        WRITE 'Sylvester is included in the list.'
    ENDIF
ENDWHILE
```

But we are to write our extra message at the *end* of the list, not as soon as we see Sylvester's name. So how about this solution?

```
Mainline
WHILE there are data
    READ name
    WRITE name
ENDWHILE
IF name = 'Sylvester'
    WRITE 'Sylvester is included in the list'
ENDIF
```

This may look pretty good, but it won't work. The problem is that we have only one variable (location in memory) called name. So every time we read another name, we lose (forget?) the previous one. The computer can only store one value at a time in a given memory location. When we check the variable name after the loop, we are really checking to see if the *last* name read was Sylvester. That's not what was intended.

One possible solution uses a flag. We initialize the flag to one value and change it to a different value when the test condition occurs. Here we'll initialize the flag to 'no.' If we see a name of Sylvester, we will change the flag to 'yes.' At the end of the loop, we can check the value of our flag to know if we should write out the message. If the flag still has a value of 'no,' we know the name Sylvester was never read.

```
Mainline
nameFound = 'no'
WHILE there are data
    READ name
    WRITE name
    IF name = 'Sylvester'
        nameFound = 'yes'
    ENDIF
ENDWHILE
IF nameFound = 'yes'
    WRITE 'Sylvester is included in the list'
ENDIF
```

Walk through the design to make sure you understand what is happening. Notice the importance of initializing nameFound to 'no' before the loop. It has to have a value so that we can check it after the loop. Actually we could have initialized it to anything other than 'yes'—'PeanutButter' would have worked since the important part is that it is changed to a value of 'yes' when the name is found and we are checking only for yes. If we had not found a Sylvester, the flag would still be 'PeanutButter,' and when we made our test IF nameFound = 'yes' the answer would be false. So why use 'no'? For the same reason we called the flag `nameFound`—because it gives more meaning to the design. We want someone else to be able to read our design and be able to understand what's happening.

Would our program work if we forgot to include the IF test inside the loop to change the flag to 'yes'? Of course not! The computer won't change the flag for us any more than my dishwasher will flip over my magnetic circle. We have to remember to initialize the flags and change their values when appropriate.

Flags help us to help make our designs clearer, more readable, more maintainable, and (in some cases) possible. Using meaningful names for our flags and meaningful values helps to achieve those goals. We could also have used a variable called test instead of nameFound, and we could have used the value 0 as the initial value and 1 as the value if a Sylvester was read. But that wouldn't have made our design very meaningful. An IF test after the loop of

```
IF test = 1
    WRITE 'Sylvester is included in the list.'
ENDIF
```

does not give much help in understanding why we're writing the message. Try to always use meaningful names and values in your designs.

Try another example. Suppose we are reading an input file of inventory data. Each record has the partNum, partName, and quantity, and we know that the partNums should be consecutive beginning with 101. That is, the number for any record should be one more than the number for the previous record. We are creating a report of the inventory, but at the end of the report we are to write a warning message if any number was skipped. We will use a flag to remember if the skipped condition has occurred, and we will test the value of the flag after the loop. This design also uses the variable lastNum to save the previous partNum for comparison.

```
Mainline
lastNum = 100
numSkipped = 'no'
WHILE there are data
    DO Process
ENDWHILE
IF numSkipped = 'yes'
    WRITE 'WARNING:  A part number was skipped in input file.'
ENDIF
```

```
Process
READ partNum, partName, quantity
WRITE partNum, partName, quantity
IF partNum < > lastNum + 1
    numSkipped = 'yes'
ENDIF
lastNum = partNum
```

Try desk checking this design. The table below shows a sample input file, the values that each variable in memory would have at the designated point in the processing, and the output at each point. Step through the entire design to be sure you understand how the flag is working.

INPUT Data

101	Washers	97
102	Nuts	98
104	Bolts	66
105	Screws	43

end of file

Memory Variables

Point in processing	part-Num	part-Name	quantity	last-Num	num-Skipped	Output
before loop				100	'no'	
after loop (1)	101	'Washers'	97	101	'no'	101 Washers 97
after loop (2)	102	'Nuts'	98	102	'no'	101 Washers 97 102 Nuts 98
after loop (3)	104	'Bolts'	66	104	'yes'	101 Washers 97 102 Nuts 98 104 Bolts 66
after loop (4)	105	'Screws'	43	105	'yes'	101 Washers 97 102 Nuts 98 104 Bolts 66 105 Screws 43

Point in processing	part-Num	part-Name	quantity	last-Num	num-Skipped	Output
end of design				105	'yes'	101 Washers 97
						102 Nuts 98
						104 Bolts 66
						105 Screws 43
						WARNING: . . . . .

PRIMING READS AND LOOP CONTROL

So far we have looked at two different kinds of loops. We have had count-controlled loops in which we knew how many times we were to do a loop and we used a counter in the design. Our loop control test was then based on the counter, for example, WHILE count < 10. We also have looked at loops in which we were to read all of a file, and our loop control was something like WHILE there are data.

Sometimes we want to control our loop based on some other condition. Assume that we are to read and write from a file of all the students enrolled at the school and that the file has an entry of "**LAST**" included to mark the end of the data to be processed. There may or may not be data following the "**LAST**" indicator. All we know is that we should not process beyond that point. Will the following design work?

```
Mainline
OPEN files
WHILE name < > '**LAST**'
    READ name
    WRITE name
ENDWHILE
CLOSE files
```

Try desk checking the design with the following sample input:

Bob
Frank
Carol
Susan
LAST
2316 2481
4498 8622
end of file

You probably found the first problem very quickly. The first time the loop control test is made we don't have a value for name! That's actually the easy problem. The more important problem is that we end up including '**LAST**' in our output list of names. We read '**LAST**' and write it, before we come back to the loop control test and exit the loop. We don't want to write the indicator, just test it to find when to exit the loop. We could fix both of these problems as follows:

```
Mainline
OPEN files
name = 'Continue'
WHILE name < > '**LAST**'
    READ name
    IF name < > '**LAST**'
        WRITE Name
    ENDIF
ENDWHILE
CLOSE files
```

This works, but it isn't a very desirable solution. We are forced to initialize name to some value other than '**LAST**' just to get into the loop the first time. (It doesn't make any difference what value we choose as long as it isn't '**LAST**' since we will assign a new value to name when we do the READ.) Second, we are testing exactly the same condition in two different places in a very short program. The conditions for the WHILE test and the IF test are identical. Redundancy is not always bad; we sometimes choose to be redundant for the purpose of clarity. But in this case, the double test is really just sloppy design. There's a better solution.

Our problem lies in the need to have our loop control test after the READ and before the WRITE. In all our loops so far, we have tested the condition for the loop, and when we entered the loop we knew we wanted to READ and WRITE the next record. This time, we don't know if we want to WRITE until after we READ and test the value. Instead of assigning a temporary value to name before the loop, we will actually READ the first value. Then, assuming we enter the loop, we can WRITE the previously read value and READ the next value in preparation for the next loop control test. Our design ends up looking like this:

```
Mainline
OPEN files
READ name
WHILE name < > '**LAST**'
    WRITE name
    READ name
ENDWHILE
CLOSE files
```

The Read before the loop is called a *priming read*; it is done once, *before* the loop, to "get things going" much like an old hand pump needed to be primed to get the water flowing. The value (like '**LAST**') that is used to signal the end of the data to be processed is called a *sentinel value*. A sentinel value must always be an otherwise impossible value since if it occurred naturally in the data file, we would stop processing early. Suppose that our sentinel value above was 'LAST' instead of '**LAST**' and that a student named 'LAST' was included in the list (unlikely, I admit, but still possible). The program would exit the loop as soon as our student 'LAST' was read. By including the asterisks here as part of the sentinel, we make sure it is an otherwise impossible value. Any time you have a sentinel value that will control the loop, you should expect to use a priming read because you need to be able to put the loop control test immediately after the read. Sentinel values aren't used very often when input comes from a data file, but they are very common when the input comes from a user at the keyboard: an interactive program. How many times have you seen some variation of the prompt "Enter your next selection or enter 'QUIT' to exit the program"? QUIT is being used as a sentinel value to exit a loop.

Try another, slightly different example. Suppose you have a file of all the students enrolled in the school along with their GPAs and that the file is ordered by GPA values from the highest GPA to the lowest. Your design is to create a list of all the students eligible for the High Achievers Club, which requires a GPA of 3.8 or better. Since the records are in order by GPA, we can just read and write from the file UNTIL we see a GPA that is less than 3.8. In this case the GPA is not a true sentinel value since it isn't included in the file only to signal the end of the data, but we can treat it like a sentinel value. So we'll have a priming read, and our loop control test will be on the just read GPA. Notice that we do not write the record that gets us out of the loop.

```
Mainline
OPEN files
READ name, GPA
WHILE GPA > = 3.8
    WRITE name, GPA
    READ name, GPA
ENDWHILE
CLOSE files
```

We can make one more modification to our priming read/sentinel value testing. We can set up a flag that will be initialized to one value and changed when the sentinel value has been read, then use the flag in the WHILE test. What follows is the same design, converted now to use a flag. The READ has been moved to a separate module since the two statements together form a unique, and separate, function. It also allows us to avoid writing the same lines in two different places in the design.

```
Mainline
OPEN files
moreData = 'yes'
DO Read
WHILE moreData = 'yes'
    WRITE name, GPA
    DO Read
ENDWHILE
CLOSE files

READ
READ name, GPA
IF GPA < 3.8
    moreData = 'no'
ENDIF
```

EXAMPLE

We want to design a program that will read an entire input file. The file contains the name, GPA, and year (1–4, where 1 = freshman, 2 = sophomore, etc.) of all students enrolled at the school. The output should be a report listing each student by name, GPA, and college year in words (Freshman, Sophomore, etc.). In addition, the report should include a final message stating if any student had a GPA of 4.0.

A sample input file could look like:

William Sweet	3.72	2
Chris Anthamum	2.04	3
Lynn Gweeny	4.00	4
Patty Fwagra	1.22	1

The output report would then look like:

William Sweet	3.72	Sophomore
Chris Anthamum	2.04	Junior
Lynn Gweeny	4.00	Senior
Patty Fwagra	1.22	Freshman

At least one student has a GPA of 4.00.

What are our major tasks?

> While
> there
> are
> data

Read input record
Check GPA
Test year
Write output line
Write GPA message

Check GPA
Compare GPA to 4.0

Test year
Convert year number to word

In pseudocode this would look something like this:

Mainline
highGPA = 'no'   *READ name, GPA, yearNum*   *changed to*
WHILE there are data *name <> EOF)*   *Priming Read*
    DO Process
ENDWHILE
IF highGPA = 'yes'
    WRITE 'At least one student has a GPA of 4.0'
ELSE
    WRITE 'No student has a GPA of 4.0'
ENDIF

Process
READ name, GPA, yearNum
DO CheckGPA
DO TestYear
WRITE name, GPA, yearWord

CheckGPA
IF GPA = 4.0
    highGPA = 'yes'
ENDIF

61

```
TestYear
IF yearNum = 1
    yearWord = 'Freshman'
ELSE
    IF yearNum = 2
        yearWord = 'Sophomore'
    ELSE
        IF yearNum = 3
            yearWord = 'Junior'
        ELSE
            IF yearNum = 4
                yearWord = 'Senior'
            ELSE
                yearWord = 'Invalid'
            ENDIF
        ENDIF
    ENDIF
ENDIF
```

Let's review what we've done. HighGPA is used as a flag to remember if we have seen a student with a GPA of 4.0. The flag is initialized at the beginning of the design and modified within the loop if a GPA of 4.0 is read. At the end of the design we test the flag to determine what message to write.

YearNum is our numeric input variable. But in our output we want to write the related word (Senior for a 4, Junior for a 3, etc.). In the TestYear module we have a nested IF that checks the possible numbers and assigns the correct word to the variable yearWord. Notice that if yearNum is not a 1, 2, 3, or 4, we write 'Invalid' as the yearWord.

Be sure you understand this design before you go on. Try creating some sample data and desk checking the design before you continue reading.

Now we'll design the same program but assume that the input file has a sentinel value of 'NoName' to mark the end of processing. This design will be the same except that it will have a priming read. We'll also take more of the details out of our mainline module (one of our long term goals) and put them all in "lower level" modules.

```
Mainline
DO StartUp
WHILE name  < > 'NoName'
    DO Process
ENDWHILE
IF highGPA = 'yes'
    WRITE 'At least one student has a GPA of 4.0'
ELSE
    WRITE 'No student has a GPA of 4.0'
ENDIF

StartUp
OPEN files
highGPA = 'no'
READ name, GPA, yearNum

Process
DO CheckGPA
DO TestYear
WRITE name, GPA, yearWord
READ name, GPA, yearNum

CheckGPA
IF GPA = 4.0
    highGPA = 'yes'
ENDIF

TestYear
IF yearNum = 1
    yearWord = 'Freshman'
ELSE
    IF yearNum = 2
        yearWord = 'Sophomore'
    ELSE
        IF yearNum = 3
            yearWord = 'Junior'
        ELSE
            IF yearNum = 4
                yearWord = 'Senior'
            ELSE
                yearWord = 'Invalid'
            ENDIF
        ENDIF
    ENDIF
ENDIF
```

And once more we modify the design so that is uses a flag to control the loop. The flag is set in StartUp and modified in a new Read module. The TestYear and CheckGPA modules are not affected, so they have not been repeated here.

```
Mainline
DO StartUp
WHILE continue = 'yes'
    DO Process
ENDWHILE
IF highGPA = 'yes'
    WRITE 'At least one student has a GPA of 4.0'
ELSE
    WRITE 'No student has a GPA of 4.0'
ENDIF

StartUp
OPEN files
highGPA = 'no'
continue = 'yes
DO Read

Process
DO CheckGPA
DO TestYear
WRITE name, GPA, yearWord
DO Read

Read
READ name, GPA, yearNum
IF name = 'NoName'
    continue = 'no'
ENDIF
```

Our design will do the same thing; we have just restructured it a bit. Create some sample data (be sure you include the sentinal value), and desk check both designs if you have any doubt that they will accomplish the same tasks.

Our Mainline module in the last two designs is a good example of a "control" module. It gives us an overview of the program with no details cluttering it up. The design does a bit of work before the loop, does a loop while there are data, then does a bit more work after the loop. This is a good outline of most designs you will have to write.

Notice how we have used modules to clarify and organize our design. The Read module is very short, but it performs a very specific task that must be completed in two locations in the design so a separate module is useful. We could even have separate people working on different parts of the design at the same time. One person could design the CheckGPA module, another the TestYear module, and so forth. With multiple people working on different parts of the same design, it becomes increasingly important to clarify what variables must be shared among modules, that is, what variables are received and what variables are returned by each module.

EXERCISES

For each of the following designs, first develop your task lists, work out your module structure using your task list, and finally complete your formal design.

1. Design a program that creates a report of sales activity for the Z-mart Store. Input comes from a file of sales, giving date, item number, quantity, and unit price for each sale item. Output should include date, item number, and total value of sale (quantity times unit price) for each item in the input file. *Use flag to control loop; Use Read module in startup & Process*

2. Design a program that creates a checking account statement listing the canceled checks by check number and amount. Input comes from a file of checks giving the check number and amount. The checks are in order by number beginning with item number 200. Checks are numbered consecutively (200, 201, 202, etc.). Output should include a message *at the end* of the statement if any check number was skipped.

3. Modify design # 2 so that instead of processing the entire file, it stops when a check number with a negative value is read.

4. Design a program that creates a report of all the salesperson totals for the Z-mart Store. Input comes from a file of salesperson data giving the salesperson ID number, salesperson name, and total sales for the past year. Output should include the salesperson ID number, salesperson name, and total sales for each salesperson in the input file. At the end of the output report, include a message giving the highest sales value for the year as well as a message if any salesperson had total sales of 0.

5. Modify design # 4 so that the program loop stops when a salesperson ID of 007 is read. (This, of course, assumes that 007 is an otherwise impossible value.)

6. Design a program that will process the payroll for the Z-mart Store. Input comes from a file including ID number, hours, payrate, and deduction percentage. Output should be the ID, the gross pay (hours * payrate), the deduction amount (gross pay * deduction percentage), and the net pay (gross pay minus deduction amount). In addition, include a message at the bottom of the report if anyone had a gross pay of over $1000.

REVIEW A: Review Exercises for Chapters 1 through 4

1. Read an input file containing the length and width of rectangles (one set of numbers per record). Calculate and write out the area and the perimeter for each rectangle. Continue to do this until all records have been processed.

2. Change design # 1 so that the loop processes exactly five rectangles.

3. Change design # 1 again so that the loop continues until it reads a length and width of 0. Do not write anything for the record with the sentinel values. HINT: Use a priming read.

4. Read an input file containing a list of insurance salespeople and their monthly sales totals. Write out the highest monthly sales figure. (Do not write out the individual figures.)

5. Modify design # 4 so that you write out the highest monthly sales total as well as the name of the salesperson with that total.

6. Use the same input file as # 4 and # 5, but create a report that gives each salesperson and his or her monthly total. At the end of the report give a message indicating whether or not any salesperson had a total of 0.

7. Design a program that reads in the name and three test scores for each of 10 students. Calculate the test average for each student and write out the name and average for each student. Assume that the input file has one piece of data per line: a name, then three scores, then a name, three scores, and so forth.

8. Modify design # 7 so that it processes 30 students, each having 10 grades. The output should be the same: name and average for each student.

9. Modify design # 8 so that it will process each student in the file without knowing in advance how many students there are. You should assume that each student included has a complete set of 10 grades.

10. Assume you have an input file that includes all the "nonworking" days for your company in the form month date, day of week (as in January 15, Sunday). Design a program that will create a list of those nonworking days that fall on Monday through Friday. HINT: It will be easier here to test for what you don't want. Use a nested IF to test for Saturday and Sunday and write the records that are *not* Saturday or Sunday.

Chapter 5

Headings
and Footers

Objectives

After completing this chapter, you should be able to:

1. Determine the line count cutoff, given the margin and headings descriptions.
2. Design a program that will print report headings plus page and column headings on every page.
3. Design a program that will print a footer at the same line on every page.
4. Design a program that will include a page number in a heading or footer.
5. Design a program that will include the system date in a heading or footer.
6. Create a check-off list of possible tasks to be completed before a loop and after a loop.
7. Determine the line count cutoff, given the desired number of detail lines per page.

INTRODUCTION

Most reports need headings. We assume that books will have titles, financial reports will have the columns of figures identified, and soup cans in the grocery store will have labels. Without the titles, column headings, labels, and so on, we would have a very hard time keeping track of what we were reading or buying. So we must start putting headings on our reports too. There are three kinds of headings we must consider: *report headings*, the overall title at the top of the first page of the report; *page headings*, that identify the report and go at the top of each page; and *column headings*, the labels identifying what each column contains.   For instance, on page one of a report, we might have headings that look like

---

XYZ Company, Flintstone, Michigan

ANNUAL REPORT
Microcomputer Division

Dec. 31, 1995   *Page 1*

Department   **Income**   **Expense**

The first two lines are the report heading and would ordinarily be printed on page one only. The third line is a page heading printed on each page. The fourth line has the column headings that would also be included with each page. Our program specifications will tell us what is needed if the user has specific requirements. If no specifications are given for headings, the designer will generally include some form of basic headings.

A printer spacing chart (see next page) is frequently a part of the specifications and will show the exact columns and format for the report. The designer/programmer will use the printer spacing chart as a guide in writing appropriate code for formatting. Since most line formatting (where a word or number goes horizontally on the line) is very specific to the particular programming language, it is more a programmer's concern than a designer's. We will not be concerned with horizontal formatting in this text. However, the vertical spacing

Sample Printer Spacing Chart:

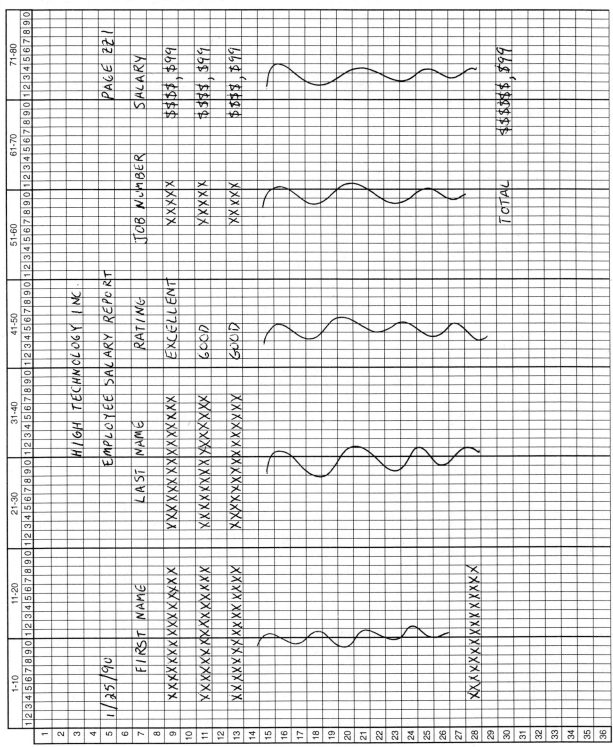

(on which line the words or numbers are written) is our concern. We need to be sure we have included in our design the necessary logic to print data on the proper line.

How do we know what line we're on? How do we get our headings at the *top* of the page? How do we know how much space is left on a page? How do we tell the printer what we want done? How much will the printer do for us, and how much must we tell it to do? Good questions!

The printer "knows" where the top of the page is (assuming that whoever is operating the printer had the paper set properly when the printer was turned on, since usually the printer just assumes that the starting point is the top of the current page). However, the printer doesn't *use* that information unless we tell it to. If we just tell the printer to print the data, it will print, line after line, right over the perforations between pages, without any top or bottom margins, without any page advances. But if we are keeping track of how much we have written and we tell the printer to advance to the top of the next page, it will! So it is up to us to know when we need to "eject" the paper and pass that information along to the printer.

How do we keep track of where we are on the page and when it is time to go to the next page? The easiest way is simply to count the lines as we use them. If we set a counter to 0 at the top of a page and add to the counter every time we "use" a line, the counter will always equal the number of "used" lines. If the counter is 39, that means we have written or skipped 39 lines and we are now ready to write on line 40. And if the counter is 55 and we know that we are to use a maximum of 55 lines per page, we know that it is time to go to the next page.

Most computer paper is 11 inches long, and most printers print at six lines per inch. So we usually have 66 (11 times 6) possible lines per page. Out of those 66 lines we may have a top margin, report headings, page headings, column headings, detail lines, blank lines, a footer line or lines, and a bottom margin. It's our job to fit all that in.

How do we "tell" the printer what to do? The actual commands are specific to the programming language and don't belong in a design. We will use a few pseudocode statements that will serve as reminders to the coder of what needs to be done:

EJECT page	to advance the paper to the top of next page
SKIP *n* lines	to advance the paper a given number of lines
WRITE (dbl spc)	to specify double spacing (a blank line *before* the write) instead of the assumed single spacing

PAGE CONTROL

Assume we want to create a report that has one inch top and bottom margins. For this first attempt we won't worry about headings, we'll just be happy to get the page breaks in the right places. (Step by step, we will later add to this design to include all our heading and footer possibilities.)

If we are printing at six lines per inch, our one inch top margin will be six lines. At the top of every page we will skip six lines before we begin writing our output. Since we also want a bottom margin of six lines, we will need to stop writing after we write on line 60 (so lines 61 through 66 will be left as the bottom margin). If we are counting the lines we have used, we need to eject the paper to a new page when we have used 60 lines. We need a line counter to know when we have used those 60 lines. To keep the example simple we will just assume that all we're going to do is read a record and write it out (no fancy processing).

Our list of tasks might look like:

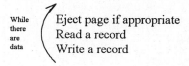

```
          ┌ Eject page if appropriate
While     │ Read a record
there     │
are       └ Write a record
data
```

"Eject page if appropriate" might be just a bit vague for you. We know we want to start on a new page so we could just start off by ejecting the page. And we also know that when the page is full, it's time to go to another page. Our revised list of tasks might look like:

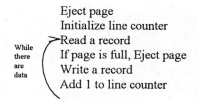

```
            Eject page
            Initialize line counter
While     ┌ Read a record
there     │ If page is full, Eject page
are       │ Write a record
data      └ Add 1 to line counter
```

Let's go ahead and put this into a formal design. Since we're ejecting the page in two different places, it makes sense to put those statements in a separate module.

```
Mainline
DO StartUp
WHILE there are data
    DO ProcessRecord
ENDWHILE
CLOSE files
```

```
StartUp
OPEN files
DO NewPage

ProcessRecord
READ a record
IF linesUsed > = 60
    DO NewPage
ENDIF
WRITE a record
ADD 1 to linesUsed

NewPage
EJECT page
SKIP 6 lines (top margin)
linesUsed = 6
```

We have called the NewPage module from StartUp to be sure we have a clean sheet of paper for the first page. In the Process module, we check the value of linesUsed (IF linesUsed > = 60) and call NewPage again if the page is "full"—remember full is defined through our specifications for margins and headings. Every time we go to a new page, we need to reset the counter so we can begin counting the lines used for the new page. What would happen if we forgot to reset it? When we started to write the second line on the next page, the line count would be 61, our test would indicate the page is full, and we would go to a new page. After the first page, we would get only one detail line per page because the line count test—IF linesUsed > = 60—would always be true!

This design works, but we can improve it. Remember, we want to keep our design as simple as possible and avoid any unnecessary overlap between modules. In this design we're calling the NewPage module from two different places, and it really isn't necessary. We called NewPage from StartUp because we knew we wanted to begin on a new page. But isn't there a way to eject for the first page using the same statements used in Process for the succeeding pages? There is if we're willing to "lie" a bit. In Process, our logic says to eject the page if the page is full (linesUsed > = 60). If we make the computer "think" that the first page is already full, we'll get our page eject. Our new design looks like this:

```
Mainline
DO StartUp
WHILE there are data
    DO ProcessRecord
ENDWHILE
CLOSE files
```

<u>**StartUp**</u>
OPEN files
linesUsed = **60**

<u>**ProcessRecord**</u>
READ a record
IF linesUsed > = 60
    DO NewPage
ENDIF
WRITE a record
ADD 1 to linesUsed

<u>**NewPage**</u>
EJECT page
SKIP 6 lines (top margin)
linesUsed = 6

Look closely, there's only one change! Instead of including DO NewPage in StartUp, we've included the line linesUsed = 60. So when we go into the loop the first time and get ready to write the first detail line, it checks the line count and says, "Whoops, that page is full, I'd better go to a new page." A sample of our output with a top and bottom margin follows.

100 meters running (M)	9.86 sec	Carl Lewis	U.S.	1991
100 meters running (W)	10.49 sec	Flo Griffith Joyner	U.S.	1988
200 meters running (M)	19.72 sec	Pietro Mennea	Italy	1979
200 meters running (M)	21.34 sec	Flo Griffith Joyner	U.S.	1988
400 meters running (M)	43.29 sec	Butch Reynolds	U.S.	1988
400 meters running (W)	47.60 sec	Marita Koch	E. Germany	1985
800 meters running (M)	1 min. 41.73 sec	Sebastian Coe	Gr. Brit.	1981
800 meters running (W)	1 min, 53.28 sec	Jarmila Kratochvilova	Czech.	1983
1000 meters running (M)	2 min, 12.18 sec	Sebastian Coe	Gr. Brit.	1981
1000 meters running (W)	2 min, 30.6 sec	Tatyana Providokhina	USSR	1978

Long jump (M)	29 ft, 4.5 in	Mike Powell	U.S.	1992
Long jump (M)	24 ft, 8.25 in	Galina Chistyakova	USSR	1988
Triple jump (M)	58 ft, 11.5 in	Willie Banks	U.S.	1985
Triple jump (M)	49 ft, 6.25 in	Ana Biryukova	Russia	1993
Pole vault (M)	20 ft, 1.5 in	Sergei Bubka	Ukraine	1992
Shot put (M)	75 ft, 10.25 in	Randy Barnes	U.S.	1990
Shot put (W)	74 ft, 3 in	Natalya Lisouskaya	USSR	1987
Discus (M)	243 ft.	Juergen Schult	E. Germany	1986
Discus (W)	252 ft.	Gabriele Reinsch	E. Germany	1988
Javelin (M)	313 ft., 10 in.	Jan Zelezny	Czech Rep.	1993
Javelin (M)	262 ft., 5 in.	Petra Felke	E. Germany	1988

HEADINGS

Now let's add page headings and column headings at the top of every page. This is a fairly simple addition. Our NewPage module will simply write the heading lines after it skips the lines for the top margin. And, of course, we will change the value we initialize linesUsed to since we have now used some additional lines. Since the only module that is affected is the NewPage module, only that module is shown below.

```
NewPage
EJECT page
SKIP 6 lines
WRITE page heading
WRITE column heading (dbl spc)
SKIP 1 line
linesUsed = 10
```

The "(dbl spc)" added to the WRITE column heading will provide a blank line between the page heading and the column heading. The SKIP 1 line adds a second blank line after the column heading, before the detail lines are written.

Let's add another element to our headings: a page counter. Since many reports contain multiple pages, it is helpful to have the pages numbered. All we really need is another counter. Our line counter was initialized in StartUp and incremented in Loop whenever we wrote a detail line. We set the line counter back to 10 in NewPage when we started a new page. But we never wrote the line counter. It was there to help us *control* our output, not to *be* output. The page counter will be a bit different. We will still initialize it in StartUp, but we will never re-initialize, since we don't want to start back at page 1 again. We will increment the page counter in NewPage, when we go to a new page, and we will write it. This counter is intended as output; we aren't using it to control anything. We'll also double space the detail lines in our revised example. That means that each time we write a detail line, we're actually using two lines, so we add 2 to linesUsed. We won't skip the blank line after writing the column heading since our double-spaced detail line will have the effect of putting a blank line between the column heading and the first detail line.

```
Mainline
DO StartUp
WHILE there are data
    DO Process
ENDWHILE
CLOSE files
```

```
StartUp
OPEN files
linesUsed = 60
pageCount = 0

Process
READ a record
IF linesUsed > = 60
    DO NewPage
ENDIF
WRITE a record (dbl spc)
ADD 2 to linesUsed

NewPage
EJECT page
SKIP 6 lines
ADD 1 to pageCount
WRITE page heading, pageCount
WRITE column heading (dbl spc)
linesUsed = 9
```

The example below shows the top of our first page with the top margin and page and column headings.

Track and Field Records   Page 1

Event	Time/Dist	Holder	Country	Year
100 meters running (M)	9.86 sec	Carl Lewis	U.S.	1991
100 meters running (W)	10.49 sec	Flo Griffith Joyner	U.S.	1988
200 meters running (M)	19.72 sec	Pietro Mennea	Italy	1979
200 meters running (W)	21.34 sec	Flo Griffith Joyner	U.S.	1988
400 meters running (M)	43.29 sec	Butch Reynolds	U.S.	1988
400 meters running (W)	47.60 sec	Marita Koch	E. Germany	1985

Now let's add a *report* heading line that gets written only on the first page. We'll need to add a test in the NewPage module to see if we should write the report heading line. The first time we go into the NewPage module is when we write the headings on the top of page 1, and that is when we want to write the report header. Since we have a page counter, we can simply test the counter to determine what page we're on. Notice that the test is IF pageCount = 0 since we are testing before we add 1 to pageCount.

```
NewPage
EJECT page
SKIP 6 lines
linesUsed = 6
IF pageCount = 0
    WRITE report heading
    SKIP 1 line
    ADD 2 to linesUsed
ENDIF
ADD 1 to pageCount
WRITE page heading, pageCount
WRITE column heading (dbl spc)
ADD 3 to linesUsed
```

Notice the changes to the initialization of linesUsed. In the previous design we were able to assign the correct value to linesUsed in one step. Since we now have a report header, we use more lines for the page 1 headings than for headings on other pages. The solution used here is to initialize linesUsed following the top margin and then to add to that value as additional lines are used.

In the above design we identified the first page using the page counter. What if we weren't numbering the pages and therefore didn't have a page counter? One solution would be to count the pages anyway. Another solution would be to use a flag to identify when we are writing headings on the first page. The following design (only the StartUp and NewPage modules are shown) uses the flag firstHeading to identify when the report header should be written.

```
StartUp
OPEN files
linesUsed = 60
firstHeading = 'yes'
```

```
NewPage
EJECT page
SKIP 6 lines
linesUsed = 6
IF firstHeading = 'yes'
    WRITE report heading
    SKIP 1 line
    ADD 2 to linesUsed
    firstHeading = 'no'
ENDIF
WRITE page heading
WRITE column heading (dbl spc)
ADD 3 to linesUsed
```

Dates in Headings

One final addition to the report headings: Frequently, we want to include the date as a part of the report heading. Most computers have an internal clock/calendar so they already know the current date (and time). We just need to get that information from the computer to the program. Most programming languages will have a way to access the "system date." We'll be very loose here and write it like an assignment statement: date = System date or time = System time, meaning that the design variable *date* should get its value from the system date. We're going to write the date when we write the headings. Where, in our design, should we access the date? If we access it in the NewPage module, we are forcing the computer to re-access the date for each page. At best, we're slowing the program down unnecessarily. At worst, we could get two different dates on our report. Imagine that we started executing the program just before midnight. Page 1 might have a date of January 29, 1995, but by the time the computer gets to page 2 it might be January 30, 1995. That should confuse whoever receives the report! A better solution is to access the date once, in the StartUp module.

```
Mainline
DO StartUp
WHILE there are data
    DO Process
ENDWHILE
CLOSE files
```

```
StartUp
OPEN files
linesUsed = 60
pageCount = 0
date = System date
```

Process
```
READ a record
IF linesUsed > = 60
    DO NewPage
ENDIF
WRITE a record (dbl spc)
ADD 2 to linesUsed
```

NewPage
```
EJECT page
SKIP 6 lines
linesUsed = 6
IF pageCount = 0
    WRITE report heading
    SKIP 1 line
    ADD 2 to linesUsed
ENDIF
ADD 1 to pageCount
WRITE date, page heading, pageCount
WRITE column heading (dbl spc)
ADD 3 to linesUsed
```

Again, look closely. There are two minor changes here. We accessed the system date in the StartUp module and wrote the date field in the NewPage module on the page heading line. A sample is shown below.

AMATEUR ATHLETIC ASSOCIATION

March 30, 1995   Track and Field Records   Page 1

Event	Time/Dist	Holder	Country	Year
100 meters running (M)	9.86 sec	Carl Lewis	U.S.	1991
100 meters running (W)	10.49 sec	Flo Griffith Joyner	U.S.	1988
200 meters running (M)	19.72 sec	Pietro Mennea	Italy	1979
200 meters running (W)	21.34 sec	Flo Griffith Joyner	U.S.	1988
400 meters running (M)	43.29 sec	Butch Reynolds	U.S.	1988
400 meters running (W)	47.60 sec	Marita Koch	E. Germany	1985

Sometimes we want a different date other than the current date as a part of our headings. If our report is our current inventory as of January 15, 1995, we probably want January 15 in the heading of the report, not the date when the report was actually printed. Since we may be printing the report on January 18 or 22 or later, we don't want to access the system date. In this case, we would get the date from some other source (the computer operator, an input file, etc.). We will look at these possibilities in the next chapter with parameter records.

When to Check for a Full Page

We have consistently checked the value of our line counter *before* we wrote the detail line, in effect asking, "Is there room to write this line?" Could we just as easily have written our detail line and then checked to be sure we have room to write the *next* line? That sounds like good Boy Scout procedure: Be Prepared for the Next Line. Well, it may sound like a good procedure, but it leads to problems. The most obvious problem is that we've lost the headings on the first page since we don't check the line counter until *after* the first write. We could take care of that problem if necessary (at the least we could go back to writing headings in StartUp). But we also have another, less obvious, problem. Suppose that by coincidence, the last line of a page is also the last line to be written in the report (that is, we have read and written all the records from the input file). We write that last detail line, and then we ask, "Is there room for the next line?" Since we're at the bottom of the page, the answer would be no, and we would go to NewPage and prepare for the next detail line. But there isn't another detail line! We have written headings unnecessarily! Our solution is to **check the line counter and call NewPage only when we *know* we have something to write**. If we have just done our read and are ready to write, now is the time to check the line counter.

In most of our designs so far we executed a READ and a WRITE each time through the loop, but that will not always be true. If we were designing a program to create a list of "G" rated movies from an input file of 1993 through 1995 movies, we would read the movie title and rating, but we would write the title only if the rating were a "G." If we are to check the line counter and call NewPage only when we know we have something to write, we would nest the test of the line counter inside the check on the movie rating.

```
READ title, rating
IF rating = 'G'
    IF linesUsed > = 60
        DO NewPage
    ENDIF
    WRITE title
    ADD 1 to linesUsed
ENDIF
```

FOOTERS

We've conquered headings. The top of all our pages looks wonderful, professional and impressive! But what about the bottom of the page? Sometimes, not nearly as often as we need headings, we also need to write a footer line. A footer, like a heading, means writing the same line or message in the same location on every page. We might want to write some text, like the company name or **"CONFIDENTIAL—No Unauthorized Access"** or simply the page number at the bottom of every page of our report. Where, in our design, do we write it? It may sound strange, but the easiest place to write it is in our NewPage module. That's the module that will be done when we have completed each page. When we go to NewPage, we can write the footer before we EJECT the page and write the headings. We only need to make sure we don't write a footer before the *first* page. Since the primary change is to NewPage, we will look first at that module. This design puts the page number in a footer at the bottom of every page.

```
NewPage
IF pageCount = 0
    EJECT page
    SKIP 6 lines
    WRITE report heading
    SKIP 1 line
    linesUsed = 8
ELSE
    DO Footer
    EJECT page
    SKIP 6 lines
    linesUsed = 6
ENDIF
ADD 1 to pageCount
WRITE date, page heading
WRITE column heading (dbl spc)
ADD 3 to linesUsed
```

Footer
```
SKIP (59-linesUsed) lines
WRITE "Page -- ", pageCount
```

We also need to change the check on the line counter in the Process module. Since we're going to write a footer on line 60, we don't want to write a detail line there. Working up from the bottom of the page, we have a bottom margin on lines 61-66, a footer on line 60, and a blank line on 59, so the last line available for a detail line is 58. The check on linesUsed in the Process module would become

```
IF linesUsed > = 58
    DO NewPage
ENDIF
```

You're probably asking "What is this 'SKIP (59-linesUsed) lines' business?" We know we want our footer on line 60, but do we "SKIP" down to that line? If we know that the last line used was 58, we could just write the footer double-spaced. But in this case, the last line used could not have been 58, it would have to be an odd number. (We set linesUsed to 9 or 11 at the end of NewPage, and we have added 2 to it for each detail line.) We could, of course, have figured all that out and said, "OK, we'll triple space the footer line." But what if the last line used is not 57? It is unlikely that on the last page of our report our last line will be on line 57. So it's easier (and safer) to let the computer figure out how many lines to skip.

If we want to write on line 60 and we have used linesUsed lines, we might think we can calculate the number of lines to skip by subtracting linesUsed from 60. For example,

```
Gap = 60-linesUsed
SKIP Gap lines
```

That's close to our final solution, but we need to make one more adjustment. The line counter tells us the last line used. If we have *used* 57 lines, our printer is now ready to write on the 58th line. We would want to "skip" the 58th and 59th lines and write on the 60th line. If we subtracted linesUsed from 60, we would be skipping an extra line. Our printer is always one ahead of the lines used, so we subtract from 59 (or one less than where we want the footer to go). The SKIP statement simply does the subtraction and then says, "Skip that many lines."

Unfortunately, we're not done yet. Our design doesn't work. Step through the design now and see if you can find the problem.

Back already? What did you find? Did you get a footer on the last page? Since we called the Footer module from the NewPage module, we only get a footer when we actually go to NewPage. That's okay for most of the pages, but we don't go to NewPage after we write the last detail line of the report, and so we never get the final footer line written. You will find, as we continue with design, that first lines and last lines are the most difficult lines to control in designs. Get in the habit of paying particular attention to the logic surrounding them. In this case, we needed to check the page number to make sure we didn't write an unnecessary footer before the first page. And now we need to "force" a footer on the last page. How? The simplest way is to call the Footer module after the loop. Right before we close the files, we should write the footer. So Mainline module looks like:

```
Mainline
DO StartUp
WHILE there are data
     DO Process
ENDWHILE
DO Footer
CLOSE files
```

We have added several tasks before the loop and after the loop to our growing design. Certainly not all of these tasks will be included in each design that you do, but you should be aware of the possibility. In Chapter 1, we looked at a series of questions that you could ask yourself in preparing the list of tasks:

What's our input?
What's our output?
Do we have a loop?
What controls the loop?
What happens in the loop?
What happens before the loop?
What happens after the loop?

Continue to keep those questions in mind as you develop your task lists and complete your formal designs. However, we can expand on it a bit. As you consider what happens before the loop, review in your mind the possibilities for typical **"before the loop"** processing:

- Open files
- Access the system date
- Initialize any counters or accumulators (line count, page count, total salary, etc.)
- Do any special processing (like load arrays—see Chapter 8)
- Read any needed parameter records (see Chapter 6)
- Do priming read (if appropriate)

"Open Files" is the only step we haven't talked about before. Any file must be opened *before* it can be used (either read from or written to). Opening a file is a command that actually stands for several steps. The computer will "prepare" the file for reading or writing and check to be sure that the file is indeed the correct file.

You can use this checklist of possibilities for **"after the loop"** processing:

- Finish processing the last record (sounds crazy but, as you will see, in some cases this is necessary)
- Print final totals (totals are covered in Chapter 6)
- Print final footer line (on last page)
- Close files (what was opened must be closed, consider it a law of nature)

Putting it all together, here's a final example. Design a program to create a report of spies who came in from the cold. The input comes from an input file containing the name, code name, assigned region, project code, and contact for each spy. The output should include a top margin of 1 inch and headings as shown below. Write two detail lines per spy (name and codename on line one and other data single-spaced on second line). Be sure both lines for a single spy fall on the same page. Double-space between spies. On line 58 of each page, write "TOP SECRET—CLASSIFICATION 1A1" double-spaced from the report.

Page 1 Headings:

United States of America

Jan. 30, 1995	Spies Who Came in From the Cold	Page 1
Spy's Name	**Spy's Codename**	
Region	**Project Code**	**Contact**

Headings for all other pages:

Jan. 30, 1995	Spies Who Came in From the Cold	Page X
Spy's Name	**Spy's Codename**	
Region	**Project Code**	**Contact**

Mainline
DO StartUp
WHILE there are data
    DO Process
ENDWHILE
DO Footer
CLOSE files

StartUp
OPEN files
linesUsed = 60
pageCount = 0
date = System date

Process
READ name, codeName, region, project, contact
IF linesUsed > = 54
    DO NewPage
ENDIF
WRITE name, codeName (dbl spc)
WRITE region, project, contact
ADD 3 to linesUsed

NewPage
IF pageCount = 0
    EJECT page
    SKIP 6 lines
    WRITE report heading
    SKIP 1 line
    linesUsed = 8
ELSE
    DO Footer
    EJECT page
    SKIP 6 lines
    linesUsed = 6
ENDIF
ADD 1 to pageCount
WRITE date, page heading, pageCount
WRITE column heading #1 (dbl spc)
WRITE column heading #2
ADD 4 to linesUsed

Footer
SKIP (57-linesUsed) lines
WRITE "TOP SECRET—CLASSIFICATION 1A1"

Where did the 54 come from in the linesUsed test in Process? Working from the bottom of the page up: The bottom margin is assumed to be everything below the footer; on line 58 we have our footer. We are to double-space between the last spy and the footer line, so 57 must be blank. Since a spy takes two lines plus the blank line before it (the spy lines are double-spaced), the last spy on the page would have to begin on line 55 with line 54 blank. If we have already used line 54, we don't have room for another spy.

Study the above design carefully to be sure you understand it.

It is possible, though not nearly as likely, that our specifications will describe our headings and include a specification line like "Include a maximum of 45 detail lines per page." All we have to do is count the detail lines (assuming we trust the analyst). We can initialize our line counter to 0 when we exit NewPage because we aren't counting the number lines used, we're counting the number of detail lines written. We still add to the line counter for each detail line. A full page would be defined as a page containing the maximum number of detail lines.

Computer Program Design

EXERCISES

Each of the following designs assumes that processing is simply reading a record from the input file and writing the equivalent line in the output report.

1. Design a program that will create a report with a two-line page heading (double-spaced) and single-line column headings. The detail lines should be single-spaced. Allow a maximum of 45 detail lines per page.

2. Modify design # 1 so that the page headings include the system date and a page number.

3. Modify the design, one more time, by adding a report heading, written on page 1 only.

4. Design a program that will create a report with a one-inch top margin, report headings on the first page only, and column headings on each page. Detail lines should be double-spaced. Write the footer "Designing is FUN" on line 61 of each page.

5. Design a program that will create a report that will include a half-inch top and bottom margin, two double-spaced page headings, and a footer with the page number as the last line before the bottom margin. The detail lines should be double-spaced, and there should be a blank line between the last detail line and the footer.

6. Modify design # 5 so that the first heading line is a report heading, written on the first page only; the second line is a page header that includes the system date; and at least two blank lines are written before the footer.

Chapter 6
Totals and Parameter Records

Objectives

After completing this chapter, you should be able to:

1. Identify when initialization and incrementation should take place for an accumulator given a design problem.
2. Identify when initialization and incrementation should take place for accumulators given a nested loop design problem.
3. Design a program to include a total line that is *always* on a separate page of the output.
4. Design a program to include a total line that is *never* on a separate page of the output.
5. Define parameter values/records.
6. Explain why values may be provided as parameter records even though they could have been "hard coded" into the program.
7. Explain the three types of input sources for parameter values and the input procedures required for each type.
8. Give several examples of types of data which might reasonably be entered as parameter values.

' TOTALS

Frequently, business reports include numeric totals at the end of the report as a summary of the detail lines. Totals are a very important and very easily implemented addition to many reports. We have already skimmed over the surface of totals, but now it is time to look at them in more depth.

The tools used to create the totals are accumulators and/or counters. An accumulator is just a numeric variable that we use to keep a running total of some other variable. Usually, this means that some value will be read within a loop, and during each pass through the loop we will add that value to our accumulator. If the accumulator started with a value of 0, it will be the sum of all the values at the end of the loop. Always remember these two essential steps in working with any accumulator: **Initialize it** before the loop and **add to it** within the loop. If we forget or misapply either of these steps, our accumulator will be useless. Without the initialization, our accumulator would have the wrong value (if it started at 23,452 instead of 0 for instance) or would be an illegal operation (if it started with no value at all or with a non-numeric value). Without the addition, our accumulator would have the same value after the loop that it had before the loop. The third step is to **use** the accumulator since we are not accumulating just for the joy of adding.

A counter is really a special form of accumulator. Counters are simply accumulators to which we add a set number (usually 1) instead of adding the current value of whatever variable is being accumulated. The line counter that we have used is, of course, a counter to which we add 1 or the number of lines actually used. Another difference between counters and other forms of accumulators is that counters frequently, but not always, are used to control designs and not for output, whereas other accumulators are almost always included for output purposes.

Let's look at a simple example—one, in fact, that should look familiar. We will read and process an input file containing name and salary for all our employees. Our output will be a report including the name and salary of each employee plus the average salary of all employees. For simplicity, we will assume the output will fit on one page so headings can be written in StartUp. The lines relevant to the accumulator and counter are in boldface.

Notice that both the counter (numEmployees) and the accumulator (total) are initialized to 0 in StartUp. Both are incremented in Process. NumEmployees is incremented by 1 to indicate that one more employee has been processed. Total is incremented by the value of that employee's salary. In the Finish module, the accumulator is divided by the counter to calculate the average salary of the company, and the average is then written out. A sample of the report is shown below the pseudocode.

Mainline
DO StartUp
WHILE there are data
    DO ProcessEmployee
ENDWHILE
DO Finish

StartUp
OPEN files
numEmployees = 0
total = 0
EJECT page
SKIP 6 lines
WRITE page heading
WRITE column heading (dbl spc)
SKIP 1 line

ProcessEmployee
READ name, salary
ADD 1 to numEmployees
ADD salary to total
WRITE name, salary

Finish
avg = total / numEmployees
WRITE 'Average Salary = ', avg
CLOSE files

SALARY REPORT

Name	Salary
Adam Brown	25,500
Clara Smith	35,750
Frances Farmer	55,250
John Quincy	42,000

Average Salary = 39,625

Usually, accumulators and counters are very straightforward, and you will have no difficulty implementing them. However, there are a few potential snags that we should mention.

Why Zero?

First, accumulators should always be initialized to 0. If the accumulator has any other value at the beginning, the value of the completed accumulator will be wrong (by the amount of the initial value). Counters, on the other hand, can be and sometimes are initialized to values other than 0. The most common alternative is 1. I strongly recommend that you stick with 0 for two reasons. One it makes your counters consistent with your accumulators. Two, if you initialize your counter to 0 and increment by 1, at the end of the loop the value of the counter will be the number of times you went through the loop. If you initialize to 1, at the end of the loop your counter would be 1 more than the number of times you "looped." That sounds confusing, but let's look at an example. Assume we want to do a loop 5 times. If we initialize to 0, our design might look like:

```
Mainline
count = 0
WHILE count < 5
    ADD 1 to count
    WRITE count
ENDWHILE
```

This is a very simple design, but it still makes the point. What is the value of count after the loop? It is 5. We entered the loop five times, when count had values of 0, 1, 2, 3, and 4. When we entered the last time, count was 4 (which is less than 5, of course); we added 1 to count making it 5. Since 5 is not less than 5, we did not go into the loop again. Count's value after the loop is exactly the number of loop iterations. The output for the loop is 1, 2, 3, 4, 5. The illustration below shows another way to check a design. It steps through the design showing the result of each statement.

Statement	Before loop	Loop Number					After loop
		1	2	3	4	5	
Count = 0	0						
WHILE count < 5		T	T	T	T	T	False
ADD 1 to count		1	2	3	4	5	
WRITE count		1	2	3	4	5	
After loop							Final value of count = 5

Now look at this example with count initialized to 1:

```
Mainline
count = 1
WHILE count < = 5
    WRITE count
    ADD 1 to count
ENDWHILE
```

This design will do the loop exactly the same number of times and will have exactly the same output, but what will be the value of count after the loop? It will be 6! We enter the loop when count equals 5 and increment count to 6. Since 6 is not less than or equal to 5, we do not go into the loop again. The output for this design is the same, but only because we moved the WRITE before the ADD. Who cares that count is one more than the number of iterations? You would if you were going to use count after the loop! Go back to our original example in which we calculated the average salary. If we had initialized the numEmployees counter to 1, our average would have been incorrect since we would have divided by one more than the actual number of employees. Compare the design check below with the previous design example.

Statement	Before loop	Loop Number					After loop
		1	2	3	4	5	
Count = 1	1						
WHILE count < = 5		T	T	T	T	T	False
WRITE count		1	2	3	4	5	
ADD 1 to count		2	3	4	5	6	
After loop							Final value of count = 6

Know What You're Counting

Sometimes, the location of our incrementation statement can be important. If we are simply counting the number of times we do a loop, the ADD 1 to count could go almost anywhere within the loop (except within an IF statement). But if we're counting how many times some condition occurs, the ADD 1 to count must be properly placed within the IF statement(s) that test for that condition. Some specifications ask for something like a count of the number of employee records read. This is really the same as asking for the number of times the loop is completed, but it sounds different and makes it tempting to associate the incrementation directly with the READ statement. What happens with this design that includes a priming read and controls the loop with a sentinel value?

```
Mainline
DO StartUp
WHILE name < > 'quit'
    WRITE name, salary
    DO Read
ENDWHILE
WRITE 'Number of records processed is ', numRecords
CLOSE files

StartUp
OPEN files
numRecords = 0
DO Read

Read
READ name, salary
ADD 1 to numRecords
```

We're really counting how many times we went into the Read module. The last time we go into the Read module, however, we are reading the sentinel value, a record that we are not processing. But we still increment numRecords. There are several ways to fix this, but the easiest way is to move the counter incrementation from the Read to the main body of the loop. The ADD 1 to numRecords statement could actually be placed before the WRITE, between the WRITE and the DO Read, or after the DO Read. As long as it is someplace in the loop, we will increment once for each loop iteration.

Beware of Nested Loops

We've looked at a design with a counter and an accumulator. But what if we have multiple accumulators or counters which aren't all working in or related to the same loop? With nested loops, we frequently have counters or accumulators for each loop. Then we must be very careful that we initialize and increment our accumulators at the proper time. Again, let's look at an example. We have an input file of student names and grades. Each student has five grades. We want the average grade for each student plus the number of students included in the file. We will assume that each grade is on a separate line and that each

READ in our design will read one line of input. That means that it will be easiest to read the grades in a loop. We will need a counter to count up to five to control the grade reading loop. And we will need an accumulator to sum the grade values for each student to calculate that student's average. Even though we are calculating the average for multiple students we will need only one counter and one accumulator for the grades because we can re-use them. Any time we "re-use" accumulators, we must be very careful about where we initialize the counter and accumulator. They must be set back to 0 for each student. Since we are to write the number of students in the file at the end of the report, we also need a counter for the number of students. Here's a solution:

```
Mainline
DO StartUp
WHILE there are data
    DO Process
ENDWHILE
DO Finish


StartUp
OPEN files
numStudents = 0


Process
READ name
ADD 1 to numStudents
numGrades = 0
gradeSum = 0
WHILE numGrades < 5
    READ grade
    ADD grade to gradeSum
    ADD 1 to numGrades
ENDWHILE
avg = gradeSum / numGrades
WRITE name, avg


Finish
WRITE 'Number of students in file = ', numStudents
CLOSE files
```

This design has two loops, one nested within the other. The "outer" loop is controlled by WHILE there are data. The body of this loop is the entire Process module. The "inner" loop is controlled by WHILE numGrades < 5. The body of the inner loop is the READ grade and the two ADDs that follow it. Our first counter (numStudents) is **initialized** before the outer loop (in StartUp), **incremented** within the outer loop, and **written** after the loop (in Finish). NumStudents counts the number of students. We could say it counts the number of times the Process loop is completed (although it does not *control* the loop).

Our second counter (numGrades) is used to control the inner loop. It is **initialized** within the Process module *before* the inner loop. Since our second counter is related to the second (inner) loop, we must reinitialize it for each *new* use of the inner loop. NumGrades is **incremented** inside the nested loop. It is **used** after the loop to calculate the average. Since we know there will be five grades we could have written the calculation as `Avg = gradeSum / 5`, but using numGrades makes the design easier to modify if the number of grades is later changed.

Our accumulator (gradeSum) has the same requirements. We are accumulating the grades for each student, not for the class as a whole, so we must start back at 0 for each student.

Assume we have the input file shown at the right. (It includes just two students.)

The illustration below traces the steps in the outer and inner loops.

INPUT
Dick
90
85
95
88
85
Jane
100
85
92
85
95
eof

Statement	Before outer loop	Outer Loop #1						Outer Loop #2					
NumStu = 0	0												
WHILE there are data		True						True					
READ name		Dick						Jane					
ADD 1 to NumStu		1						2					
NumGrade = 0		0						0					
GradeSum = 0		0						0					
WHILE NumGrade < 5		T	T	T	T	T	F	T	T	T	T	T	F
READ grade		90	85	95	88	85		100	85	92	85	95	
ADD grade to GradeSum		90	175	270	358	443		100	185	277	362	457	
ADD 1 to NumGrade		1	2	3	4	5		1	2	3	4	5	
Avg							87						91

Notice the importance of setting numGrades and gradeSum back to 0 for each student. If numGrades were initialized to 0 before the outer loop and not set back to 0 again, we would not be able to process Jane's grades. The test WHILE numGrades < 5 would be false since numGrades would still be equal to 5 from processing Dick's grades. If gradeSum were not set back to 0, the average for each student after the first would be wrong because the total would include more than that student's five grades. The inner loop processes the grades for *one* student so the counter and accumulator must be reset for each student.

Where Should We Write the Total?

Some specifications are very particular about where the total line should be written. Let's look at a few possibilities.

The simplest method is to say that the totals will go directly below the detail lines (usually double-spaced from the last detail line) and can extend into the bottom margin if necessary to keep them on the same page. In this case, when we get to Finish, we simply write the total line or lines. We don't have to check the line count to see if there is space because we are not concerned with preserving the bottom margin. This method would only be used when the total line is one or two lines (we certainly wouldn't want to try writing many lines without checking the line count) and when the bottom margin is not critical. With some reports, the output will be used within some other document or as an overlay in a form, and the bottom margin is critical.

The next simplest method is to say that all totals will go on a separate, last page of the report. That is, before we write the total line, we go to a new page, even if the previous page isn't full. Often with this method the total page will have different headings (or the same page headings but no column headings). Our Finish module might look like:

```
Finish
DO FinalHeads
WRITE total
CLOSE files
```

The FinalHeads module would advance the paper and write whatever special headings are required for the total page. We still don't need to be concerned with the line count since we know we will be advancing to a new page. Generally, this method would be used only if there are multiple total lines to be written.

Another method is to say that the total line should be double-spaced from the last detail line if there is room but that the bottom margin must be maintained. If there is sufficient room left on the last page for the final total line(s), the result of this method will look identical to that of the first method. But since we may not continue into the bottom margin, we need to check the line count value (in the Finish module) before we write the total line. If there isn't room on the page, we will call the Heads module. Heads will advance the paper and write the headings so that when control returns to Finish, we can just write the total line. Finish would then look something like this (we check for a line count of 59, making sure there is room for two lines above the one inch bottom margin, since the total line is double-spaced):

```
Finish
IF lineCount > = 59
    DO Heads
ENDIF
WRITE total (dbl spc)
CLOSE files
```

The final possibility is just a bit more complex. The specifications might say that the total line is to be double-spaced from the last detail line with a one inch bottom margin but that the total line must not be on a page by itself. In other words, you should not have the last detail line of the report fit at the very bottom of the page and then go to the top of a new page for the total line. How do you control for it? Usually when we do a line check before a write we are asking, "Do I have room to write this detail line?" If it happens that this is the last detail line, we need room not just for the detail line but also for the total line and so would have to ask, "Do I have room for three lines, the detail line, a blank line, and the total line?" But when we write a detail line, we do not know if it is the last detail line that will be written. So we have to assume that any detail line *could* be the last line and always ask if there is room for both the detail line and the total line. In our example, that means our check in the Loop module before writing a detail line would be IF lineCount > = 58 (instead of IF lineCount > = 60). When we are ready to write the total line then in Finish, we don't even check the lineCount value. We *know* there is room to write the line. The downside of this style is that we would never use the full 60 lines on the page unless on the last page the last detail just happened to be on line 58. On all previous pages and, most likely, on the last page, too, we are effectively increasing the bottom margin to allow expansion room for the total.

If we have multiple total lines, we certainly don't want to increase the bottom margin to allow for all those extra lines. There is a way around this problem if we are willing to include an extra test in the line check. Remember, we are assuming that any detail line *could* be the last line, so with each detail line we make sure there is also room to write the total line. If we know that the detail line we are writing is not the last detail line, we would not need to reserve the extra lines. Essentially we then have two line cutoff figures, one for the last detail line of the report and another for all other lines. We would decide which cutoff figure to use based on whether there were additional data to be read in the input file (IF there are data). Our loop module might then look something like the following:

```
READ name, salary
ADD salary to totalSalary
IF there are data
    IF linesUsed >= 60
        DO Heads
    ENDIF
ELSE
    IF linesUsed >= 58
        DO Heads
    ENDIF
ENDIF
WRITE name, salary
ADD 1 to linesUsed
```

In our Finish module, we know we have room to write the total line, so we do not need to check the line counter before we write.

Subtotals

Taking the totals idea a step further leads us to the question of subtotals. Subtotals are simply a total for a subgroup of the file. If we are doing a design with total salary for our entire company, we might also want to write a subtotal of the salary for each department within the company. We will handle subtotals as a separate topic in Chapters 12 and 13.

PARAMETER RECORDS

What is a parameter? My *Random House Dictionary* defines parameter as "a determining factor, characteristic, etc." In computer terms, parameter is frequently used to mean a selected option or a qualifier. If you are an MS-DOS user, you are probably aware of the variations on the DIR command. When we add the /W or /P to modify the output form of the DIR command, we are adding a parameter. Airlines use a similar qualifier when they write airline tickets. Next to the flight number is a letter which is used as a parameter to designate the seating class of the ticket holder.

What does all that have to do with us? We can use parameters in our designs in somewhat the same way. In our case, a parameter will be a value or values which we read in from an external input source and use within the design to control the operation of the program (e.g., in loop control) or use in processing our detail records. Another way of saying it is that the parameter record or records provide values that are not available at the time the design is done (or at least aren't included in the design), but are needed for the processing. Some examples will help.

Assume we are designing a count-controlled loop. Our loops so far have specified the ending value of the counter within the design (WHILE count < 10, for example). But what if we want to be able to vary the number of times we do the loop? Perhaps we want to be able to do the exact same processing, but sometimes we want to do the loop 10 times and other times we will want to do it 20 times. If the 10 is actually written into the design, we can change the number of times the loop is done only by changing the program itself. Parameter record to the rescue! We can design our program so that the loop control uses a variable instead of a literal number (WHILE count < totalNum, for example). Now all we have to do is read in the value that will be held in the variable. Here's a partial design:

```
Mainline
READ totalNum
count = 0
WHILE count < totalNum
    DO Process
ENDWHILE
```

TotalNum is our parameter value here. It controls the loop in that it states the ending point. The value for totalNum will come from an external source (more on this in a bit). We read the parameter record in at the beginning of the design. What have we gained? FLEXIBILITY! Without a parameter record, we would have had to put the literal number in the design. That is called "hard coding" the parameter; the loop control value is specified within the design/program. When we code the program, the literal number would be given. That means that to change the loop control number that has been hard-coded in the program to a different value, we would have to go back to the source code and change the value, recompile the source code, and reexecute the resulting object code. And if we want then to go back to the original number, we must repeat the procedure. With the parameter record, totalNum can have a different value (so we complete the loop a different number of times) with each execution of the program, and we don't have to change anything but the value provided as input.

A parameter record could be used with a program that computes the bank account interest. Interest rates vary frequently, and banks certainly don't want to have to recompile their programs every time they change the interest rate. So they can write the program so that the interest rate is read in as a parameter record. At the beginning of the program, the interest rate would be read in as input. That rate would then be available for the rest of the program to use in processing the input detail record.

We may work for a company that pays workers on an hourly rate using four different pay rates. Hopefully, those pay rates increase now and then. The company could design their payroll program so that the rates are read in as parameter records—then we could easily get a raise every week. Here's an example:

```
Mainline
DO StartUp
WHILE there is a record
    DO ProcessEmployee
ENDWHILE
CLOSE files
```

within the same file

```
StartUp
OPEN files
READ rate1, rate2, rate3, rate4
```

```
ProcessEmployee
READ name, rateCode, hours
IF rateCode = 1
    pay = rate1 * hours
ELSE
    IF rateCode = 2
        pay = rate2 * hours
    ELSE
        IF rateCode = 3
            pay = rate3 * hours
        ELSE
            pay = rate4 * hours
        ENDIF
    ENDIF
ENDIF
WRITE name, hours, pay
```

> **Warning:** Please notice that this design assumes that if the rateCode is not a 1, 2, or 3 it must be equal to 4. If there is a chance that the rateCode would be outside the range of 1 through 4, the design would need to include the additional test IF rateCode = 4. In a later chapter we will look at designs that edit an input file so that we can confidently make assumptions about the validity of the input data.

With this design, the employee input records contain a code that would be a 1, 2, 3, or 4 and would identify the pay rate for that employee. In the ProcessEmployee module, the code is checked to select the proper pay rate, the pay is then calculated, and the output is written. Since the pay rates are not included as literal numbers (such as Pay = 6.26 * hours) but are read in as parameter values, the company could adjust the rates by just changing the input without any changes to the program code.

Sources for Parameter Values

The question that we have ignored for a while is: Where do these parameter values come from? We know that we are reading the parameter values from an external input source. What's the source? There are three possibilities.

First, the program could have the **computer operator** input the values. Someone is running the program. If it is a microcomputer system, we have a person sitting in front of the machine, and that person could enter the values when asked. If it is a mainframe computer, there is an operator who has responsibility for tasks such as running the programs and mounting the proper tape or disk files for input and output. That operator has a "console" that can be used for entering input to the program. If we are expecting to have the user or operator input the parameter values, we must write a message to the operator's screen asking for the input. Otherwise, our program would pause waiting for the input, but the operator would just have a blank screen and no way of knowing what was expected. All we need to do is write a "prompt" message to the screen immediately before the read. Since we now have a write that goes to a different output device (other writes go to the printer) and a read that is reading from a different input source, we have to clarify our devices. The simplest method is to assume that input is from our usual input source (disk?) and output is to the printer unless we say otherwise. When we are reading from or writing to a different device, we can note it in parentheses. Our StartUp module then becomes something like this:

StartUp
OPEN files
WRITE 'Enter the current pay rates, starting with rate one' (to screen)
READ rate1, rate2, rate3, rate4 (from keyboard)

A second possible input source for the parameter values is **the same input file** that contains the detail records. Our assumption here would be that the first record contains the parameter values, and all succeeding records contain the detail (employee) data. The good news is that this method does not require any changes to our design. The original design that we gave assumes this form of input. The bad news is that the method has some inherent problems. Usually, a data file is used by more than one program. If we modify the nature of the data file for one of the programs, we are probably creating trouble for the other programs. Unless all programs using the data file will need the same parameter values, we're better off not putting them in the primary data file.

The final possible input source is **a separate input file.** If our detail records are in a disk file, we could create a second disk file that contains the parameter values. Now we have two different input files: one that contains only the parameter values and the second that

102

is our detail record input file. When we open the files, we open both input files. In StartUp, we would read the parameter record(s) from their file (and we would have to indicate that somehow). In Process, we would read the detail records from their file. The only problem here is that there is a lot of "overhead" for any file, no matter how small. We may be wasting more storage space than the file is worth. So why would we use this method? If we reject the second method because it makes the data file unusable for other programs, we are left with either operator input or a second input file. We may decide that some data should not be left to operator input. In our pay rate example above, a simple typing error by the operator (say an extra 0) could mean that many pay checks are incorrect. It also might be very tempting for the operator to grant himself or herself a raise by simply typing in a different pay rate. By putting "sensitive data" in a file, we are protecting it somewhat from those accidents and temptations. Even better protection is to "hard code" the values in the program and with very sensitive data, that is exactly what would be done.

In the previous chapter we looked at including the run date from the system in the heading of a report. We agreed (you did agree, didn't you?) that there will be times when we want a date other than the current system date in the heading, for example, the effective date for a new price list or the actual date of an inventory count. The appropriate date would then be entered as a parameter record in the StartUp module.

EXERCISES

1. Design a program that will calculate the tuition for all students at your school. Per credit tuition fluctuates depending on the current price of computer disks and the mood of the business manager, so it will be read in as a parameter value from a separate file. The detail record input file contains student ID number and credits enrolled. Output should be ID number, credits, and total tuition.

2. Modify the above design so that the total tuition is written at the end of the report. The total should be double-spaced from the last detail line and may extend into the bottom margin if necessary to print on the same page. The report should have one-inch top and bottom margins, a page heading, and column heading.

3. Design a program that will calculate the quantity discounts for all sales records in an input file. The input file contains purchase order (PO) number, item number, quantity ordered, and unit price. Output should be PO number, item number, gross price, discount amount, net price. Gross price is quantity times unit price. Discount amount is based on a percentage of the gross price. Net price is gross price minus discount amount. Discounts are given for quantities of 10-49, 50-99, 100-200, and over 200. Discount percentages vary, so the four percentages will be read in as parameter values from the operator.

4. Modify the above design to add totals for the gross price and net price and counts of the number of orders that fall into each of the quantity categories: 10-49, 50-99, and so on. The final totals and counts should be written on a separate page with separate headings.

5. Design a program that can be used at livestock sales to create pricing sheets. Input will be from a disk file and will contain animal category (hog, lamb, steer, or cow) and the animal's weight. Output will be the category, weight, and price. Livestock prices vary daily, so the per pound prices will be entered as parameter values as the first four values in the input file (hog, then lamb, then steer, then cow in cents per pound). Include four price totals at the end of the report, total price for hog, for lamb, for steer, and for cow. Final totals should be written double-spaced below the last detail line and must be on a page that includes at least one detail line. The report should have one-inch top and bottom margins and reasonable headings.

6. Modify the above design so that instead of printing final totals of the prices, the report gives average weights for each of the four animal categories. In addition, add a date to the heading that reflects the date of the prices (read in as a parameter value from the operator).

Chapter 7

Structured Design and Interactive Programs

Objectives

After completing this chapter, you should be able to:

1. List the requirements of structured design.
2. Identify the techniques of structured design that make the above requirements possible.
3. List the primary goals of structured design.
4. Identify the unstructured elements in a design and rewrite the design into a structured design.
5. Define interactive programs and explain how they differ from batch programs.
6. List the design questions that must be answered in interactive programs that are not relevant in batch programs.
7. Give examples of appropriate interactive input routines.
8. Design a program that includes input from the keyboard and a file as well as output to the screen and a printer.

INTRODUCTION

We have, by now, looked at the major aspects of program design. We can implement the major elements of a design, and we are familiar with two of the major formal design tools. It is time to take a step back and place our knowledge within a broader framework. What makes one design "good" and another "bad" (or at least "less good")? How do we recognize a "good" design? How can we define a "good" design so that others can recognize one? It is not enough to say, "I know it when I see it." We must be able to define our design goals and requirements.

STRUCTURED DESIGN

One of the terms we will use here is "structured" design. What are we adding by the term "structured"? Over the past 25 years, a form of program design has been developed that emphasizes a certain methodology of design and specific requirements for the completed design. Designs that meet those requirements are said to be structured. Designs that followed the earlier process of design are said to be unstructured. We will look at the methodology and requirements of structured design.

Requirements of Structured Design

TOP-DOWN DESIGN—We have looked at our design problems so far by asking first what are the major tasks, then breaking those tasks down into subtasks, and continuing that process until we had complete lists of *what* needed to be done. The key point is that we started with a broad view of the design and continued to break that broad view down into smaller and smaller sections until we were down to the level of the smallest detail needed. This process is Top-Down Design. It is also known as Step-Wise Refinement and Functional Decomposition. However, top-down design goes further than just creating our task lists. We also write our formal design in the same manner, starting with the broad view (our Mainline module) and working down to the small detail modules. Our completed design has the same "look" as our original task lists because we present it from major tasks broken down to minor tasks. We continue in the same manner to code and implement our design. Rather than code the entire program and try to run it all at once, we code it in sections (our Mainline module, then add the input and output modules, then add the calculation modules, etc.). We continue to use the top-down philosophy with our program documentation. We begin to create our documentation package when we begin to list our tasks. The completed package will show the completed design, the source code, the results of test runs, and any notes accumulated about the program.

LIMITED TO THE THREE MAIN STRUCTURES—We use the sequence, selection, and loop structures, as well as the few accepted variations of those structures (UNTIL loop as a variation of the WHILE loop, case structure as a variation of the nested IF). You are probably asking, "What else is there?" As you will see later in this chapter, it is possible to create designs (and programs) that ignore the requirements we have set up for the three structures. The designs may even work, but they will almost always be difficult to follow and therefore difficult to modify.

PROGRAMMER TEAMS—Major programs should be created by programmer teams working cooperatively under a team leader. Programming teams provide several advantages to the designers. Instead of one designer working months or years on one program, a team can complete the program in much less time. A single programmer has no one who is already familiar with the program to help resolve particular problems. A team will be in regular consultation and will be able to put their heads together quickly and efficiently to solve design/programming problems.

STRUCTURED WALK-THROUGHS—A structured walk-through, a formal review of the design (and perhaps code) by a review team of peers, should be used with major programs. The goal is to identify potential problems before the design is cast in concrete. The walk-through team should be given copies of the design in advance and "walked through" the design by the primary designer. The goal is to find the potential errors, not to fix them. Identified problems are referred back to the design/programming team for revision.

MODULAR CONSTRUCTION—Designs are written using a modular construction. Each module is dedicated to a single function (or at times to a particular set of lesser functions grouped because they occur at the same time). Within a module, statements should be tightly related with a clear and obvious reason for the inclusion of each statement. Very loose relationships should exist between modules. We have looked at modules before, but the use of programming teams makes modularity much more important. One programmer may write one module, and another programmer (perhaps working at a different site) may write another module, and the two modules may need to share data. The way in which a program is broken into modules may make it easier (or more difficult) for the two programmers to coordinate their work. The structured walk-through is where the team makes sure the modules fit together.

SINGLE ENTRANCE–SINGLE EXIT—Every structure, every module, and every program should be limited to a single entrance and a single exit. This is really a restatement of earlier rules, but it is important to emphasize. Early designs were often made to work by one-way branching. When we call a module, the return from the module is automatic. It is a round-trip ticket since when the module is completed, control automatically returns to the statement following the call. Earlier designs used a "GO TO" that branched to another location without any return implied. The GO TO was often used for multiple exits from IF statements and from loops rather than controlling for data variations within the IF or loop.

FLAGS, SWITCHES, AND IFs—The use of flags, switches, and IF statements make the single entrance/single exit rule possible.

Goals of Structured Design

As we will see when we look at some of the history of structured design, the rules given above were developed in direct response to the then current problems in the computer program development world. The goals essentially were to correct those problems. The goals of structured design continue to be practical, production-oriented goals.

LESS TESTING/DEBUGGING TIME—By spending more up-front design time creating a complete top-down design for the program, designers should be able to cut in half the time needed to test (and debug) the completed program. Less testing time means lower development costs.

LESS MAINTENANCE TIME— All programs will need to be changed during their time of use. Programs that can be modified quickly and put back into use immediately will save the company time and therefore money.

These first two goals are both related to certain characteristics of structured designs. Structured designs are simple, clear, readable, and follow the same guidelines (within a company) no matter who did the design. Since all designers are following the same standards, any designer should be able to follow easily someone else's design. This concept, ego-less programming, means that a design should follow the style of the company, not an individual designer's style.

MAINTAINABILITY, NOT EFFICIENCY, AS PRIMARY GOAL—Program efficiency is no longer the final and major criterion for judging all programs as it once was. A program which executes very quickly but takes five times longer than other programs to modify every time a change is needed is not an efficient program. The first goal of design (and coding) is to make the design work through clear, simple, maintainable logic. Once that goal is met, the designer can investigate means to make the program run more efficiently as long as the efficiency does not come at the cost of the clarity and maintainability of the program. Because most business application programs follow our overall outline of something before the loop, a loop, and something after the loop, it is common for a very few lines to account for most of the execution time. Optimization of those few lines in the loop can have a major increase in efficiency without hurting the maintainability of the program.

History of Structured Design

A typical unstructured design of 25 years ago might look like the flowchart on the following page (although this is a very small design). This flowchart is a design solution for a program to create an inventory list from a current holdings input file. The file is to be in order by inventory number and contains inventory number and quantity on hand for each item in inventory. The report should include all items in the input file unless an item is found to be out of order, in which case an error message should be written and the execution stopped. If the quantity on hand is less than 10, the message "Immediate Action Needed" should be written along with a message to reorder the item. If the quantity on hand is 10 to 50, the message "Action Required" should be written along with a message to reorder the item. If the quantity on hand is greater than 50, the part number should be written with no message. "Reasonable" headings are also included in the report. The design is given in flowchart because we can show a GO TO using a flowline. Remember that pseudocode was developed along with structured design to correct some of the weaknesses of flowcharting. It would be much harder to create the same unstructured design in pseudocode.

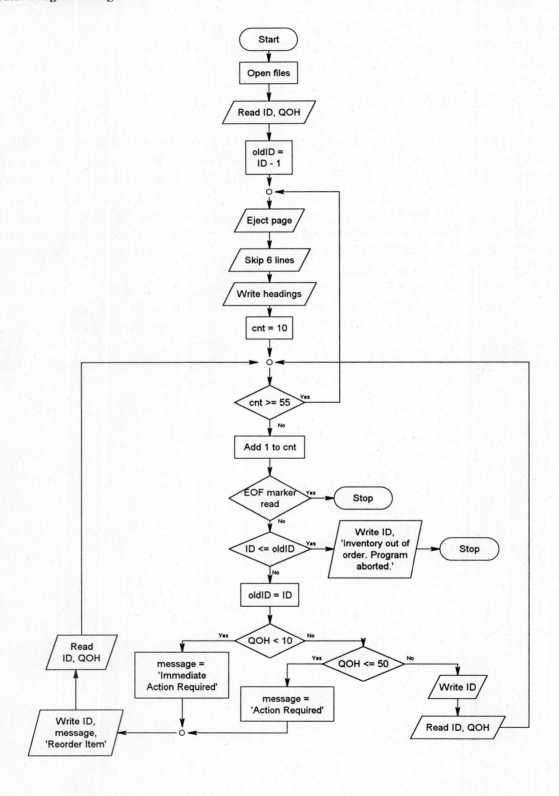

What's wrong with the design? You should be able to find several things that are wrong. The design does not use modular construction—everything is in the same module. The design has two exits (two Stops). There are several selection structures and none has a clear end (single exit). There is a loop (the flowline loops back to before the test) that is really intended to act as a selection. The "real" loop test is not at the beginning or end of the loop, but in the middle. The design uses "GO TOs" to branch to other locations in the design without any return. In larger designs that included GO TO flowlines branching throughout the design, the page resembled a plate of spaghetti. That is why unstructured code was often referred to as "spaghetti code."

A structured solution follows below and on the next page. Notice that it uses modules to separate the details from the main structure. It uses a flag (continue) to control the loop. Since there are two reasons to exit the loop, there are two locations where the value of continue can be changed.

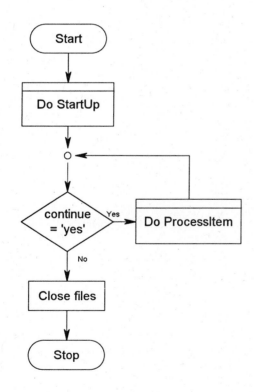

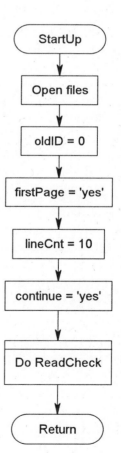

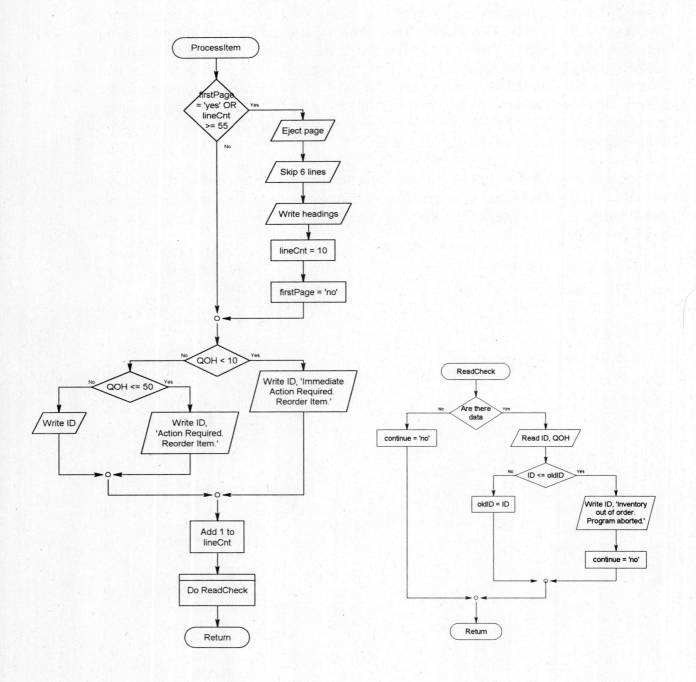

Try to take the image of the unstructured design and expand it into a much longer program. Programs that were thousands of lines long and still used the same unstructured "spaghetti code" were almost impossible to follow once they were written. In the early days of programming, programmers were left pretty much to themselves. As long as their programs worked (and no matter how they worked), the programmers were left, rather like artists, to produce their creations. The problem was that their creations were so individualistic, so difficult to follow, and so poorly documented that maintaining them became an increasingly time-consuming task. Some programmers had to be retained on staff because they were the only ones who could modify the programs they had written. In many companies, the backlog for maintenance became so great that there was no new program development. In most companies, the majority of programmer time was spent on program maintenance.

In 1964, Bohm and Jacopini, two mathematicians, presented a mathematical proof that all programming could be completed using the three basic structures (sequence, selection, and loop). Conspicuously absent from their list of structures was the GO TO. Unfortunately, their paper did not receive much notice in the United States (for one thing, it was written in Italian). In 1966, an English translation was written in a U.S. journal, but the article still did not receive the attention it deserved. In 1968, E. W. Dijkstra wrote a letter to the editor of the *Association for Computing Machinery Journal* outlining the "harmful" effects of the use of the GO TO statement in programming. The letter served to focus attention on the ideas of structured design presented earlier by Bohm and Jacopini. From these beginnings, structured design was born, but it still didn't flourish.

In the early 1970s two major programming projects received major attention in the programming world. One was an IBM project completed for the *New York Times* and the other was a NASA project. Both utilized the concepts of structured design as we have outlined them here; both were major, multiyear projects completed on time, within budget, and judged to be highly reliable. Structured design gained acceptance in the United States partly because of the attention given to these two projects. By the mid-to-late seventies, structured design had become the standard design philosophy.

We are now going through a new upheaval in program design. Currently most programming is done with third-generation programming languages called *procedural languages*. With these languages we must define not only *what* is to be done, but also *how* it is to be done. The planning of the design is critical to defining the *how*. Newer, fourth-generation, nonprocedural languages take a different approach to program creation. With these languages it is no longer necessary to define *how;* the system establishes the how, once we tell it the *what*. Does that mean program design is no longer going to be important? No!

It means that program design will (as fourth generation languages become more prevalent) become more specialized for a few. But it is true now and will continue to be true that most students of design will never be programmers; they will utilize their design skills in their work with application programs (spreadsheets, data base packages, etc.), in systems analysis, and other related occupations.

INTERACTIVE PROGRAMS

The programs we have designed so far are *batch* programs. The input is "collected" and stored in a file of some kind. When the program is executed, it opens the file and processes the input one record at a time. Once the command to execute the program is given, no further intervention from the user is needed because *all* the input are already gathered in the file. The program runs on its own, processing the stored batch of data.

In an *interactive* program, the user interacts with the computer during the execution of the program. Usually the interaction is in the form of providing the input. Data for a read statement would be typed in at the keyboard at the time it is needed for the program. There are many advantages (and some disadvantages) to interactive programs. For many purposes, interactive programs are the only way for us to get our output within the needed time frame. Suppose you are telephoning in an order to a catalog store. When you provide the catalog number, the operator can check the availability of the item immediately using an interactive ordering program. If the item is not available, you can make a decision about ordering a different item, waiting until the item is available, or choosing a different color. Because the order program is interactive, you can make ordering decisions and modify the input while the order is being processed. If the program were a batch program, your order would be stored in a file until the end of the day (or whenever the orders were processed), and all orders would be processed sequentially. A sequential process of the stored orders is actually a more efficient use of the computer, but a less satisfactory way for you to order. By the time the computer checks your order and finds that the item is out of stock, it is too late for you to make a change. With interactive programs, we get timely input and output, and we get the opportunity to control the execution of the program based on our input.

From our perspective, interactive programs present some unique design considerations. When our input comes from the disk or some other computer-controlled peripheral, we don't have to worry much about the interface between the two pieces of hardware. Our program will give commands to the computer which will relay them to the input/output devices. But when the input comes from a human being sitting at the keyboard, the interface is between the program/computer and the user. Now we have the program interfacing with the human, and it must be done so that the human understands what is needed and in what form. In a sense, the program is having a conversation with the human user. The program asks a question and the user answers it. The program must be designed so that it makes the best and clearest use of the human user. There are two major design issues that concern us.

Loop Control

Most of our loops have been controlled indirectly by the end-of-file marker in the input file. We have used the loop test WHILE there are data which instructs the computer to check the data file to see if the input file contains another record or if the end-of-file marker is the next value to be read. When the input comes from the keyboard, there isn't an end-of-file marker because there really isn't a file. How will we control the loop? It needs to be controlled based on user input; essentially, does the user want to repeat the loop? One solution is to ask a question at the end of each loop ("Do you have more information to process?") and exit or repeat the loop based on the answer. This is a condition controlled loop much like our flag controlled loops. Another solution is to have the loop continue until the user enters a sentinel value. Perhaps we have an interactive college registration program that asks for a name and tells us to enter Quit as the name if we want to exit the program. The loop is controlled by the value of the name entered. If the name is "Quit," the program exits the loop; if the name is anything other than Quit, the loop is entered and the name is processed. One of the last statements within the loop would be to Read the next name. In both cases, the loop is controlled by user input. With the condition controlled loop that asks if the user wants to repeat the loop, a generalized task list might look like the following:

```
REPEAT
    Prompt for input
    Read input
    Process input
    Write output
    Ask user if loop should be repeated
    Read user response
UNTIL user says don't repeat loop
```

If the loop is controlled by a sentinel value, the task list will change because, as you know, sentinel value processing requires a priming read. If we use an UNTIL loop we are assuming that the first piece of input is not the sentinel value. All future input is then read at the bottom of the loop and is tested to see if the sentinel value has been entered. The generalized task list could be:

Prompt for input
Read input
REPEAT
    Process input
    Write output
    Prompt for input
    Read input
UNTIL user enters sentinel value

You probably noticed the use of UNTIL loops in the above task lists. With interactive input, UNTIL loops will be much more common. Remember that the UNTIL loop is always executed at least once since the controlling condition is not tested until *after* the first execution. Usually, we can assume the user wants to do the loop at least once in an interactive program. We will look in a moment at editing loops that often seem more logical when designed as UNTIL loops. Any loop that can be done as an UNTIL loop, though, can also be done as a WHILE loop.

Editing the Input

When our input comes from a file, our design frequently just assumes that the input is in the correct form and is valid. But when the input comes from the keyboard, we must assume just the opposite. We must always account for the possibility that the user has made a typing error or skipped a line and typed in the wrong data, or made some other input mistake. Most input will need to be "verified" by the user or checked against some standard before we accept it. The advantage is that because the program is interactive, invalid data can be corrected immediately. Much of this editing will be done in series of small UNTIL loops (read the name *until* you get a correct name; read the address *until* you get a correct address; read the course number *until* you get a valid course number, etc.). The more catastrophic an incorrect entry would be the more important it is to check the input. If a typo in a product number will only mean that a search is unsuccessful and the user gets a warning and a prompt to enter the next number, then the user can just correct the entry on the next loop iteration. But if the typo in the product number means that a customer is automatically charged for the purchase of some other product, some form of check needs to be done.

In the examples that follow, we will check virtually all the user input. Most users would consider such an extreme more of a hindrance than a help. As the designer you must be able to find an appropriate balance between checking the input to prevent errors and slowing down the user with constant prompts for verification. Where the balance point is will depend on such factors as the complexity of the input, how well trained the users are likely to be, how often they use the program, and the source of the user's input data.

In addition to these two major issues, interactive programs present a variety of other design questions. We will not address all these issues in the design examples because some fall in the domain of the systems analyst rather than that of the program designer.

What will the visual display look like? Remember, the visual display is the interface with the user, and any information that needs to be communicated to the user must go on that display. Where on the screen should the data be displayed? What data should be displayed together? When and how often should the screen be cleared? How should the input and output be intermixed on the screen? Should one piece of input be cleared before the next piece is requested? There are, of course, no single answers to these questions. Often the screen design will be partly determined by a printed input source form to which the user is referring. Novice users are often more confused by a screen that shows or requests many pieces of data, but experienced users may find a screen holding all the data easier to use. The visual design of the screen, colors used, location on the screen of prompts and error messages, and a variety of other issues may all be field-tested before the program is finalized.

Every piece of input must be preceded by some form of "prompt" for the input—remember, this is a conversation with the user. The user needs to know what is expected of him or her next. What form of prompt should be used? How detailed a prompt is needed? For an experienced user the prompt "Code?" may be sufficient, but a novice or infrequent user may need to have the possible entries listed. Alternatively, instead of asking the user to enter a code or other entry, you could list all the possibilities on the screen and have the user "highlight" the desired entry. Long, explanatory prompts just get in the way of an experienced user, but may be essential for new users.

When the user needs to make selections to control the program, the program can present a menu, can assume the user knows the options and will type one in, or can do some compromise between the two. Should a menu be used? If yes, what form of menu? How many menu options can reasonably be included on the screen at once? A hierarchy of menus can keep any single menu from getting too complex with too many options, but it may force the user to work through many layers to get to the desired option. Pull-down menus, particularly when used with mouse input, are popular, but they may be distracting for typists doing primarily text entry.

Some of these questions will be answered by the designer's understanding of the intended audience of the program. If the anticipated user will be a computer-trained person who will use the program every day, much more understanding of the program can be assumed than if the user has no computer background and will only use the program once a month. Prompts that are appropriate for the very casual user would be annoying for the experienced user. Always remember that the interactive program is a dialogue between the user and the program. You would describe your last program design quiz differently to a fellow programming student than you would to your Aunt Hilda who has never used a computer. The audience dictates the tone.

EXAMPLES

Let's look at two examples of interactive programs.

First, design a program that will control a computerized cash register at a store. Our visual output is a single line "screen." Our input comes from a modified keyboard. The user should get a prompt to enter P (Purchase), R (Return), or X (exit), and the program should remain in the loop until an X is entered. Purchases should invoke a separate loop that is repeated until the user enters a purchase of 0. The total of one user's purchases should be calculated along with the tax amount, the total amount due, and the change due for the amount paid. Returns should read in the amount of the original purchase, calculate the tax, and write out the amount to be refunded. Write your own task lists, then compare yours to mine below. The pseudocode follows the task list.

Task List

until
exit

{ Prompt for and read transaction type
  Process action   either Purchase
                          or   Return

Purchase
Initialize sum

until
0

{ Prompt for purchase amount
  Read purchase amount
  Add purchase amount to sum
Calculate tax amount and add to sum
Write sum
Prompt for and read amount paid
Calculate and write change due

Return
Prompt for and read purchase amount
Calculate tax and add to amount
Write refund due

Pseudocode

Mainline
```
REPEAT
    REPEAT
        WRITE 'Enter P, R, or X' (on screen)
        READ transType (from keyboard)
    UNTIL transType = P, R, or X
    IF transType = 'P'
        DO Purchase
    ELSE
        IF transType = 'R'
            DO Return
        ENDIF
    ENDIF
UNTIL transType = 'X'
```

Purchase
```
sum = 0
REPEAT
    WRITE 'Enter amount of purchase—enter 0 if done' (to screen)
    READ amtPur (from keyboard)
    sum = sum + amtPur
UNTIL amtPur = 0
tax = sum * .045
total = sum + tax
WRITE 'Total Due is ' total (on screen)
WRITE 'Enter amount paid' (on screen)
READ paid (from keyboard)
change = paid - total
WRITE 'Change due = ' change (on screen)
```

Return
```
WRITE 'Enter amount of purchase returned' (on screen)
READ amt (from keyboard)
tax = amt * .045
total = amt + tax
WRITE 'Total amount of refund = ', total
```

Note the use of the UNTIL loops for most of the input. The Mainline module includes a nested UNTIL loop that checks the code entered to select the operation. If the code is not one of the three acceptable letters, the loop repeats. Our design uses two sentinel values: when transType = 'X' the program exits the mainline loop and when amtPur = 0 the program exits the Purchase loop. Note also that we are making a lot of assumptions about the validity of the user's input. I'm assuming that the user is the salesclerk in a store who would be familiar with the operation and the keyboard. If the user were an infrequent user, additional edit checks would be necessary, particularly on the numeric values.

A second example. We'll design an interactive student registration system. The system should continue to register students until someone (a college official, we hope) enters a code to shut down the registration. For each student, the system should read in the student's name and student identification number and the course ID for each course desired. We want to make it possible for a student to register for more than one course, so we will have to have a nested loop that is repeated for each course the student desires. In a true registration system, of course, we would have many checks to make, but we will include just two checks here: First, we'll check a list of the student identification numbers of all students at the school to make sure the student should be allowed to enroll, and second, we'll check a list of available courses to be sure the registration should be accepted. Since we have not yet covered the processes required to do those two checks, they will be included here as calls to undefined modules. The modules will return a flag that our design can test to determine if registration should continue. My task list is shown here with my pseudocode below. Try yours first and then compare it with mine.

Task List:

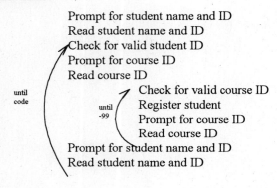

There are many ways that you could organize these tasks. I've used a priming read for the outer loop to read the student name and ID so that the until condition test will occur immediately after the read that is included in the loop. The check for a valid student ID is done at the top of the loop. That way we are sure we will not be checking the sentinel value as though it were a student ID. I have also used a priming read for the inner loop since it also is controlled by a sentinel value.

Pseudocode:

Mainline

```
DO GetStudent
REPEAT
    DO CheckStu
    IF studentOK = 'yes'
        DO GetCourse
        REPEAT
            DO CheckCourse
            IF courseOK = 'yes'
                DO Register
            ELSE
                WRITE 'Sorry, that is not a valid course.  Please try again.'  (to scr)
            ENDIF
            DO GetCourse
        UNTIL courseID = -99
    ELSE
        WRITE 'Sorry, that is not a valid ID.  Please try again.' (to scr)
    ENDIF
    DO GetStudent
UNTIL stuName = shutDown Code
```

GetStudent

```
REPEAT
    WRITE 'Please enter your first name, then a space, then your last name.'  (to scr)
    READ first, last (from keybrd)
    WRITE 'Thank you, ', first, 'now please enter your student ID.'  (to scr)
    READ stuID  (from keybrd)
    WRITE 'You have entered: ', first, last, stuID (to scr)
    WRITE 'Are the entries correct?  Y / N '  (to scr)
    READ resp  (from keybrd)
UNTIL resp = 'Y' or resp = 'y'
```

GetCourse

```
REPEAT
    WRITE 'Please enter the ID for the course you want.'  (to scr)
    WRITE 'Enter an ID of -99 if you do not wish to continue.' (to scr)
    READ crsID  (from keybrd)
    WRITE 'You have entered: ', crsID  (to scr)
    WRITE 'Is that entry correct?  Y / N'  (to scr)
    READ resp  (from keybrd)
UNTIL resp = 'Y' or resp = 'y'
```

The CheckStu and CheckCourse modules would take the input values and check them against the lists of valid IDs. Both modules set a flag (studentOK and courseOK) to 'yes' if the value is found in the list. After a few more chapters, we'll be ready to write those modules too.

EXERCISES

1. In interactive programs that ask the user to verify the input, there is a lot of duplication of small routines. Design an interactive program that asks the user to enter (one entry at a time) his or her name, a color, a name for a pet giraffe, and a "magic word." Each entry should be verified by the user with a Y or N response. Design a "utility" module that can be called after each entry to ask for and read the Y or N response. The utility module will ask if the input is correct and will read the user's response. Finally, you might as well do something with all that input you read in, so write the following sentence on the screen: "When <userName> waves a magic wand and says <magicWord> a <color> giraffe named <petName> will appear."

2. Design an interactive program that will replace the cashier at the movie theater ticket window. The output will be to a speech synthesizer. Input will be from a small keyboard (all digits, a decimal point, the letters A – D, Y, and N, and an ENTER key). User will be asked which movie (theater A, B, C, or D) and how many adult and child tickets. The price will be calculated and payment asked for. User should key in the amount offered in payment (only honest patrons are allowed at this theater), and the machine will calculate and announce the change due. (At that point a cashier takes over and makes the change.) Movies in theaters A and B are $6 for adults and $4 for children. Movies in theaters C and D are $5 for adults and $2.50 for children. The program should continue until someone enters a 0 for the number of tickets desired. (This theater has a policy that all families must stick together, all tickets purchased together must be for the same theater.)

3. Design an interactive program that will take dinner reservations for a popular, and very high-tech, restaurant. Assume that an input file is available storing the count of any existing reservations. Reservations are only taken for 5:00, 6:00, 7:00, 8:00, 9:00, and 10:00 (six different times available per evening) and only 20 reservations are available for a given time. The program will read in from a disk file the six numbers representing the reservations already made for the available time slots. It will then continue, interactively, to take reservations. If a slot is available for the time requested, the counter for that time slot should be incremented and an appropriate message given. If a slot is not available, an alternate time should be suggested. Continue until all slots are full or the user indicates there are no more reservations to enter. After all reservations are taken, write the number of reservations for each time slot back to the disk file. Don't worry about saving names or numbers in dinner parties (that's too low-tech).

4. Convert the flowchart on the next page from an unstructured design to a structured design. (Your structured solution can be either flowchart or pseudocode.)

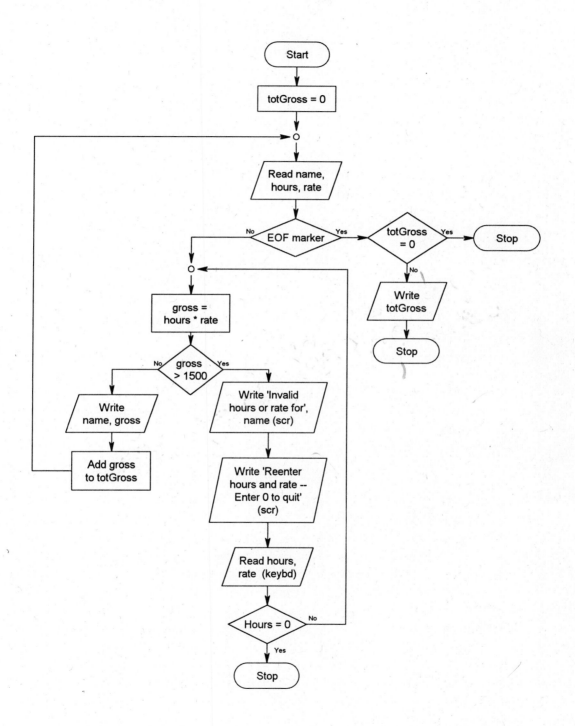

REVIEW B: Review Exercises for Chapters 5 through 7

1. Design a program that will print all even numbers from 2 to 250 along with their square and cube. The output should have a page heading, including page number, and column headings. Do not print beyond the 55th line of the page.

2. Change design # 1 so that it prints the page number on the 60th line of each page.

3. Design a program that reads and processes an entire student input file. Each record of the input file contains a name, SSN, major code (0 means no declared major, 1 means a major has been declared), GPA, and degree code (A = Associate Degree, B = Bachelor's Degree, N = No Degree status yet). The report should have one-inch top and bottom margins, report, page, and column headings and a detail line in the form shown below:

George Johnson	3.21	Has Major	Associate Degree
Muriel Templeton	2.99	No Major	No Degree

You may assume that the input file has been checked to ensure the major code has only a 0 or a 1 and the degree code has only A, B, or N.

4. Modify design # 3 so that only students with a declared major are printed out. At the end of the report print a count of the total number of students and a count of those students included in the report (those with a declared major). The totals should not be on a separate page (a page without detail lines) but may extend into the bottom margin if necessary. Headings and margins should remain the same.

5. Design an *interactive* program that will "interview" the student to see if he or she is ready to graduate. The program should ask the following questions and give appropriate responses as follows. A student who answers yes to all questions should be congratulated and directed to the counseling center to complete the graduate application process.

Total credits >= 120? --------no-------------> need to complete more classes

GPA >= 2.0? ------------no------------------> need to raise GPA

Signed off by faculty advisor? -----no-------> meet with advisor

All library fines paid? --------no-------------> go pay up

"Congratulations"

6. Design a program that reads and writes the *first* 400 students (names only) in the student file for your school. (You are assured that there are more than 400 students in the file.) The output should have a page heading and column headings on each page including the date of the close of registration (which is read in from a separate input file) and a report heading on the first page. The report should have a top margin of one inch and a bottom margin of one half inch. Detail lines (student names) should be double-spaced.

7. Modify design # 6 so that it now uses an input file holding name and credits for each student. Read the name and credits enrolled for each student and at the end write the total number of credits for the listing. The total line should *not* be on a page without detail lines and may not be written in the bottom margin. Headings and margins should remain the same, but you should now single space the detail lines.

8. Design a program that will count how many books the city public library has from a given publisher. The publisher whose books are to be counted will be read in from the user at the time of program execution. The input file holds title, author, and publisher for each book held in the library. The only output is the count of the books. It should be written to the user's screen.

9. Design a program that will create a grade report for an elementary school class. The program will use a disk file as input source for student names and will read an academic grade and a conduct grade interactively from the teacher. Output is a printed report that will include "reasonable" headings and margins.

10. Modify design # 9 so that the following information is entered by the teacher and included in the report headings: term and year for grades (e.g., Fall 1995) and class grade number (e.g., third grade).

Chapter 8
Single
Dimension Arrays

Objectives

After completing this chapter, you should be able to:

1. Define an array and describe the advantages of using an array.
2. Define a subscript.
3. Explain why an array *must* be declared prior to use.
4. Define "hard coding" an array.
5. Describe the differences between loading an array of known size and of unknown size.
6. Describe the differences between loading an array from a separate input file and from an input file that contains array data and other data.
7. Design a program that loads data into an array with known and/or unknown size from a separate and/or combined file.
8. Explain why the number of elements loaded into an array must be saved.
9. Design a program that writes the data from an array.
10. Define parallel arrays.
11. Design a program that loads data into parallel arrays.
12. Design a program that accesses data from parallel arrays.

INTRODUCTION

Single dimension arrays sounds pretty fancy. If you want to impress whoever asks you what you're studying right now, answer casually, "Oh, we're studying loading and processing single dimension arrays." But all we're really doing is looking at how we can store lists in the computer. List doesn't sound high-tech enough, so the computer lingo is "array." To a mathematician, "vector" would mean the same thing and sound more familiar. We'll continue to use array because you have to learn to speak the native language.

So what is an array? Our official definition is that an array is multiple values stored under a single name. So far, all of our variables have represented one location in memory: one name, storing one value. When we used those variables in a loop, we knew that loading a second value into the variable meant that we lost the first value—only one value was stored. But sometimes we have related values that we want to store as a group. Those values can be stored in an array and referred to by a single name.

Did you ever write a shopping list? Yes?—Good, then you have real life experience with an array! You might even have written up at the top "Grocery List;" that's the single name for the whole list. And the groceries that you intend to buy are the multiple values contained in the array. Each item in the list is one part of the array, and the items together make up the whole array. We could refer to the list as a whole ("Here's the grocery list") or to particular elements in the list ("You look for the last two items, I'll get the rest").

> Grocery List
> millk
> chocolate chips
> bread
> cereal
> raisins
> apples

Why do we need arrays (and we do need them)? Let's say we want to design a program that will read in 10 scores and write out the scores in reverse order. That doesn't sound too difficult, but how would you do it? We can't read the scores in a loop because when we repeat the read statement for the second score, we lose the first one. And we can't write out the first score until we have written out the tenth through the second scores. In other words, we need to save the first nine scores before we can write anything out. Without arrays, that would mean having 10 different variables (score1, score2, score3, etc.). We would have to read the 10 variables (READ score1, score2, score3, score4, etc.), and then we could write out the variables (WRITE score10, score9, score8, etc.). Yes, that will work, but what if we were doing the same thing with 100 scores? There has to be a better way, and arrays are it.

Since arrays can hold multiple values, we can set up an array to hold 10 scores, read the scores in from the top (the first score) to the bottom (the last score), and then write them out from the bottom up. The beauty of this is that since all the scores are stored under the same name, we can do the reading and writing in a loop. We'll come back to this in a bit.

Suppose someone put five different children's blocks in front of you and asked you to identify the one pointed to. That wouldn't be too difficult. Since the blocks are different, you could just say the "K block."

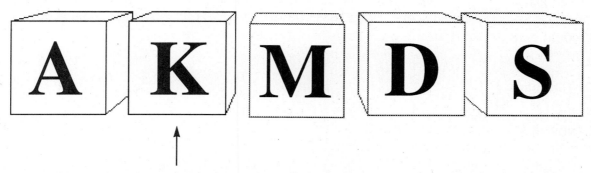

But what if the blocks all looked alike? Now you can't just say the "A block" because they are all A blocks. But you could define the block by its position, "the second block from the left."

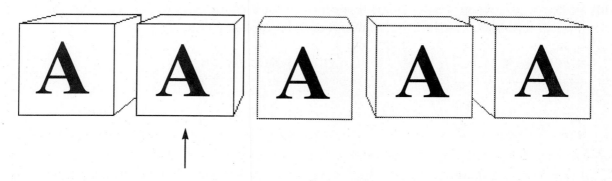

If you think of those blocks as a list, we are identifying the desired block by giving its location or position within the list: the second block. That's exactly how we deal with arrays. Since all the elements in the array have the same name, we identify a particular element by telling its position within the array. In our grocery list we could say "bread" is the third item in the list. In computer terms we would say Groceries(3), where the 3 in parenthesis is indicating the position of the desired element within the array Groceries. The 3 is a *subscript*, meaning a pointer to a particular element in an array by the element's position.

Subscripts can be "literal" numbers, like the 3 above. We could say names(4) meaning the fourth name in an array called NAMES. Subscripts can also be variables. Assume that *ptr* is a variable that holds a number. If we say WRITE names(ptr), we are saying to use the value stored in ptr to identify which name should be written. If ptr has a value of 3, the third name is written. If ptr has a value of 6, the sixth name is written. We could keep the exact same statement (WRITE names(ptr)) and be "pointing" to different names by changing the value of ptr.

Let's go back to our need to save those 10 scores and write them out in reverse order. We will use an array called scores and a subscript called ptr. Here is sample pseudocode that would read the 10 scores into the array.

```
ptr = 0
WHILE ptr < 10
    ADD 1 to ptr
    READ scores(ptr)
ENDWHILE
```

We use a count-controlled WHILE loop so that we "execute" the READ statement 10 times. Each time we execute it, ptr has a different value, so we're pointing to a different location in the array scores. Our read statement says: "Go to the input file, get the next value available, and store it in the array called scores in the position pointed to by ptr." As with all our reads, when we say READ scores(ptr), we are identifying where the input value should be stored *after* it is read, not where it is to be read from.

Input File	**Scores**

Input File	Scores
295	295
299	299
265	265
277	277
300	300
195	195
204	204
266	266
271	271
286	286
EOF marker	

Once we have the scores all stored in the array, we can easily write them out in reverse order:

```
ptr = 10
WHILE ptr > 0
    WRITE scores(ptr)
    SUBTRACT 1 from ptr
ENDWHILE
```

Some of you may be thinking that those loops look a lot longer than just doing

```
READ score1, score2, score3, score4, score5, score6, score7, score8, score9, score10
WRITE score10, score9, score8, score7, score6, score5, score4, score3, score2, score1
```

But how would we change the design to read/write 100 scores? If we used the individual names in the READ and WRITE statements, we would have to list 100 names in each statement. But if we used the count-controlled loops, we only need to change the number of times we go through the loops!

In this chapter and the next we will look at how to declare, load, write, access, and search single dimension arrays and single dimension arrays used in parallel. In a later chapter, we will look at how to do all those things with multidimension arrays.

DECLARING ARRAYS

Arrays must be declared prior to their use within a design or program. Until now we have just used variables and let the computer assume that if we were using the variable within the design/program, it must be a variable that needs to be stored. When we said something like count = 0, we were saying: "Set up a memory location that we can call count and put a value of 0 in that location." But we didn't "declare" the variable in advance. We never said anything like "I'm going to have the following variables in my program; get ready for them."

Why would we need to declare arrays? Remember that all our other variables just stored one value. There was no confusion: When we first used the variable name, the computer just grabbed a handy memory location and that was it. But with an array, we're storing multiple values. And not only that, we're assuming that those values are all stored together because we are referring to a particular value by giving its position within the list. That means the memory locations reserved for the array must be contiguous. The computer can't just grab whatever memory location is handy; it must have a memory location with enough free space after it to store the entire array. And, therefore, it must know how much free space the array will take up. We give it that warning by "declaring" the array. (Some programming languages do require us to declare *all* our variables, but most often the declaration is for the purpose of identifying the type of value the variable will hold, such as numeric or character.)

We'll just use the word DECLARE as a pseudocode statement, give the array name, and, in parenthesis, give the number of elements the array could or will have. In flowcharts we would use a process box or preparation symbol and put the declare statement within the box.

```
DECLARE scores(10)
```

What if we don't know how many elements will be in the array? We must set a maximum size. If we aren't sure how many items will be on the grocery list, but we know it will be less than 50, we can declare the array with a size of 50. The only problem with setting the size larger than we actually need is that we have reserved some memory space that we didn't use. But if we declare the array as smaller than we actually need, we will run out of room for the array and have to terminate the program.

LOADING ARRAYS

The simplest way to load an array is to "hard code" the values within the design/program. With hard coding, we actually include the values to be stored in the design itself. When we say count = 0, we are storing the value 0 in the memory location count. You will remember that we also looked at hard coding when we discussed parameter records. We could do the same thing with an array by including an assignment statement for each element within the array:

```
DECLARE rate(5)
rate(1) = 6.75
rate(2) = 7.25
rate(3) = 7.75
rate(4) = 8.50
rate(5) = 9.35
```

Hard coding means that our design does not have to go to an external data file to get the values for the array. If our values will not change, it is simplest to hard code the array in the program since otherwise our program has to read the data from the external file every time the program is run. For example, we could have an array that held the 12 names of the months. Probably those names won't change within the life of the computer program (or within our lives either for that matter). We can hard code the names into the array. Our

hard coding would look like the pseudocode on the left. The result in memory might look like the array on the right.

<table>
<tr><td>

PSEUDOCODE

DECLARE months (12)
months (1) = 'January'
months (2) = 'February'
months (3) = 'March
months (4) = 'April'
months (5) = 'May'
months (6) = 'June'
months (7) = 'July'
months (8) = 'August'
months (9) = 'September'
months (10) = 'October'
months (11) = 'November'
months (12) = 'December'

</td><td>

MEMORY
months

months
January
February
March
April
May
June
July
August
September
October
November
December

</td></tr>
</table>

Array values that aren't going to change can be hard coded. But if the values *are* going to change frequently, we would need to edit and recompile the program source code every time we needed to change one of the array values. For arrays with changing values, it is much easier to read the values in from an external data file since it is easier to change the values in an input file than to change the code in a program and recompile the program. The way in which we load the values will vary depending on two questions: (1) Do we know how many values there will be? and (2) What is the source of the values? Let's look at both of these questions.

In the example we already looked at (reading and writing the 10 scores), we knew that there would be 10 scores. When we wrote the loop to read the scores, we could write the loop as a count-controlled loop. Sometimes, we only know the maximum possible number of elements, but we don't know exactly how many elements there will be. We might be reading the names of the students present in a class into an array. We know that the class has an enrollment of 25, but we don't know if everyone will be present at that particular class. So we can declare our array to hold 25 elements, but how will we control the loop?

133

```
READ class(ptr)
    READ code
ENDWHILE
numClass = ptr
```

This option leads to another complexity. When we read the first record that is not a record code of 1, what is it? Well, presumably it's the record code for the first detail record! So by the time we exit from the loop to load the array, we have already read the

135

If we do the loop 25 times and not everyone is present, we will run out of input data before we finish the loop. Usually, we can just do the loop until we see the end-of-file marker. Of course, that could lead to another problem. What if one student, for some strange and inexplicable reason, has brought 5 guests to the class? We might run out of space in the array before we see the end-of-file marker! If there is any possibility of exceeding the array limits, our loop has to have two conditions to check: the first, to make sure there are data to store and the second, to make sure there is room to store it.

record code for the first detail record. All the designs we have done so far read an entire line of input in one read. Most programming languages allow us to read part of a line in one read statement and the rest of the line in a separate read statement. We have avoided the question to avoid the details of specific languages, but some design solutions almost require that we read a single line in two separate reads. This is one of those cases.

There is a third option for the source of the input values. We've looked at a separate file as source and a file combining the array values with the detail records. We could also read the array values in from the computer operator. That part of our program would then become an interactive program, communicating with the operator:

```
DECLARE class(25)
ptr = 0
continue = 'yes'
WHILE continue = 'yes' AND ptr < 25
    ADD 1 to ptr
    WRITE 'Please enter name #', ptr
    READ class(ptr)
    WRITE 'Do you have another name to enter? '
    REPEAT
        WRITE "Enter 'Y' for yes, 'N' for no"
        READ resp
    UNTIL resp = 'Y' 'y', 'N', OR 'n'
    IF resp = 'N' OR 'n'
        continue = 'no'
    ENDIF
ENDWHILE
numClass = ptr
```

This design looks much more complicated, but most of it just handles the communication with the operator. The first write (WRITE 'Please enter name #', ptr) is a prompt asking for the operator to enter a name and using the ptr as a numbering variable. After reading and storing a name, the design asks the operator if there is another name. An UNTIL loop checks to be sure the operator has entered a valid response to the prompt (it accepts upper-case or lowercase letters). If the operator entered N or n, the flag, continue, is changed to 'no.' Continue controls the loop to load the array.

Let's try to organize all of this. We have three different sources for the array data: a separate file, a combined file, or the operator. We may or may not know how many input values will be given. If we are sure that we know exactly how many elements will be loaded in the array, we can (and should) load with a count-controlled loop. If we don't know the number of elements, we must use a loop testing another condition: sentinel value, record code (which is really a variation of a sentinel value), end-of-file, or operator response to a prompt. We must also remember to be sure we don't exceed the size of the array and to save the count of array positions actually used. We can summarize these points in the following chart.

Source	Number of values known	Number of values not known
Combined file	Count loop	Loop controlled by sentinel value or record code Check for full array Save length of array
Separate file	Count loop	Loop controlled by end-of-file marker Check for full array Save length of array
Operator	Count loop	Loop controlled by operator response to prompt Check for full array Save length of array

WRITING ARRAYS

Writing arrays is a lot like loading arrays, but much easier. Why is it easier?—Because you already know how many elements are in the array (assuming you remembered to save the length when you loaded it)! Writing can always be done with a count-controlled loop. Remember, the declared length does not control the writing loop. It is the actual length, how many elements are really stored in the array, that controls the writing. We don't want to try to write more elements than we actually have.

Assume we have an array named *courses* that we declared with a length of 50. We loaded the values from a separate input file, so we used an end-of-file check and saved the number of elements in the variable numCrs. Here's what both the load and the write segments would look like:

```
LoadArray
ptr = 0
WHILE there are data AND ptr < 50
    ADD 1 to ptr
    READ courses(ptr)
ENDWHILE
numCrs = ptr
```

```
WriteArray
ptr = 0
WHILE ptr < cumCrs
    ADD 1 to ptr
    WRITE courses(ptr)
ENDWHILE
```

That writes out the entire array (or at least that part of the array that has data). Can we write out just part of the loaded array? Sure, if we want to write out the first 10 courses in the array, we just change the loop control on the write loop from WHILE ptr < numCrs to WHILE ptr < 10. What if we want to write out the 11th through the 20th courses? We would initialize ptr to 10 (one less than the first one to be written) and use 20 to control the loop:

```
ptr = 10
WHILE ptr < 20
    ADD 1 to ptr
    WRITE courses(ptr)
ENDWHILE
```

Could we write out just the even numbered courses (2, 4, 6, etc.)? Just add 2 to ptr instead of adding 1!

ACCESSING ARRAYS

In reality, everything we've done so far has been accessing the arrays. We certainly accessed the array elements to write them. But how would we access a particular element in the array? Suppose we had our array of courses, and we wanted to write out the name of the ninth course.

```
WRITE courses(9)
```

OK, that was too easy. Suppose we wanted to be able to read in the position of the element to be written?

```
READ ptr
WRITE courses(ptr)
```

I know, that was easy too. The point is that if you understand the concept of arrays, accessing them *is* easy.

PARALLEL ARRAYS

Frequently, we want to store more than one piece of information about each element in our list. Even for our class list, we might have a second value for each person (like a GPA). Our array can only store one value in each slot. We can't squeeze in both a name and a GPA. And, even if we could, that would be two different kinds of information. The array cannot hold both character data (like names) and numeric data (like GPAs). Our solution is to make two arrays. One array will continue to hold the names, and the other array will hold the GPAs. But how can we make sure that we will know which GPA goes with which name? We set up the arrays so that the first element in one array goes with the first element in the other array, the second goes with the second, and so on. If we know that Robert is the 5th person in the name array, we also know that his GPA will be in the 5th position in the GPA array.

NAMES		GPA
Ted	←——————→	3.21
Sam		2.25
Harvey		3.72
Carole		2.10
Robert		2.89
Marilyn		3.91
Quentin		1.00
Denise		2.55
Betty Lou		4.00
Walter		1.78

These are called parallel arrays. They are completely separate arrays which are *logically* related and which we maintain so that they are always related. If we add a value to one array, we must add the related value to the other array in the same position. If we delete a value from one array, we must delete the related value from the other array. Parallel arrays will be very important to us when we get into array searching.

EXAMPLES

We want to design a program that will have an array holding the 12 names of the months. We will then use the array in our processing loop to convert a date from the form 2/12/95 to the form February 12, 1995. For simplicity, our design will assume that all dates have a valid day number and have a year in the 1900s.

```
Mainline
DECLARE months(12)
DO StartUp
WHILE there are data
    DO Process
ENDWHILE
CLOSE files

StartUp
OPEN files
months(1) = 'January'
months(2) = 'February'
months(3) = 'March'
months(4) = 'April'
months(5) = 'May'
months(6) = 'June'
months(7) = 'July'
months(8) = 'August'
months(9) = 'September'
months(10) = 'October'
months(11) = 'November'
months(12) = 'December'

Process
READ mon,day,year
WRITE months(mon), day, ', 19', year
```

The array values are hard coded because we know they won't change. This array is also a good example of a *positional array*, meaning that a value's *position* in the array communicates some meaning. In this array, the position in the array corresponds to the month's position in the calendar year; the third month is in position 3 in the array. The next chapter will look at positional arrays again.

Another example. We want to design a program that will access part names and prices for the cashier in our store. We will use two parallel arrays: one to hold the part names and the other to hold the prices. Each item that we sell is marked with a part number that (coincidentally) is also the position of that part within the parallel arrays (another positional array). Assume we have a maximum of 100 items for sale in our store. We will load the arrays from a separate data file that has a part name then a price for each item. Our input file looks something like the following file:

chocolate sauce	1.49
vanilla ice cream	2.25
yucky white bread	.99
whole wheat bread	.99
.	
.	
chicken legs	4.37
(end-of-file marker)	

The pseudocode to implement the task is below:

```
Mainline
DECLARE names(100), prices(100)
DO StartUp
WHILE there are data
    DO Process
ENDWHILE
CLOSE files

StartUp
OPEN files
ptr = 0
WHILE there are data (array file) AND ptr < 100
    ADD 1 to ptr
    READ names(ptr), prices(ptr)  (array file)
ENDWHILE
IF there are data (array file)
    WRITE 'ERROR -- more than 100 items in input file'
ENDIF
numItems = ptr

Process
READ partNum
WRITE names(partNum), prices(partNum)
```

Obviously, for these programs, the complex part is loading the array. Accessing the information in the array is easy. Don't get too contented. In the next chapter we'll access the information by using a search to locate the desired values. Notice the check in StartUp to see if the array is full before the entire input file has been processed. If there are still data in the input file after the loading loop, it means the loop was exited because the array was full (ptr = 100). We write an error message as a warning that the input file contained more items than expected and, therefore, not all data are loaded into the array.

EXERCISES

1. Write the portion of a StartUp module needed to load two parallel arrays, one with the names of the 50 states and one with the two-letter abbreviations for the 50 states. You may assume that the data file has a name and abbreviation in each record and that it has exactly 50 records.

2. Design a program that will test dates by making sure that the day number given within the date is a valid date. Prior to any checking, you should hardcode an array with the number of days in each month from January to December (31, 29, 31, 30, etc.). In your loop, read in a date in the form 3/5/90. Compare the date's day to the maximum number of days for that month and write out a message stating if the date value is legal or illegal.

3. Write the portion of a StartUp module needed to load student names into an array named Students. The maximum number of students is 3000, but the exact number is not known. Input data are in a separate file.

4. Modify design # 3 above so that the input data come from a combined file. Array values are separated from detail records by a sentinel value of 'NotAName.'

5. Modify design # 3 again. This time the file includes the students' GPAs and telephone numbers in addition to their names. The file has all the data for one student on a line (name, GPA, phone). You should load the data into parallel arrays.

6. Assume that the arrays you loaded in design # 5 are positional based on a student ID number. Add a module to your design that will read in a student ID and write out the name, GPA, and phone number for that student.

Chapter 9
Searching Arrays

Objectives

After completing this chapter, you should be able to:

1. Describe the process for searching ordered and unordered lists.
2. Describe the algorithms for the main search types (sequential, sequential with early exit, and binary) and tell when each is most appropriate.
3. List the conditions for stopping a search for the three main search types.
4. Design at least one search algorithm in each of the search types.
5. Given an array description, identify the most appropriate search type to use.
6. Given a need for information and an array description, determine if a search is needed and, if so, identify the most appropriate search type.

INTRODUCTION

If we were only going to use arrays as we used them in the last chapter, we wouldn't be gaining much. Our real advantage with arrays comes from the ability to search through the array for a particular value. Since we have one name for the entire array, we can write a very efficient search using a loop and varying only the subscript value. Searching is the most common use of an array in the data processing world.

Sometimes in a search we are simply trying to find out if a given value is included in the array. Given an array holding the names of those present in class, we might ask if John Jones attended class. At other times, we want to know where in the list the value occurs. When we are using parallel arrays, it is common to search one list to locate the position and then use that position (subscript) to access the needed value in the parallel array. If we have two parallel arrays, one holding sales item names and the other the price of each item, we might search the name array looking for the position of a particular item. Once we know the position of the item's name, we also know the position of the item's price, and we can use the subscript to access the price.

With either type of search, we are using essentially the same process. We have a variable that holds our key value: the value for which we are searching in the array. One at a time, we compare the value of the key variable with the values stored in the array. When we have a match, we know the item is in the array and we know its position. Remember that we are not comparing the *subscript* to the stored values or to the key value. The subscript is simply a pointer to the stored values telling us the *position* of the value within the array. The order in which we compare the values and how we know when to stop searching are the points that separate one search type from another.

SEARCH TYPES

The actual method we use for searching depends on how the values are ordered within the array. We will look at four ways to order the data and the search type or types that should be used with that order. If we don't know the order, we must assume that there is no order.

NO ORDER—Naturally, the data will have an order, but it might not be a meaningful order for a search. Names may be in the list in the order in which the people arrived. That doesn't help us much with a search. Even if we know that John Jones is usually early, we can't assume he'll be at the top of the list. He could have arrived late for this meeting. If we have no usable order, we must search the array from one end to the other. This is a **Sequential Search**. Usually we start at the beginning (subscript of 1) of the array and search toward the end of the array, but we could start at the end and work back toward the beginning. When do we stop searching? We certainly stop when we have found a match. But if we never find a match, we continue to search as long as there is something left in the array to check. Remember that when we loaded the array, we saved the count of the number of elements that we loaded. That was so we would know when to stop searching.

Data Order	Search Type	When to End Search
No Order	Sequential	1. When match is found 2. When entire array is searched

With the data at the right, if we were searching for the number 23, we would find it almost immediately. But if we were searching for the number 5, we would have to search down to the last value in the array before we found a match. And if we were searching for 16, we would have to check every element in the array before we could know that there is not a 16 in the array.

23
13
2
81
14
5

SEQUENTIAL ORDER—It seems logical that sequential order would call for a sequential search, but don't be too hasty. If our data are in sequential order, we have a lot more information. Assume that we are searching the list at the right for the value 16. We certainly can do a sequential search down through the first three items (2, 5, and 14). But what happens when we get to the fourth item (18)? Since we know that the values are in order, and we know that 18 is larger than the value we are searching for, we also know that our value (16) is not going to be in the list. If it were in the array, it would be *before* the 18. So with sequential data, we can go one step further, what we'll call a **Sequential Search with Early Exit**. We *may not* have to search the entire array. When we pass the position where the value would be, we can stop the search. Does that mean we never have to search the entire array? Suppose we're searching for the value 99. Will we ever pass the position where the 99 would be? No. When the value would occur (or does occur) at the end of the array, we still need to search to the end.

2
5
14
18
31
42
49
58

Data Order	Search Type	When to End Search
No Order	Sequential	1. When match is found 2. When entire array is searched
Sequential	Seq. w/ Early Exit	1. When match is found 2. When sequence indicates value cannot be there 3. When entire array is searched

There is a second type of search that we could use with sequentially ordered arrays: the **Binary Search**. The binary search is a much more efficient search because for each comparison to a value in the array it asks two questions: Is this the item we're searching for? and, if not, Is the item before or after this point in the array? We can determine if it is before or after because the data are sequentially ordered. If we start the search by comparing our key (desired) item to the middle value in the array, we will either find a match or limit the array left to be searched by 50 percent. Each check divides the remaining array in half. We'll look at the details later. Even though the binary search is very efficient, it requires extra processing for each search, so it is usually used only if there are over 50 elements in the array to be searched. We stop the search if we find a match. But what if we don't find a match? As we will see when we look at the search algorithm, because of the sequence of the data we will be able to prove that the match isn't present.

POSITIONAL ORDER—In the last chapter we looked at an array holding the names of the months used in a program to convert a numeric date form to a text date form (p. 140). But we didn't do any searching! Why didn't we have to search? Because we already knew where the month name that we needed would be. Our array was ordered so that each element was in a "meaningful" position: The first month was in position 1, the second month in position 2, and so on. So when we read in a month value of 7, we knew exactly where it was: in the seventh position. In fact, we used the input month value as the subscript for the array access. With positional arrays, we usually don't have any search. It is possible to conceive of an access to a positional array that would require a search (for example, a check to see if "February" is in the array). In such cases, we use a sequential search.

Data Order	Search Type	When to End Search
No Order	Sequential	1. When match is found 2. When entire array is searched
Sequential	Seq. w/ Early Exit	1. When match is found 2. When sequence indicates value cannot be there. 3. When entire array is searched
Sequential	Binary	1. When match is found 2. When proved value is not there
Positional	None	N/A

SEARCH ALGORITHMS

Let's go back and look at how we could implement each of the search types we have discussed. For each we will assume that we have two parallel arrays: one holding student names (nameList) and the other holding grade point averages (gpaList). Both have been declared with a length of 50, but the number of values actually loaded is stored in numNames. We will read a key name into the field nameIn and search the nameList array for a match. If we have a match, we will write out the GPA from the parallel array. If we cannot find a match, we will write out a message that the student is not in the array.

SEQUENTIAL SEARCH—Remember we have two reasons to stop our search: We have a match (the search is successful) or we have searched the entire array without a match (the search is unsuccessful). Our loop conditions must reflect those two reasons. This design uses a flag (searching) to help control the loop. Searching will be 'Yes' if we haven't found a match. It will be changed to 'Found' if we find a match.

```
    searching = 'Yes'
    READ namein
    ptr = 0
    WHILE ptr < numNames AND searching = 'Yes'
        ADD 1 to ptr
        IF namein = nameList(ptr)                    Sequential Search
            searching = 'Found'                      Method #1
        ENDIF
    ENDWHILE
    IF searching = 'Found'
        WRITE gpaList(ptr)
    ELSE
        WRITE 'Name not found in list'
    ENDIF
```

We can extend the use of the searching flag so that our WHILE condition is simplified but the flag has three possible values: 'Yes' means we are still in the midst of a search; 'Found' means that we have found a match and should exit the search; 'No' means that we have searched the entire array without a match.

```
    searching = 'Yes'
    READ namein
    ptr = 0
    WHILE searching = 'Yes'
        ADD 1 to ptr
        IF nameList(ptr) = namein                    Sequential Search
            searching = 'Found'                      Method #2
        ELSE
            IF ptr = numNames
                searching = 'No'
            ENDIF
        ENDIF
    ENDWHILE
    IF searching = 'Found'
        WRITE gpaList(ptr)
    ELSE
        WRITE 'Name not found in list'
    ENDIF
```

Notice that in the above design, we compare the "ptr-ith" value in nameList to nameIn to see if we have a match, *and* we compare the value of ptr itself to numNames to see if we're at the end of our array. Don't get these two comparisons confused. Would it make any sense to compare ptr to nameIn or ptr to nameList(ptr)? No, in each case it would mean comparing a name with a numeric value used as a subscript. Notice also the order of the comparisons. We compare the ptr-ith value in nameList to nameIn *first*, and only if we don't have a match do we test the value of ptr to see if we have searched the entire array. If we switched the order of the tests, we wouldn't check the last element in the array.

We'll look at one more variation of this sequential search. This one is the shortest, but perhaps least easily followed. It does not use a flag, so it saves the lines needed to set the flag and puts the complete "burden" for testing for the match in the WHILE condition.

```
ptr = 1
READ nameIn
WHILE ptr < numNames AND nameIn < > nameList(ptr)
      ADD 1 to ptr
ENDWHILE
IF nameIn = nameList(ptr)
      WRITE gpaList(ptr)
ELSE
      WRITE 'Name not found in list'
ENDIF
```

Sequential Search Method #3

The loop in this design is much shorter, but notice that when we exit the loop, there is no flag to identify why we exited. Therefore, we must again check to see if we have found a match. Notice that we initialize ptr to 1, instead of 0. If we initialize ptr to 0, the first time we check the loop conditions we will be testing nameList(0), a position outside the array boundaries.

Each of the above designs is workable and there are other possible variations. It is not necessary for you to be able to design 10 slightly different sequential searches. Get one down well and stick with it.

SEQUENTIAL SEARCH WITH EARLY EXIT—This search is very much like our plain vanilla sequential search except that we add one more condition for exiting the loop. Assuming our array values are in ascending order, if our subscript is currently pointing to a value that is greater than the key value (the value we are searching for), we know that the key value will not be in the array.

Our first design is a revision of the first sequential search design—adding one more test in the loop that changes the value of our flag, searching.

```
searching = 'yes'
READ nameIn
ptr = 0
WHILE ptr < numNames AND searching = 'yes'
    ADD 1 to ptr
    IF nameList(ptr) = nameIn
        searching = 'found'
    ELSE
        IF nameList(ptr) > nameIn
            searching = 'stop'
        ENDIF
    ENDIF
ENDWHILE
IF searching = 'found'
    WRITE gpaList(ptr)
ELSE
    WRITE 'Name not found in list'
ENDIF
```

**Sequential Search
with Early Exit
Method #1**

The next design is the sequential search with early exit version of the second sequential search given, in which the loop condition tests only the value of the flag, searching.

```
ptr = 0
searching = 'Yes'
READ nameIn
WHILE searching = 'Yes'
    ADD 1 to ptr
    IF nameList(ptr) = nameIn
        searching = 'Found'
    ELSE
        IF nameList(ptr) > nameIn
            searching = 'No'
        ELSE
            IF ptr = numNames
                searching = 'No'
            ENDIF
        ENDIF
    ENDIF
ENDWHILE
IF searching = 'Found'
    WRITE gpaList(ptr)
ELSE
    WRITE 'Name not found in list'
ENDIF
```

**Sequential Search
with Early Exit
Method #2**

Our final sequential search with early exit design is a revision of the third sequential design given above. This one puts most of the test responsibility in the WHILE condition.

```
ptr = 1
READ nameIn
WHILE ptr < numNames AND nameList(ptr) < nameIn
    ADD 1 to ptr
ENDWHILE
IF nameList(ptr) = nameIn
    WRITE gpaList(ptr)
ELSE
    WRITE 'Name not found in list'
ENDIF
```

**Sequential Search
with Early Exit
Method #3**

The WHILE condition here is a little tricky. If nameList(ptr) is equal to nameIn, our search is successful and we should exit the loop. If nameList(ptr) is greater than nameIn, we know our value is not in the array because we have passed the position where it would be stored, so we should exit the loop. Only if nameList(ptr) is less than nameIn should we stay in the loop. But we still have to do some checking after we exit the loop to determine why we exited. We might have exited because we found a match. We might have exited because we discovered the value could not be in the list. We might have exited because we checked the entire array. We must test again to see if nameList(ptr) is equal to nameIn before we can write the output line.

These designs work equally well. Your choice.

BINARY SEARCH—Our final search type is the binary search which is built on the "divide and conquer" theme. Instead of checking the elements in the array one by one, the binary search checks to see if the key value would be in the top half or the bottom half of the array. In one check, the binary search reduces the portion of the array to be searched by half! (With our sequential searches, one check reduced the portion to be searched by only one position.) By applying the same logic to the portion that remains to be checked, the search range is repeatedly cut in half, until we either have a match or have nothing left to halve. Remember, the binary search can *only* be done with an array that is sequentially ordered. Otherwise, we could not tell if the value would be in the top or bottom half.

The search first finds the middle element (the value in the middle position) and tests to see if that is a match with the key. If it isn't, the search determines if the key value would be in the top or bottom half. Using whichever half is identified, it again finds the middle element (this time of only half) and tests to see if that is a match. This cycle continues. Let's look at the design.

```
lowPtr = 1
highPtr = numNames
READ nameIn
search = 'Yes'
WHILE lowPtr < = highPtr AND search = 'Yes'
    midPtr = (lowPtr + highPtr) / 2
    IF nameList(midPtr) = nameIn
        search = 'Found'
    ELSE
        IF nameList(midPtr) < nameIn
            lowPtr = midPtr + 1
        ELSE
            highPtr = midPtr - 1
        ENDIF
    ENDIF
ENDWHILE
IF search = 'Found'
    WRITE gpaList(midPtr)
ELSE
    WRITE 'Name not found in list'
ENDIF
```

Binary Search

This design might look longer, but actually it is much shorter and faster than a sequential search or even a sequential search with early exit. The reason is that the loop will not have to be repeated nearly as many times. If we are sequentially searching an array of 1000 elements, we might have to do 1000 accesses to the array, meaning 1000 times through the loop to determine the value isn't in the array. Our average number with a sequential search would be 500 times through the loop. With a sequential search with early exit, we might still have to go through the loop 1000 times to determine that the value isn't there. Our average would be somewhat better that 500 times but still not great. With the binary search, however, our absolute worst situation would not take more than 10 times through the loop. The first check reduces the range to test to 500 elements, the second check takes it down to 250, the third to 125, the fourth to 62, the fifth to 31, the sixth to 15, the seventh to 7, the eighth to 3, the ninth tests the middle of those three, and we are down to one possible position left for the tenth test.

And what if we double the number of elements in the array to 2000? With the sequential and sequential with early exit, our worst case scenario would also be doubled: up to 2000 times through the loop. But with the binary search, we just add one: up to 11 times through the loop. After the first access we have cut the array in half, and we're back to the 10 accesses for an array of 1000 elements.

Notice that the loop condition test includes WHILE lowPtr < = highPtr. Certainly when the search begins, lowPtr will be less than highPtr, but why use this condition to control whether we enter the loop? Each time through the loop we change the value of either lowPtr or highPtr (assuming we haven't found our match). These two values get closer and closer as we narrow the range of the array left to be searched. If we never find a match, the values not only get closer, they cross! If the highPtr is less than the lowPtr, we know that there is no range in the array left to be searched.

The only problem with the binary search is that the search itself requires extra variables (lowPtr, highPtr, midPtr) and calculations (finding the midPtr, checking for which half). For small arrays, the extra variables and calculations actually slow the search down enough so that a sequential search is faster. Most people recommend a cutoff of 50 elements. If the array has fewer than 50 elements, use a sequential search with early exit.

EXAMPLE

We have designed a program for We Fly 'Em Airlines. The program will read in a city name and write out the fare for a flight from Washington Dulles International Airport to that city and the in-flight time for the flight. In order to complete that task, we will need to load three parallel arrays: city, fare, flight time in minutes. Our array input comes from a separate file containing at least 100 records (each record holds city, fare, and flight time), but not more than 500 records. There are two additional tasks for the program. Airline prices fluctuate dramatically, and We Fly 'Em never wants to be too much lower than the competition. So the program first needs to read in (from the operator) a minimum fare level. Then after loading our three arrays, we will check each fare and increase any fare that is below the minimum so that it is set to the minimum fare. Second, after the loop we should write out all the arrays as a separate report (since we may have changed the fare values). Our pseudocode solution is shown below and on the next pages.

```
Mainline
DECLARE city(500), fare(500), time(500)
DO StartUp
WHILE there are data
    DO Process
ENDWHILE
DO Finish
```

155

StartUp
OPEN files
ptr = 0
WHILE there are data (array file) AND ptr < 500
    DO LoadArray
ENDWHILE
IF there are data   (array file)
    WRITE 'More array records in input file than expected'
    WRITE 'Output from program is suspect'
ENDIF
flightCnt = ptr
REPEAT
    WRITE 'Please enter new minimum fare level' (to screen)
    READ fareMin (from keybrd)
    WRITE 'You have entered ', fareMin, '. Is that correct? Y or N?' (to screen)
    READ resp
UNTIL resp = 'Y' or 'y'
ptr = 0
WHILE ptr < flightCnt
    DO RaiseFare
ENDWHILE

Process
READ cityIn
lowPtr = 1
highPtr = flightCnt
search = 'Yes'
WHILE lowPtr < = highPtr AND search = 'Yes'
    midPtr = (lowPtr + highPtr) / 2
    IF city(midPtr) = cityIn
        search = 'Found'
    ELSE
        IF cityIn > city(midPtr)
            lowPtr = midPtr + 1
        ELSE
            highPtr = midPtr - 1
        ENDIF
    ENDIF
ENDWHILE
IF search = 'Found'
    WRITE cityIn, fare(midPtr), time(midPtr)
ELSE
    WRITE 'Sorry, We Fly 'Em does not fly to ', cityIn
ENDIF

```
Finish
lineCnt = 55
ptr = 0
WHILE ptr < flightCnt
    ADD 1 to ptr
    IF lineCnt > = 55
        EJECT Page
        SKIP 6 lines
        WRITE page heading
        WRITE column heading (dbl spc)
        SKIP 1 line
        lineCnt = 0
    ENDIF
    WRITE city(ptr), fare(ptr), time(ptr)
    ADD 1 to lineCnt
ENDWHILE
CLOSE files


LoadArray
ADD 1 to ptr
READ city(ptr), fare(ptr), time(ptr)  (array file)


RaiseFare
ADD 1 to ptr
IF fare(ptr) < fareMin
    fare(ptr) = fareMin
ENDIF
```

EXERCISES

1. Given the arrays loaded in the example program on the previous pages, write a module to read in a flight time and write out all the cities that could be reached in that length of time or less.

2. Rewrite the example program using the assumption that there are a maximum of 40 flights in the input array file.

3. Design a program to test the membership applications for the DIP Club. There are two criteria for membership: First, the applicant *must not* have the same first name as any current member in the Club and second, the applicant *must have* the same telephone exchange (first three numbers) as at least one current member in the Club. The input file to be processed contains the first name and telephone exchange of all applicants. You should write a message for each applicant telling if the application is accepted. A separate data file contains the first names of all the current members (less than 50 members) in alphabetic (sequential) order. The end of the names is marked by the sentinel value 'STOP.' After all of the names (and the 'STOP'), but still in the same file, are all the telephone exchanges of the current members (in no particular order). You may assume that no two applicants have the same first name.

4. A large hotel uses parallel arrays to help in scheduling its conference rooms. A total of four arrays are used: **Room** (the name of the room), **Max** (the maximum occupancy for the room), **AV** ('yes' if the room has audio-visual connections and 'no' if it does not), **Food** ('yes' if the room is connected to the kitchen for food service and 'no' if not). The data file from which the arrays are loaded has all the data for one room together and the rooms ordered by room number. For example:

201	30	yes	yes
205	45	yes	no
209	75	no	yes
333	20	yes	no
335	20	yes	no

A. Design a program to load the arrays and then write out a report (with reasonable headings and margins) of the input (array) data. The hotel has a total of 35 conference rooms.

B. Modify the design so that after the arrays are loaded, a room number can be read in (interactively) and the maximum occupancy and the availability of A-V connections can be displayed on the screen. Do not include the report to write out all the array data.

C. Modify the design so that after you load the arrays you can read in (interactively) the number of seats required and whether you need food service, and then create a list of all the rooms that could be used.

D. Assume that the hotel had a total of 100 conference rooms. How would that increase change your designs for steps B and C?

Chapter 10
More IFs
Plus Extracts

Objectives

After completing this chapter, you should be able to:

1. Explain the meaning and use of the logical operators AND, OR, and NOT.
2. Convert IF statements using AND and OR into nested IFs.
3. Convert nested IFs into IF statements using AND and OR.
4. Structure AND/OR nested IFs so that they will be most efficient.
5. Convert a nested IF into an IF-ELSE IF structure and into a CASE structure.
6. Describe the design impact of having two output files in a program.
7. Define an extract program.
8. Design an extract program that selects records according to specifications using AND and OR logic.
9. Design an extract program that selects records according to specifications and provides a count of the number of records selected and the number not selected.

NOT IFs AGAIN!

Logical Operators

We have already studied IF statements, but there are more details that we have to add to the picture. We know that a nested IF is one IF structure contained within the true portion or the false portion of an "outer" IF structure. Now it's time to refine our understanding of nested IFs and look at a few variations.

We have used the term "condition" to mean that part of the statement following the IF, WHILE, or UNTIL. The condition is the expression that will be evaluated resulting in a true or false value. For the most part, our conditions have been made up of single logical expressions. If we can think of (8 * 5) as an arithmetic expression, we should be able to think of (A > B) as a logical expression. And those single logical expressions have been our conditions. We know that we can take multiple arithmetic expressions and combine them into larger expressions, something like (8 * 5) + (6 * 4). The + symbol here is an arithmetic operator that combines the two arithmetic expressions. The result of the total expression is the sum of the two smaller arithmetic expressions. We can also use an arithmetic operator to "modify" the result of an arithmetic expression. Adding a minus sign before an expression reverses the sign of the result of the expression, as in –(8 * 5). The minus or negative sign is still an arithmetic operator, but it is used to modify the expression rather than to combine two expressions.

We can combine and modify logical expressions in the same way by using *logical operators*. Our first logical operator modifies the result of a logical expression. If we precede the expression with NOT, we are saying the result of the expression should be reversed. Remember that logical expressions can only have one of two results: true or false (yes or no). Reversing a result simply means that a true becomes false. If we had a test IF Name = 'Harold', the test would be true for anyone with a name of Harold and false for everyone else. If we add the logical operator NOT before the expression IF NOT (Name = 'Harold'), we reverse the results. Now the condition will be false for anyone named Harold and true for everyone else, or the equivalent of IF Name < > 'Harold' where < > means "not equal."

If we have the test IF A > = B, we could make a logically equivalent test by using IF NOT (A < B). The way in which you write the condition depends on how it will "read" best. Perhaps we've been brainwashed into the power of positive thinking, but most of us have trouble following logic peppered with NOTs. Use them sparingly, but on occasion they will be important.

Our other two logical operators are used to combine logical expressions. Suppose we want to write headings only if two conditions are both true: The current page is full and the flag moreData has a value of 'yes.' We can write this in an IF statement using the logical operator AND: IF lineCnt > = 50 AND moreData = 'yes'. The AND operator says that the combined condition is true only if *both* of the individual expressions are true. We can show this in a "truth table" of the expression.

lineCnt > = 50	moreData = 'yes'	lineCnt > = 50 AND moreData = 'yes'
true	true	true
true	false	false
false	true	false
false	false	false

We can see that there are four possible combinations of the two conditions (since each condition has two possible values, true or false). But of the four combinations, only one will result in a TRUE. Only if both conditions are true will the combined expression lineCnt > = 50 AND moreData = 'yes' be true.

Our combined expression is really just taking two logical conditions and joining them, so it makes sense that we could consider them as separate conditions and come up with an equivalent nested IF structure. To convert an AND expression into a nested IF, we must remember that we want both conditions to be true for the action to be taken. Therefore, the second IF should be nested in the true portion of the first IF.

Using the AND operator we have

```
IF lineCnt > = 50 AND moreData = 'yes'
    DO Heads
ENDIF
```

Converting that into a nested IF structure, we get

```
IF lineCnt > = 50
    IF moreData = 'yes'
        DO Heads
    ENDIF
ENDIF
```

Which is better? There's no simple answer to that question. Sometimes we *must* use the nested IF structure because we must not check the second condition until we know the first condition is true. Sometimes it's our choice. In this text, we will use primarily the nested IF structure because it is clearer and easier to desk check. However, in conditions used in WHILE or UNTIL loops, we have no choice. If we need to test two conditions for the same loop, we must use the combined test. For example:

```
ptr = 0
WHILE there are data AND ptr < 20
    ADD 1 to ptr
    READ name(ptr)
ENDWHILE
```

We execute the above loop a maximum of 20 times, but we have fewer than 20 iterations if we run out of input data first. Compare this loop to the one that follows.

```
WHILE there are data
    ptr = 0
    WHILE ptr < 20                    WARNING: Don't follow this example!
        ADD 1 to ptr
        READ name(ptr)
    ENDWHILE
ENDWHILE
```

With this design we have two loops. We will do the inner loop 20 times (regardless of the data file), then exit to the outer loop test. If, by chance, there are still data, we will go back to the inner loop again for another 20 iterations!

Our final logical operator is also used to combine logical expressions. Let's vary our expression a bit. We still want to write headings if the current page is full, but we have another reason to write them: if the current page is the first page. We want to write headings if *either* condition is true. For this we use the OR logical operator: IF lineCnt > = 50 OR pageCnt = 0. The OR operator says that the combined condition is true if either condition *or* both conditions are true. In a truth table, it looks like this:

lineCnt > = 50	pageCnt = 0	lineCnt > = 50 OR pageCnt = 0
true	true	true
true	false	true
false	true	true
false	false	false

We still have our four possible combinations of the two conditions. But now our combined condition will be true for three of the four possible combinations. Only when both conditions are false will the combined condition be false.

We can convert this combined condition into a nested IF structure also. With the OR combination, the second expression becomes important only if the first expression is false. If the first expression is true we *already* know that the combined expression is true—there's no need to check the second expression. Check the truth table to confirm this statement. If the first expression is false, we need to check the second expression because there is still one chance that the combined expression will be true. Using the OR operator the structure looks like

```
IF lineCnt > = 50 OR pageCnt = 0
    DO Heads
ENDIF
```

Converting this into our nested IF structure, we get

```
IF lineCnt > = 50
    DO Heads
ELSE
    IF pageCnt = 0
        DO Heads
    ENDIF
ENDIF
```

Obviously, the nested structure is much longer (more lines), but that doesn't necessarily mean that it is more "work" for the computer. It probably ends up being more efficient for the computer to use the nested IF! We'll look at efficiency in these nested IF structures.

Be careful with both these combined conditions. Their meaning in a logical sense is very specific. Unfortunately, we are a bit "sloppy" when we use them conversationally. If I addressed a group of people and asked everyone born in November and December to please stand, probably about a sixth of the people present would stand up. But it is very unlikely that those standing were really born in November AND born in December. We also use the OR sometimes to mean an "exclusive OR" in which either condition could be true, but both conditions could not be true. We might say, "I'm going to go to the movie tonight or staying home and watch TV." We don't mean there is a possibility that we will do both. (Of course, those people who are able to be born in two different months might also have the ability to be in two places at once!) Don't let this casual use of the logical operators confuse you when you are using them in a formal design usage.

Nested IF Efficiency

Suppose we are trying to identify all freshmen with a GPA of 3.5 or higher. We have two conditions, and both conditions must be true for the record to meet our criteria. In nested logic, our test would look like

```
IF gpa > = 3.5
    IF class = 'Freshman'
        WRITE name
    ENDIF
ENDIF
```

Would it make any difference if we wrote the test like this?

```
IF class = 'Freshman'
    IF gpa > = 3.5
        WRITE name
    ENDIF
ENDIF
```

It wouldn't make any difference in what names we get written. (In math, 3 + 4 is the same as 4 + 3.) But it might make a difference in how much work the computer has to do. Let's add a bit more information. Let's assume that 60 percent of our students are Freshmen and that 15 percent of our students have a GPA greater than or equal to 3.5. If we have 5000 students, how many IF tests will the computer have to do? Check it for testing the GPA value first:

```
IF gpa > = 3.5                          done for each student
    IF class = 'Freshman'        done for those with a GPA > = 3.5
        WRITE name
    ENDIF
ENDIF                                   Total of 5750 IFs
```

The first IF, of course, is tested for everyone, so that's 5000 IFs. Only the students who have a GPA > = 3.5 will continue onto the second test. Since 15 percent meet the first test, 15 percent of 5000 students will have the second test: 750 students. So we have a total of 5750 IFs with this logic. Now let's try it testing the class value first:

```
IF class = 'Freshman'                   again done for each student
    IF gpa > = 3.5                           done for Freshmen
        WRITE name
    ENDIF
ENDIF                                   Total of 8000 IFs
```

166

We still have our 5000 IFs on the first test. All students who are Freshman (first test = true) will also have the second test. So 60 percent of the students will continue on to the nested IF: 3000 tests. We have a total of 8000 IFs with this logic.

What can we conclude? For efficiency, our goal would be to lower the number of IF tests. We lower the number of IFs by avoiding the second IF as often as possible. When the first IF is true, we continue on to the second IF. When the first IF is false, we fall out of the IF structure and avoid the second IF. So our efficiency goal is to make the first IF false as much as possible. In other words, **with AND logic, test the least likely condition first.**

Try it with the OR logic. Now we want a list including two groups of students: those with a GPA of 3.8 or higher and those who are members of any sports team. We know that 6 percent of our students have a GPA of 3.8 or higher and that 32 percent are a member of an intercollegiate or intramural sports team. Let's count how many IFs we have with our two possible orders. Try testing the GPA value first:

```
IF gpa > = 3.8                          Done for all students
    WRITE name
ELSE
    IF teamMember = 'yes'               Done for students with GPA < 3.8
        WRITE name
    ENDIF
ENDIF                                   Total of 9700 IFs
```

The above order gives us a total of 9700 IFs since all 5000 students would be tested in the first IF, and those students who don't have a GPA > = 3.8 (which is 94 percent of our student body or 4700) would also be tested in the second test. Now try it with the team member test first:

```
IF teamMember = 'yes'                   Again, done for all 5000 students
    WRITE name
ELSE
    IF gpa > = 3.8                      Done for nonteam members
        WRITE name
    ENDIF
ENDIF                                   Total of 8400 IFs
```

Our second order totals 8400 IFs. We still have the first 5000 IFs (there's no way to save there), and we have 3400 IFs in the second round because 68 percent of our students are not on any team, and the first IF will be false for them. Our first version requires 1300 IFs more than the second.

What do we conclude? Again, our goal is to avoid the second IF. With OR logic we avoid the second IF when the first IF condition is true. So if we can order the two tests so that more students evaluate to true on the first IF, they don't have to be tested on the second IF. In other words, **with OR logic, test the most likely condition first.**

CASE STRUCTURE

There is another variation on the nested IF that we haven't looked at yet. Let's assume that we have a variable named code that should hold a 1, 2, or 3. We want to write out "One," "Two," "Three," or "Error" based on the value of code. How would the following design work?

```
IF code = 1
    WRITE 'One'
ENDIF
IF code = 2
    WRITE 'Two'
ENDIF
IF code = 3
    WRITE 'Three'
ELSE
    WRITE 'Error'
ENDIF
```

There are two problems with this design. First, when will we write "Error"? Every time code is anything but 3! If code is equal to 1, we will write One, but we continue to test each of the following Ifs, and when we test IF code = 3, the answer is false, and the ELSE section is executed. That's a major problem. The second problem is the lack of efficiency. We have to continue to test the IFs, even after we have found the value. No matter what value code holds, we will execute three IFs.

OK, let's try to fix it up a bit. See the nested IF structure on the next page.

```
    IF code = 1
        WRITE 'One'
    ELSE
        IF code = 2
            WRITE 'Two'
        ELSE
            IF code = 3
                WRITE 'Three'
            ELSE
                WRITE 'Error'
            ENDIF
        ENDIF
    ENDIF
```

This one works though it can get a bit lopsided if we have too many values to check. (Imagine how far we would have to indent if code could go up to 20.) This is our plain-vanilla nested IF. But because each of our IF tests is checking the same variable, our tests are mutually exclusive, only one of them can be true at a time. With nested IFs testing multiple values of the same variable, we frequently rewrite the IF into what is called an IF-ELSE IF structure. It would look like this:

```
    IF code = 1
        WRITE 'One'
    ELSE IF code = 2
        WRITE 'Two'
    ELSE IF code = 3
        WRITE 'Three'
    ELSE
        WRITE 'Error'
    ENDIF
```

This is word for word the same as the previous version except the indentation is different, and we only have one ENDIF. The ELSE IF structure is a bit easier to read because we can scan quickly down the column looking for the one condition that will be true. Use it only when you are testing the same variable in each test, or, put another way, when the tests are mutually exclusive so that when one condition is true, *all* the other conditions must be false.

From the ELSE IF structure, it is only a short jump to the CASE structure. The CASE would be used in exactly the same situations the ELSE IF would be used, testing multiple possible values of the same variable. There is no agreement at all on what a CASE should look like in pseudocode (or in flowcharts for that matter). We'll use the pseudocode format shown on the next page.

```
CASE code
    = 1 - WRITE 'One'
    = 2 - WRITE 'Two'
    = 3 - WRITE 'Three'
    ELSE - WRITE 'Error'
ENDCASE
```

Suppose we wanted to write a message based on the value of the department field. We might end up with something like this:

```
CASE department
    = 'Sales' - WRITE 'Be sure to set new sales goals.'
    = 'Mgmt' - WRITE 'Team work leads to good work.'
    = 'Manuf' - WRITE '100 accident-free days and counting!'
    ELSE - WRITE 'Are you sure you work here?'
ENDCASE
```

In both designs, we started with the word CASE followed by the variable being tested. On each line below, we give a partial logical expression which assumes the case variable as the missing side of the expression (*code* "=1" or *department* "= 'Sales'") and the action to be taken if the expression was true. We could have listed multiple statements to be executed for one expression. At the end, we have the option of including the ELSE which works just like the ELSE in an IF structure. Naturally the structure must be closed with an ENDCASE.

For flowcharts, we'll use the following (nonstandardized) form:

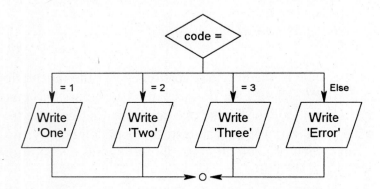

Don't feel that you have to use a case structure. It doesn't do anything you can't do with a nested IF. In addition, not all languages implement the case structure. You should use a case in your design only if you *know* the design will be eventually coded in a language using a case. Remember that one of our goals is to keep our designs language independent. Most often, you should design a test of multiple conditions with a nested IF and let the coder decide if the tests should be implemented with a traditional nested IF, an IF-ELSE, or a case.

TWO OUTPUT FILES

Most of the programs we have looked at so far have had a single output file: usually the printer. Frequently though, we have programs that require two output files. One output file might in a computer readable form (such as a disk file or tape file), and the other output might be in a human readable form (such as a printed report). What impact will two output files have on our design? Not too much as it turns out! Mostly it just means that we need to specify the destination with each WRITE. Our output to a printer will still have our line control, headings, and so on. Output to a disk or tape file will usually not have such extras because those files are generally being created for use as input for another computer program. We've actually already done programs like this when we had some output going to the screen and some going to the printer. It's the same concept, different devices.

EXTRACT PROGRAMS

An extract program does exactly what it sounds like it should do: It extracts data from an input file. We are extracting specified records from the data file to create a report or a new data file. An extract could be as simple as creating a list of all the employees who have been with the company for 10 or more years. The list, presumably, would not include everyone in the input file, just those employees who meet the extract criteria. Frequently, extract criteria are much more complex and involve tests on multiple variables.

The basis for any extract program is the IF test. Our specifications will provide the criteria for selection. We must convert those criteria into the conditions for our IF tests. Usually, a record which meets all the criteria is written to a report file or a data file. A record which does not meet the criteria is usually ignored. The complexity of an extract program is based on the complexity of the selection criteria. If we can write the IF conditions, extracts will be a breeze.

Let us assume for our examples that we have a file of all houses for sale in the Washington, D.C., suburbs. Each record in the input file has the following form:

Variable name	Description
Name	Owner's name
Price	Asking sales price

Addr	Street address
City	City or town
ZIP	ZIP code
Bath	Number of bathrooms in house
Bedrm	Number of bedrooms in house
Lot	Lot size in acres
Firepl	Whether or not there is a fireplace (Y/N)
Deck	Whether or not there is a deck (Y/N)
Pool	Whether or not there is a swimming pool (Y/N)
Tennis	Whether or not there is a tennis court (Y/N)

If we wanted a list of homes for sale in Reston, our design could look like this:

```
Mainline        Read All variable names (name, Price, Addr
OPEN files
WHILE there are data    name <? EOF
    DO Process
ENDWHILE
CLOSE files


Process
READ record (name, price, addr, city, zip, bath, etc.)
IF city = 'Reston'
    WRITE record (name, price, addr, city, zip, bath, etc.)
ENDIF
```

Not too much to that design. (Of course, we are ignoring headings.) We could make it a bit more complex by adding the additional specification that we want to count the number of houses identified and write the count out at the end of the loop. Then it becomes:

```
Mainline
OPEN files
count = 0
WHILE there are data
    DO Process
ENDWHILE
WRITE 'Number of homes identified: ', count
CLOSE files

Process
READ record (name, price, addr, city, zip, bath, etc.)
IF city = 'Reston'
    WRITE record (name, price, addr, city, zip, bath, etc.)
    ADD 1 to count
ENDIF
```

Notice that we increment count within the IF structure. If we incremented within the Process module but outside the IF, we would be counting the number of records read, not the number of records selected.

Occasionally, we also want to know how many records were *not* selected. In the previous design we could simply add an ELSE and increment the nonselected count in the ELSE section. But as our designs become more complicated, it will be more difficult to find the best location in the design to increment the nonselected count. The easiest solution is to count the selected records (incrementing any place you write a selected record) and to count the total number of records checked. Then, after the loop, you can easily subtract the selected count from the total count to get the nonselected count.

Our extract can get more complex by specifying additional criteria. Suppose we want a list of all houses in Reston with an asking price of less than $200,000 and with at least three bedrooms. First, we must ask ourselves if our conditions should be combined with AND or combined with OR; in other words: Must all the conditions be true, or just any one or more of them? In this case, we are combining the conditions with AND since to be selected, the house must meet all of the criteria. Our loop module now becomes:

```
Process
READ record
IF city = 'Reston'
    IF price < 200,000
        IF bedrm > = 3
            WRITE record
            ADD 1 to count
        ENDIF
    ENDIF
ENDIF
```

Try another. We want all the houses in Reston or Herndon with a swimming pool and a deck. This time we are combining some of the conditions with AND, but we are combining the two conditions testing the city with OR. One possible solution is shown on the next page.

```
Process
READ record
IF city = 'Reston'
    IF pool = 'Y'
        IF deck = 'Y'
            WRITE record
            ADD 1 to count
        ENDIF
    ENDIF
ELSE
    IF city = 'Herndon'
        IF pool = 'Y'
            IF deck = 'Y'
                WRITE record
                ADD 1 to count
            ENDIF
        ENDIF
    ENDIF
ENDIF
```

That design looks pretty long. It is possible to write it with fewer lines by switching the order of the tests. If we test the AND conditions first and then finish with the OR condition, we don't have to repeat the tests for pool and deck.

```
Process
READ record
IF pool = 'Y'
    IF deck = 'Y'
        IF city = 'Reston'
            WRITE record
            ADD 1 to count
        ELSE
            IF city = 'Herndon'
                WRITE record
                ADD 1 to count
            ENDIF
        ENDIF
    ENDIF
ENDIF
```

This version is shorter, but is it more efficient? Maybe. The efficiency is based on the likelihood of each condition being true. Our specifications didn't give us that information so we had to guess. Probably, a house is less likely to have a pool than to have a deck. By testing for the pool first, we avoid the additional IFs for all the records that don't have a pool.

Try one more. We're looking for houses in the 22132 ZIP code. The house must either have a fireplace and be on a lot of three acres or more or have a pool and be on a lot of two acres or more. We still don't have any information about the frequency of these characteristics so we just guess.

```
Process
READ record
IF zip = 22132
    IF lot > = 3
        IF fireplace = 'Y'
            WRITE record
            ADD 1 to count
        ENDIF
    ELSE
        IF lot > = 2
            IF pool = 'Y'
                WRITE record
                ADD 1 to count
            ENDIF
        ENDIF
    ENDIF
ENDIF
```

WARNING: This design will not work!

Can you figure out why the above design doesn't work? What if we have a house with 10 acres, a pool, but no fireplace? It won't be selected but it should have been. Because the three acres was tested first along with the fireplace and the two acre test was in the ELSE portion of the three acre test, anything that was three or more acres was not tested for a pool. We can fix the design with something like the following:

```
Process
READ record
IF zip = 22132
    IF lot > = 2
        IF pool = 'Y'
            WRITE record
            ADD 1 to count
        ELSE
            IF lot > = 3
                IF fireplace = 'Y'
                    WRITE record
                    ADD 1 to count
                ENDIF
            ENDIF
        ENDIF
    ENDIF
ENDIF
```

Notice that the test for lot > = 3 is in the ELSE portion of the test on pool, not the test for lot > = 2. If we put it in an ELSE section under lot > = 2, we would only have the lots of less than two acres, not the lots of three or more acres. This isn't the only way to do it, but this one does work.

EXERCISES

For all of the exercises below, assume the same input file described in the example.

1. Design a program to identify all houses in the Washington, D.C., suburbs with four or more bedrooms, three bathrooms, and no pool on a lot of exactly a half acre. After the loop, provide a count of the number of records selected and the number of records checked, but not selected.

2. Design a program to identify all houses in the 22090 or 22091 ZIP codes with a fireplace and a half acre lot.

3. Design a program to identify all houses in the 22075 or 22070 ZIP codes costing less than $175,000 or costing less than $180,000 but with a fireplace. Provide a count of the number of selected and unselected houses.

4. Design a program to identify all houses in the D.C. suburbs with a fireplace and a two acre lot costing between $250,000 and $300,000.

5. Design a program to create a new disk file of all house listings in all ZIP code areas beginning with 22 (that is 22000 to 22999). Selected houses must have a tennis court, a deck, and at least two acres, but must not have a pool. Price is unlimited.

6. Design a program to create a report listing all homes on five to 10 acres. The house must have a fireplace and at least three bedrooms, but cannot have a deck. (We're afraid of heights.) The selection conditions should be printed at the top of every page of the report as a heading.

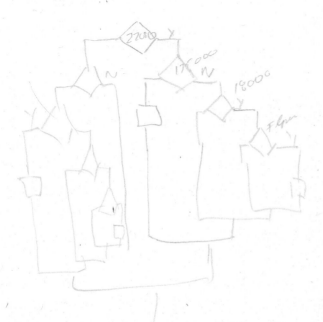

Chapter 11

Input
Editing

Objectives

After completing this chapter, you should be able to:

1.   Describe the goals of an input editing program.
2.   List and describe at least seven types of input errors.
3.   Explain the importance of a flag in input editing programs.
4.   Design an input editing program that identifies the input record once and writes a message for each field error found.
5.   Design an input editing program that provides a count of valid and invalid records as a final line.

INTRODUCTION

Is it possible that an error exists in an input data file? (Is it possible that apples grow on apple trees?) Of course! So far we've ignored the possibility, but that doesn't make it any less real. We can, in fact, look at input errors at any of three levels: file, record, or field. File errors could be problems like an empty file or the wrong file provided (wrong disk/tape). We control for these errors in our OPEN files statement. As we know, the OPEN statement actually represents a set of commands that the computer will complete. Usually, in a programming language, the OPEN statement will include the name of the file or files and the type of usage the file will have (input or output). When we issue the OPEN command, we are telling the computer to be sure the proper file is available and to prepare the file for use.

Record errors usually assume that we have different types of records within the design/program. If our program requires a parameter record as the first record in the input file and the record is not present, we could have a record error. We will come back to another type of record error later in our readings.

Field errors are our primary concern now. A field error means that within the record, some field (variable) does not have what we expect it to have. How could that happen? Obviously, the primary source is a data entry "typo." It is certainly easy to hit the wrong key during data entry and just as easy to miss the mistake during proofreading. Some typos may not make much difference. If John Smith's name is entered as John Snith, he may not like it much, but he'll still get his pay check and still be able to cash it. But if his pay amount is entered as 2179 instead of 1279, his company has a much more serious problem. It is possible that field errors result from hardware problems, particularly if the data are being transmitted over telephone lines, but it is much less likely. It's more comfortable to blame "the computer," but usually neither the computer, nor the transmission lines, nor the storage devices made the error.

What's the consequence of a field input error? You have probably heard the phrase "Garbage In/Garbage Out." If our input data are wrong, our output will be wrong. So one consequence is certainly invalid output. A second potential consequence is that the program won't work at all. If we have a field that is supposed to hold numbers but contains a letter by mistake, the computer can no longer process that field as a number. The computer can easily add, multiply, or do whatever you want with 48.37. But it can't do any arithmetic operation with 4B.37. When it sees the letter, it will give us an invalid input error message and stop the program. Which of these two consequences (program termination or invalid output) is the more serious? Program termination may sound more serious at first, but at least we know we have a problem. Too often, invalid output is not noticed, so the input isn't corrected. We can send out bills, write paychecks, build buildings, reserve airline tickets, all based on invalid input.

What's our solution? One possibility is to have every program "check" each field (or at least each critical field) before it uses the field. Our program loop task list would look something like

```
Read a record
Check the fields in the record
IF record is OK
    Process the record
    Write the output
ENDIF
```

This could work, but it raises two questions. First, how many times are we going to end up checking the same record? Many, I would guess. If we have multiple programs using the same data file and each program uses the file multiple times, every use would end up checking each record. Second, what happens with the records that have errors? There is no provision in our task list above for fixing the errors; we're concerned just with avoiding the records with invalid fields. Does that mean John Smith never gets paid because there is a typo in his input record? Obviously, we need another system.

Our second possibility is to separate the input editing functions from the rest of the program(s). Before a data file is used as input to any of the processing programs, we edit it. The edit program does two things: (1) it pulls out all the "valid" records, creating a separate file of valid records and (2) it identifies all "invalid" records so that they can be corrected. We have two forms of output from the editing program: the newly created "valid" file that can be used as input to all the programs needing this file and the error list that can be used to correct the errors in the invalid records. After correction, these previously invalid records would again be "run through" the edit program and presumably added to the file of valid records.

What follows is a system flowchart describing the edit process. Appendix B describes system flowcharts, but you can probably interpret this one fairly easily. Each symbol in the flowchart stands for a program, operation, or input/output "file." Different symbols are used to indicate different forms of input or output. Notice in this flowchart that the Error Report is used to correct the errors, and the corrected records are cycled back as input to the edit program again.

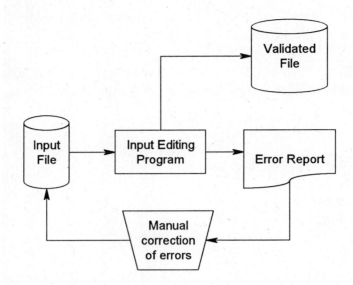

It is important to remember that we have two goals for an input editing program: (1) to create a file of "validated" records and (2) to create a report of identified errors for correction. Our validated file will be in a computer-readable medium, not a printout. This file is output from the edit program, but it is intended as input to other computer programs. Our second output from the edit program is the error report. This output must be in a human-readable medium, almost always a printout, so that the user can take the listing of errors and use it to correct the invalid input records.

If we all agree on the two goals given above, then we should also agree that our input editing program will not stop checking a file when we find the first invalid record. If our goal were to determine if this file contains any errors, we could answer the question when we find the first error. But we want to identify the valid *records* and all the *field* or *variable* errors, not just make a "yes/no" statement about the *file*. We should also be able to agree that our input editing program will not stop checking a record when we find the first field error. If our goal were only to create the file of valid records, we could stop there since we would know the record didn't belong in the new file. But we want also to identify the errors for correction, so we must keep checking the other variables in the record.

Our general process will follow these steps:
1. Obtain from our design specifications the variables or fields and types of errors to check.
2. For each record:
    A. Check the record, one field at a time, and write an error message for each identified error.

B. After all fields in one record have been checked, decide if the record should be written to the file of valid records.

TYPES OF EDIT CHECKS

There's a large area we've been skipping over. What kinds of field errors are we talking about? All but one of the following errors are errors that affect one field only. For each edit check description that follows, a pseudocode example is given which identifies an error message to be printed and then calls an error module. The error module, which we will look at soon, will print the error message as another line in the error report. Notice that most tests are written in the negative. We want to do something if the test shows an error, but if the field is OK we don't need to do anything.

SPECIFIC VALUE—Frequently our specifications call for a given field to have only a few possible values. A field identifying the employee's sex could be only M or F. A field identifying your driver's license restrictions could have only Y or N for Glasses Required. Our edit program could be written to look for the acceptable values and write an error message if the value is not in the acceptable list. We are really saying that the value *looks* valid, not that it *is* valid. Your license might have Y in Glasses Required when in fact you don't need glasses, but at least it has an "acceptable" value. Our edit program will identify any letter other than a Y or an N, but it won't guarantee that the correct letter is there.

```
IF sex < > 'M'
    IF sex < > 'F'
        message = 'Invalid letter in Sex Field'
        DO WriteError
    ENDIF
ENDIF
```

A variation on the specific value test allows for more than a few values. We might want to check the Social Security Number on all the time cards before we write the paychecks. We certainly wouldn't want to write a nested IF checking the input SSN against the SSN of each of our employees. And we wouldn't want to have to recompile the program to add an SSN when we hire a new employee. But we could create an array holding the valid SSNs and search the array. If the input SSN is not in the array, the time card does not represent one of our employees.

DATA TYPE—A field can be identified as a numeric field, an alphabetic field, or an alphanumeric field. If alphabetic characters are entered in a numeric field, the computer can't process it. If numeric characters are entered in an alphabetic field, the computer is equally stuck. Any character is acceptable in an alphanumeric field. Numeric calculations can only be performed on numeric fields (even though the alphanumeric field could be all numbers). We can do an editing test to be sure that the field contains only data of the allowed type. We could check a numeric field to be sure it contains only numeric data or check an alphabetic field to be sure it contains only alphabetic data.

```
IF hrsWorked not numeric
    message = 'Hours worked not numeric'
    DO WriteError
ENDIF
```

ABSOLUTE LIMIT—Some numeric fields have an absolute limit based on predefined and accepted conditions. For example, a month within a date has an absolute limit of 1 through 12. We all accept that there is no 13th month. Any record that includes a value outside this range is flat-out wrong, no excuses, no explanations.

```
IF month < 1
    message = 'Zero or negative value in month field'
    DO WriteError
ELSE
    IF month > 12
        message = 'Value above 12 in month field'
        DO WriteError
    ENDIF
ENDIF
```

REASONABLENESS LIMIT—There is another kind of numeric range or limit test. Frequently, companies will establish a reasonableness limit for numeric fields. Hours worked per week may be tested against a reasonableness limit, or annual salary may be compared to our reasonableness limit on salary. But the company has simply established these limits by policy and may change them. Furthermore, there may be exceptional cases that are not errors but do exceed the reasonableness limit. (If the Chairman of the Board raises her salary to a value beyond the "reasonable" limit, I don't want to be the one to tell her she can't because it isn't "reasonable"!) A complete editing system must have a way to override reasonableness checks.

```
IF salary > 100,000
    message = 'Salary above 100,000'
    DO WriteError
ENDIF
```

It is common to combine a type check for numeric data with a range check. This is one of the few occasions when nested IFs are used in input editing. If the field is not numeric, we want to avoid the range check, so the second test is nested within the numeric test.

```
IF salary not numeric
    message = 'Salary not numeric'
    DO WriteError
ELSE
    IF salary > 100,000
        message = 'Salary above 100,000'
        DO WriteError
    ENDIF
ENDIF
```

PRESENCE OF DATA—Some fields may be identified as essential for processing. If our data file contains new subscriptions to our magazine, we must have a value in the name field. (Who would we bill otherwise?) We can't check the name to be sure it is correct, but we can, at least, make sure it is there.

```
IF name = spaces
    message = 'Name is missing'
    DO WriteError
ENDIF
```

ABSENCE OF DATA—Some input records have blank space between fields. We can check to be sure that the portion of an input record that is supposed to be blank is, in fact, blank. What do we care? If it isn't blank, it *may* mean that the data entry person began entering the field which follows the blank space one or two columns early. The result could be that all fields that follow the blank space would be invalid. In order to check this, we must have a name for the portion of the record that is supposed to be blank.

```
IF blank1 < > spaces
    message = 'Unexpected data in space following name'
    DO WriteError
ENDIF
```

DATA SIGN—"Sign" in this case refers to positive or negative. Testing the sign of a numeric field is really a variation of testing the range. To say a field must be negative is the same as saying that it must have a range less than 0. However, we will include it as a separate test because it will allow a simple test of positive (greater than 0) or negative (less than 0).

```
IF length not positive
    message = 'Length dimension less than or equal to 0'
    DO WriteError
ENDIF
```

SEQUENCE—Our file may have the records ordered by some field within the record. If a record has a value that is not greater than the value of the previous record, those two records are not properly sequenced (assuming we expect ascending order). Sequence is checked by comparing the value of the current record to the value of the previous record (which must have been saved). The problem with this check is that it frequently identifies the wrong record. If we have inventory records in a file, sequenced on the part number, our sequence might be 101, 102, 777, 104, 105, and so on. We can look at this sequence and the 777 jumps out as the most likely error. But our sequence check may identify the 104. The 777 will meet our criteria: it is greater than the previous value. The 104 that follows it will not meet the criteria!

```
IF ssn < = oldSsn
    message = 'Social Security Number out of sequence'
    DO WriteError
ENDIF
oldSsn = ssn
```

Notice that in this design even if the SSN is out of sequence, we save it in the compare field (oldSsn). What error messages do we get when we save every number in the compare field? For the series of numbers given above, the 777 will appear valid because it is greater than the previous number. But we will get an error message for 104 since it is not greater than the previous number. Since we still go ahead and save 104 in the compare field, 105 will appear valid; it is greater than the number before it.

When the number comes after its correct sequential position (as in the list 101, 102, **63**, 104, 105), we will get an error message on the incorrectly placed value because it is not greater than the previous value. And the numbers that follow it will not lead to error messages because they are greater than the previous value. Notice that if our criteria is for an order that is ascending and unique (that is, a number cannot be repeated), we would not detect a duplicate number if the misplaced number fell between the duplicates as in 101, 102, 63, 102, 103. The second 102 would appear valid.

With a descending sequence, we have the same two possibilities: The misplaced number is too early or too late, for example, 66, 65, 14, 63, 62 or 66, 65, 74, 63, 62. And we have the same results. When the misplaced number is early, it appears valid but the number that follows it appears invalid. When the number is after its current position, it will be correctly detected as misplaced.

It is also possible to write our design so that the tested value is saved in the compare field only if it passes the sequence test. But as we have seen, we do not always detect the misplaced value, so we would not always be ignoring the errant record. Consider the following design:

```
IF ssn < = oldSsn
    message = 'Social Security Number out of sequence'
    DO WriteError
ELSE
    oldSsn = ssn
ENDIF
```

With the sequence 101, 102, 777, 104, 105, not only do we not get an error message for the number which really is out of sequence, we save the out of order number and get false messages for *all* the numbers that follow until we reach the position at which the misplaced number should have been. With this sequence, we would get an error message for 104, 105, and any number that follows that is less than or equal to 777.

With an ascending sequence and the misplaced number later than its correct position (as in 101, 102, 63, 104, 105), the 63 would be identified as an error. The 104 would still be compared to 102, and it will not be incorrectly identified as an error.

With descending sequences, we have the same results. A number that is earlier than it should be (as in 66, 65, 14, 63, 62) will appear correct and therefore will be saved. The next number (63) will be compared to 14 and will appear out of order. All numbers that follow will appear out of order and will not be saved in the compare field until we reach the position in the list where the out of place number should have been. With a descending sequence and a number that comes after its correct position, the number is correctly detected.

The good news is that computers (given the correct software) do an excellent job sorting files, and we should not have to do a sequence check as part of the edit process. Of course, if a human did the original sorting, we should still go ahead and check the sequence.

CONSISTENCY—This check is different in two ways. First, it involves two (or more) fields from the same record and checks to see if the two are consistent. Second, it can tell us that the values are actually wrong, not just that they look like they might be wrong. If an area code field has 703 (which is a Virginia area code) and the state field has AZ (whose area code is 602), we *know* there is an error because the two fields are not consistent. Notice that an individual check on either of the fields would not have identified an error. The problem is that many consistency checks are very time consuming.

Our example checks the consistency between graduation honors and the GPA.

```
        IF honors = 'Summa Cum Laude'
            IF gpa < = 3.8
                message = 'Inconsistent Fields, GPA must be above 3.8 for the Summa Honor'
                DO WriteError
            ENDIF
        ELSE
            IF honors = 'Magna Cum Laude'
                IF gpa < = 3.5
                    message = 'Inconsistent Fields, GPA must be above 3.5 for the Magna Honor'
                    DO WriteError
                ENDIF
            ELSE
                IF honors = 'Cum Laude'
                    IF gpa < = 3.2
                        message = 'Inconsistent Fields, GPA must be above 3.2 for the Cum Laude
                        Honor'
                        DO WriteError
                    ENDIF
                ENDIF
            ENDIF
        ENDIF
```

Presumably we are also doing field checks on the honors field (to make sure it holds a valid entry) and GPA (to make sure it is numeric and within the acceptable range). But neither of these separate checks would identify the error of the inconsistency of the two fields.

If we had many more graduation honors, we would end up with a very lengthy nested IF. Often a simpler solution is parallel arrays. Assume that we have five possible honors and that two parallel arrays have been declared and loaded. One holds the honors and another the minimum GPA for that honor. Then, instead of a long nested IF, we can search the honors array looking for a match and then use the same position in the GPA array to test for that minimum value.

The example that follows also includes the test to be sure the GPA is numeric. The test for numeric is done separately since it should be done for every record. The test for a valid GPA level is done only if the GPA is numeric *and* the honor was found in the list.

```
        IF gpa not numeric
            message = 'GPA is not numeric'
            DO WriteError
            gpaNumeric = 'no'
        ELSE
            gpaNumeric = 'yes'
        ENDIF
        search = 'yes'
        ptr = 0
        WHILE ptr < length AND search = 'yes'
            ADD 1 to ptr
            IF honorsChk(ptr) = honorIn
                search = 'found'
            ENDIF
        ENDWHILE
        IF search = 'no'
            message = 'Honor is not in list of honors'
            DO WriteError
        ELSE
            IF gpaNumeric = 'yes'
                IF gpa < gpaChk(ptr)
                    message = 'GPA is below minimum level required for honor'
                    DO WriteError
                ENDIF
            ENDIF
        ENDIF
```

ERROR REPORTS

Now to put all this together. We know that we want to write valid records to a file. But we can't do that WRITE until after we have checked all the appropriate fields in the record. And we must have some way to "remember" if an error was found. A flag will serve that purpose nicely.

We also want an error report identifying all the errors found in the invalid records. It won't be enough to list the errors. A printout with error message after error message without any way to tell which record the messages refer to would be useless. Usually, an error report identifies the record in question by copying some identifying field (an SSN or name, for example) or by copying the entire record. The record may take up a lot of room in the report, but it avoids the problem of identifying a record with a field value that is itself invalid. We'll use the entire record for identification purposes.

Our example edits an input file of students containing name, age, sex, and GPA according to the following specifications:

Name	Must be present
Age	Must be numeric and positive
Sex	Must be M or F
GPA	Must be numeric and within 0 to 4.0

Note that if the age and GPA are not numeric, we do not want to check their range.

```
Mainline
DO Start
WHILE there are data
    DO EditRecord
ENDWHILE
DO Finish

Start
OPEN files
lineCnt = 60
pageCnt = 0

EditRecord
errorFound = 'no'
READ name, age, sex, gpa
IF name = spaces
    msg = 'Name missing'
    DO WriteError
ENDIF
IF sex < > 'M'
    IF sex < > 'F'
        msg = 'Invalid sex field'
        DO WriteError
    ENDIF
ENDIF
DO AgeCheck
DO GPACheck
IF errorFound = 'no'
    WRITE name, age, sex, gpa  (to valid file)
ENDIF

Finish
CLOSE files
```

```
AgeCheck
IF age not numeric
    msg = 'Age not numeric'
    DO WriteError
ELSE
    IF age < = 0
        msg = 'Age less than or equal to zero'
        DO WriteError
    ENDIF
ENDIF


GpaCheck
IF gpa not numeric
    msg = 'GPA not numeric'
    DO WriteError
ELSE
    IF gpa < 0
        msg = 'GPA too low—cannot be below zero'
        DO WriteError
    ELSE
        IF gpa > 4
            msg = 'GPA too high—cannot be above 4'
            DO WriteError
        ENDIF
    ENDIF
ENDIF



WriteError
IF lineCnt > = 60
    DO Heads
ENDIF
WRITE name, age, sex, gpa, msg
ADD 1 to lineCnt
errorFound = 'yes'

Heads
EJECT page
ADD 1 to pageCnt
SKIP 6 lines
WRITE page heading, pageCnt
WRITE column heading (dbl spc)
SKIP 1 line
lineCnt = 10
```

Study the previous design carefully so that you are sure you understand everything that is being done in it. (We will modify it several times, and you need to understand this version before you continue.) Pay particular attention to the relation between the field

editing and the WriteError module. Any writing to the error report is done in the
WriteError module (or the Heads module called from WriteError). The other thing that
happens in the WriteError is that the flag (errorFound) is set to 'yes' indicating that at least
one error has been found for this record. ErrorFound is later checked in the EditRecord
module to determine if the record should be written to the valid file.

Sometimes the specifications call for a count of the valid and invalid records to be
written at the end of the error report. We would need to add two counters to our program
and initialize them in StartUp. But where do we increment them? What happens if we
increment the invalidCnt within the WriteError module? Every time we find an error we go
to that module, but we would be counting how many *field errors* we found, not how many
invalid *records* we found. Some records may have more than one error, and our counter
would be incremented too often. One solution is to increment at the end of the loop based
on the value of the flag. The IF test at the end of loop now becomes:

```
IF errorFound = 'no'
    WRITE name, age, sex, gpa  (to valid file)
    ADD 1 to validCnt
ELSE
    ADD 1 to invalidCnt
ENDIF
```

The counters would be written out in the Finish module.

Let's add another option. The error report that was created by the previous design had a
line written for each error. If a record had three errors, each line would repeat the input
record. Furthermore, the whole report was single-spaced. Let's rewrite it so that the input
record is only written for the first error of a given record; subsequent errors will contain
only the message. Let's also double-space between records and single-space within records.
How are we going to do that? How do we know by the time we are in WriteError if this is
the first error for a record or a subsequent error? Remember our flag? ErrorFound is set
back to 'no' for each record. It only becomes 'yes' after an error is found and we go to the
WriteError. If errorFound is 'no' when we enter the WriteError module, that means we
haven't been to WriteError before for *this* record so this must be the first error for the
record. If it's the first error, we should write the input record and the message and double-
space the WRITE. If it isn't the first error, we write only the message, single-spaced. (The
line count check for Heads has been changed to 59 because we are double-spacing the first
line for a record.) On the next page we have our revised WriteError. (Nothing else in the
design changes.) A sample of the output is shown on the same page.

```
WriteError
IF lineCnt > = 59
    DO Heads
ENDIF
IF errorFound = 'No'
    WRITE name, age, sex, gpa, msg (dbl spc)
    ADD 2 to lineCnt
    errorFound = 'Yes'
ELSE
    WRITE spaces, msg (single spc)
    ADD 1 to lineCnt
ENDIF
```

Sample Output:

XYZ University Student File—Editing Error Report   Page 1

Input Record				Error Message
John Jones	32	N	5.31	Invalid Sex Field GPA too high—cannot be above 4
Frances Smith	XX	F	2.3L	Age not numeric GPA not numeric
Quentin Pearson	19	M	-.14	GPA too low—cannot be below 0
	32	F	3.18	Name Missing

One more change. If a record has more than one error, we will, of course, write more than one error message. But those messages may end up on two different pages! It is certainly possible that the first message will fit at the bottom of a page, but the next message will have to go on a new page. Since we're now writing the input record only with the first error message, the subsequent messages will appear unidentified on the next page. It also looks misleading when the reader sees just one error message down at the bottom of the page. He or she may not realize that the messages for that record continue on the next page. Let's rewrite the WriteError module one final time to be sure all the error messages for one record are on the same page. We can ensure that by only checking the line count at the first error message. We are in effect asking, Is there room here for *all* the error messages I might have for the current record? With this program, we have a maximum of four error messages, so we would check to see if there is room for five lines to be written (four error messages plus the blank line). Since we don't know when we write the first message if there will be any more errors for that record, we have to check for the maximum. Our new WriteError module looks like this:

```
WriteError
IF errorFound = 'no'
    IF lineCnt > = 46
        DO Heads
    ENDIF
    WRITE name, age, sex, gpa, msg (dbl spc)
    ADD 2 to lineCnt
    errorFound = 'yes'
ELSE
    WRITE spaces, msg (single spc)
    ADD 1 to lineCnt
ENDIF
```

EXAMPLE

Design an edit program to check an input file for the following errors:

Name	Must be present
Hours	Must be numeric and less than or equal to 75
Rate	Must be numeric and less than or equal to 100
SSN	Must be included in list of valid SSNs

Valid SSNs will be loaded in ascending order from a separate file—there is a maximum of 1000 SSNs. Valid records should be written to a new disk file. All identified errors should be written to an error report and identified by the input record. The error report should have one-inch top and bottom margins, a report header, and column headings. Double-space between records; single space error lines for one record. Give a count of the number of valid and invalid records at the end of the error report.

```
Mainline
DECLARE ssnList(1000)
DO Start
WHILE there are data
    DO EditRecord
ENDWHILE
DO Finish
```

```
Start
OPEN ssn data file
lineCnt = 60
firstPage = 'yes'
invalidCnt = 0
validCnt = 0
ptr = 0
WHILE ptr < 1000 AND there are data
    ADD 1 to ptr
    READ ssnList(ptr)
ENDWHILE
numSsn = ptr
CLOSE ssn data file
OPEN Employee Payroll File, valid data file

EditRecord
errorFound = 'no'
READ name, hours, rate, ssn
IF name = spaces
    msg = 'Name is missing'
    DO ProcessError
ENDIF
DO HourCheck
DO RateCheck
DO SSNCheck
IF errorFound = 'no'
    WRITE name, hours, rate, ssn    (to valid data file)
    ADD 1 to validCnt
ELSE
    ADD 1 to invalidCnt
ENDIF

Finish
WRITE 'Number of Valid Records in File:'  validCnt (dbl spc)
WRITE 'Number of Invalid Records in File:' invalidCnt
CLOSE files

HourCheck
IF hours not numeric
    msg = 'Hours figure not numeric'
    DO ProcessError
ELSE
    IF hours > 75
        msg = 'Hours figure too high -- over 75'
        DO ProcessError
    ENDIF
ENDIF
```

<u>RateCheck</u>
```
IF rate not numeric
    msg = 'Pay rate figure not numeric'
    DO ProcessError
ELSE
    IF rate > 100
        msg = 'Pay rate figure too high -- over 100'
        DO ProcessError
    ENDIF
ENDIF
```

<u>ProcessError</u>
```
IF errorFound = 'no'
    IF lineCnt > = 56
        DO Heads
    ENDIF
    WRITE name, hours, rate, ssn, msg (dbl spc)
    ADD 2 to lineCnt
    errorFound = 'Yes'
ELSE
    WRITE spaces, msg
    ADD 1 to lineCnt
ENDIF
```

<u>SsnCheck</u>
```
lowPtr = 0
highPtr = numSsn
search = 'yes'
WHILE search = 'yes' AND lowPtr < = highPtr
    midPtr = (lowPtr + highPtr) / 2
    IF ssn = ssnList(midPtr)
        search = 'Found'
    ELSE
        IF ssn < ssnList(midPtr)
            highPtr = midPtr - 1
        ELSE
            lowPtr = midPtr + 1
        ENDIF
    ENDIF
ENDWHILE
IF search = 'yes'
    msg = 'SSN not found in list of valid SSNs'
    DO ProcessError
ENDIF
```

```
Heads
EJECT page
SKIP 6 lines
IF firstPage = 'yes'
    WRITE Report Heading
    SKIP 1 line
    lineCnt = 8
    firstPage = 'no'
ELSE
    lineCnt = 6
ENDIF
WRITE column heading
ADD 1 to lineCnt
```

EXERCISES

Each of the following exercises is based on an input file of supply orders with the following fields:

partName	partID
partPrice	quantity
supplierCode	deptCode

1. Design a program to provide the following edit checks:

partName	Must be alphabetic
partID	Must be in list of valid IDs provided in separate file
partPrice	Must be numeric and positive

Provide a count of the number of valid and invalid records. Valid records should be written to a new disk file. All identified errors should be described and identified by the input record in an error report.

2. Design a program to provide the following edit checks:

partID	Must be sequential (ascending order, no duplicates)
quantity	Must be numeric
supplierCode	Must be 1 through 10 inclusive
deptCode	Must be A, B, or C

Provide a count of the number of valid and invalid records. Write valid records to a new disk file. Identify invalid records on an error report with the input record written for the first error only.

3. Design a program to provide the following edit checks:

supplierCode	Must be numeric
quantity	Must be numeric
partPrice	Must be numeric

supplierCode and deptCode must be consistent (supplierCode of 1 or 2 goes with Dept of A; supplierCode of 3 or 4 goes with Dept of B; and so forth. SupplierCodes range from 1 through 10.) *Use table(s) ("hard coded" in StartUp) to implement this check.*

Identify invalid records with an appropriate error message and the complete input record.

4. Design a program to provide the following edit checks:

partID	Must be included in list contained in separate file (see below)
partName	Must be the name that goes with ID in separate file
partPrice	Must be numeric
quantity	Must be numeric

If quantity is over 100, the partPrice must be less than 50.

A separate file is available that holds a list of all the parts the company purchases from suppliers. The file is in order by partID and has the format: ID   Name
ID   Name
and so forth

Reasonable headings should be included.

5. Design a program to provide the following edit checks:

partID	Must be in descending (non-unique) order
supplierCode	Must be code associated with partID in separate file
deptCode	Must be code associated with partID in separate file

A separate file is available of all partIDs that the company purchases. This file is in *descending* order by partID. Along with the ID, the file contains the code for the supplier the company uses for this part and the code for the department that uses this part. The format of the file is: partID   supplierCode   deptCode
partID   supplierCode   deptCode
partID   supplierCode   deptCode

You can assume that data are included in complete sets. The company purchases up to 1,000 different parts from a total of 50 different suppliers.

REVIEW C: Review Exercises for Chapters 8 through 11

1. Design an interactive program that can be used to convert two-letter state abbreviations to the full state name. A file contains the abbreviations and names, with an abbreviation and a name in each record. The records are in alphabetical order by the abbreviations.

2. Design a program that will edit the personnel data file. The file contains the following fields and should be edited as noted:

name	Must be present
deptCode	Must be alphabetic
yearsExpr	Must be numeric, must be $> = 0$
skillCode	Must be numeric, must be in range 1 through 5
langCode	Must be F, G, or S

Valid records should be written to a file of validated records. All identified errors should be written to an error report and identified by the input record. Write the input record only once regardless of how many errors are found for that record. Be sure all error messages for one record are on the same page.

3. Design a program to use your newly validated personnel file to select employees who are qualified for a new special assignment in Germany. To qualify an employee must speak German (langCode = G), have programming skills (skillCode = 2) with at least seven years of experience or analyst skills (skillCode = 4) with at least five years of experience. At the end of the listing of qualified employees, include a count of the number qualified and the number not qualified.

4. Modify your edit program (design #2) to include the following two additional checks:
    deptCode   Must be ACCT, CIS, RESCH, SALES, or MANUF
    consistency of deptCode and skillCode:
                    skillCode of 1 must go with RESCH or MANUF deptCode
                    skillCode of 2 or 4 must go with CIS deptCode
                    skillCode of 3 must go with ACCT deptCode
                    skillCode of 5 must go with SALES deptCode
                    (Do check only if deptCode and skillCode pass previous checks.)

5. Design a program to select all students who are eligible for a special work-study program. Students must be enrolled in one of the "high need" curricula, have a GPA of 3.5 or greater, be at least 20 years old and have completed 30 credits, or be at least 24 years old with 25 credits completed. The student file includes name, GPA, age, credits completed, and major. For the purposes of this program additional records will be inserted at the beginning of the student file containing the names of the "high need" curricula (not more than 20, but exact number is unknown). The curricula list will be separated from the student data by a record

containing "SentinelRec." Names of all qualified students should be written in a printed report (with appropriate headings and spacing). HINT: Put the "high need" curricula in an array.

6. The FBI is developing a file of all students who harass teachers of computer program design. The file contains the student's name, SSN, ZIP code, age, and whether or not the student owns a car (Y/N). Design a program to edit this file using the following criteria:

Name	Must be present
SSN	Must be unique and ascending
Age	Must be numeric and $>= 15$
Car	Must be Y or N

All identified errors should be identified by the record number (the position of the errant record in the file), the field with the error, and a description of the error as shown in the following sample report.

ERROR REPORT—Teacher Harassment File

Field in Error	Error Message
Error(s) found in record number: 3	
Name	Must be present
Age	Must be numeric
Error(s) found in record number: 22	
Car	Must be Y or N

Chapter 12

Single Level Control Breaks

Objectives

After completing this chapter, you should be able to:

1. Define a control break.
2. Give examples of typical "special processing" in a control break.
3. Design a control break program that goes to a new page when the test field changes.
4. Design a control break program that writes a subtotal after each test field grouping.
5. Design a control break program that writes a subtotal after each test field grouping and a final total at the end of the output.
6. Design a control break program with and without a priming read.

INTRODUCTION

In the programs we have designed so far, we have treated each record of the input file the same. Even with extract programs, we made the same tests on each record. But, sometimes, we want to change what we're doing at certain points through the input file. Let's look at several examples. First, assume we have an input file of all the employees who work for our company in order by their department. We want to create an employee list for each department, which is really just writing the list of the whole company but beginning each department on a new page. So, for the first employee in a department, we want to go to a new page, but for all subsequent employees in the department we stay on the same page.

Or, as another example, we may have an input file that includes all students and their final exam grades for all classes of Programming I. We could create a printed report listing all the students and for each class give the average exam grade. We know how to calculate an exam average. When would we write it? We write it *after* writing the last student in one class and *before* writing the first student in the next class.

As a final example, assume we have a file of the scores from all the entries in a dog obedience show, by entry class. We want to write out the highest score in each class. For each record we read, we would check to see if that score is the highest so far, but we wouldn't write the high score until we have finished processing all the records *from that class*. Then, before we write the first entry in the next class, we would write out the highest score for the previous class.

Each of these is an example of a *control break* program. As the name implies we are breaking the usual flow of control through the program. Instead of going through the loop and doing the same processing for each record, we are breaking that flow when certain conditions occur. We can define control break processing as an interruption of the normal sequential processing, whenever there is a change in a specified field, to handle some special form of processing. The trick is to be sure you know what is the normal sequential processing and what is the special processing.

Normal sequential processing is the processing that we do for each record. In our first example above, the normal processing was just to read and write the record. In the second example, the normal processing was to read the record, add to the accumulators (needed to calculate the average grade), and write the record. In the last example, the normal processing was to read the record, check to see if that score was higher than our current high, and write the record.

The special processing is whatever we do when that specified test field changes. In our first example, we go to a new page when the department field changes. In the second example, we calculate and write the average grade when the class number field changes. In the third example, we write the highest score when the entry class changes.

How do we do this? There are three points to notice. First, we must have a compare field to be able to test if the field has changed. We need to be able to ask "Is this department different from the department in the previous record?" We can ask that question by saving the value from the previous record in a compare field. Second, we don't know that it is time to process the break until we have read the first record from the next group. Until we read the first employee in the second department, we don't know that we're finished with the first department. It is only when we compare the department values and see that the record we have just read has a value that is different from the previous record that we know we must go to a new page. That means that we must check for the special break processing *after reading* a record but *before processing* the record. In our second example, we would read a record and then immediately check to see if the class number has changed. If the number is different from the previous record, we go into our special processing (calculate and write the average) and then we return to our normal sequential processing and write the new record.

Our third point to notice is the importance of the order of our input file. We are assuming that the file is in order using our test field. If we are going to a new page every time we read a record with a new department, our file must be in order by department. That is, we must have all the employees in the accounting department together, all the employees in the personnel department together, and so forth. What would happen if the file were not ordered like that? Suppose we have a person from accounting, then one from personnel, then two from sales, and another from accounting, two from personnel, and so on. What would happen? The employee from accounting would be on the first page. The next record has a new department so we would give the command to eject the page and the personnel employee would be at the top of page 2. Next we would read the employee from sales, another new department so we would go to the top of page 3. Our fourth record is also from sales, so we stay on the same page. Then we read another employee from accounting. But we're only comparing this employee to the previous record. It looks like a new department, so we go to another new page. If all the employees from accounting were together, they would all have been read in order and the department wouldn't change until we read the first employee from another department.

When you are designing a control break program, ask yourself three questions:

> **What is my "normal sequential processing"?**
> **What field am I testing to see if it has changed?**
> **What is my "special processing"?**

A First Attempt: New Page

The following example processes our file of employees to create a report with each department on a new page. Our normal sequential processing is just reading a record, checking for a full page, and writing the record. Our test field is the department. Our special processing is to go to a new page (when the department changes). Notice that we have two reasons to go to a new page: if the current page is full or if the department field has changed.

```
Mainline
DO StartUp
WHILE there are data
    DO ProcessEmployee
ENDWHILE
CLOSE files

StartUp
OPEN files
lastDept = 'AAAAA'
pageCnt = 0

ProcessEmployee
READ name, department, salary
IF department < > lastDept
    DO DeptBreak
ELSE
    IF lineCnt > = 60
        DO Heads
    ENDIF
ENDIF
WRITE name, salary
ADD 1 to lineCnt

DeptBreak
DO Heads
lastDept = department
```

```
Heads
EJECT page
ADD 1 to pageCnt
SKIP 6 lines
WRITE page heading, department, pageCnt
WRITE column heading (dbl spc)
SKIP 1 line
lineCnt = 10
```

In any control break program, we must pay particular attention to the first record and the last record. What happens with our first record here? Since we have initialized lastDept to 'AAAAA' in the StartUp module, our test in ProcessEmployee will indicate a break. We will go to the DeptBreak module, write the headings, and reset the lastDept compare field to the value of the first record's department.

Why don't we have to initialize lineCnt in the StartUp module? Linecnt is set to 10 in the Heads module. We go into the DeptBreak module (which calls the Heads module) before the first test of lineCnt. And finally, why is the test for lineCnt nested within the test for the change in department? It doesn't need to be. We could have written the test as two separate IFs.

```
READ name, department, salary
IF department < > lastDept
    DO DeptBreak
ENDIF
IF lineCnt > = 60
    DO Heads
ENDIF
```

Both methods will get us exactly the same output; the first is just a tad bit more efficient. We know that if we have a change in department we will be going to a new page, so there's no need to check if the previous page is full. We only need to check for a full page if this current record did not cause a control break. That's why we nested the lineCnt test in the false portion of the break test. Later in this chapter we will see a good reason to keep the two tests separate.

How would this design change if we used a priming read? There is one important difference. If we read the first record in the StartUp module, we can initialize the compare field to the actual value of the first department. We don't get the "false" control break on the first record.

```
Mainline
DO StartUp
WHILE moreData = 'yes'
    DO ProcessEmployee
ENDWHILE
CLOSE files

StartUp
OPEN files
moreData = 'yes'
DO Read
lastDept = department
lineCnt = 60
pageCnt = 0

ProcessEmployee
IF department < > lastDept
    DO DeptBreak
ELSE
    IF lineCnt > = 60
        DO Heads
    ENDIF
ENDIF
WRITE name, salary
ADD 1 to lineCnt
DO Read

Read
IF there are data
    READ name, department, salary
ELSE
    moreData = 'no'
ENDIF

DeptBreak
DO Heads
lastDept = department

HEADS
EJECT page
ADD 1 to pageCnt
SKIP 6 lines
WRITE page heading, department, pageCnt
WRITE column heading (dbl spc)
SKIP 1 line
lineCnt = 10
```

With this example, we get our headings on the first page because we have initialized lineCnt to 60, not because we have a "false" control break.

A Revision: Adding a Subtotal Line

Now let's add the next layer of complexity to our program. We want the same kind of listing, but this time we want to write the number of employees in each department at the end of each department listing. Obviously, we need a counter, but do we need a counter for each department? No, because we can use the same counter over and over again. Once we have counted the employees in one department and written out that value, we don't need to save the value any more. We can set the counter back to 0 and use the same variable to count the employees in the next department. Also keep in mind that we need to write the value of the counter *before* we do the headings for the new department. It's tempting (but wrong) to just add a simple write in our break module so that the revision looks like this.

<u>Mainline</u>
DO StartUp
WHILE there are data   **WARNING: This design does not work!**
    DO ProcessEmployee
ENDWHILE
CLOSE files

<u>StartUp</u>
OPEN files
emplCnt = 0
pageCnt = 0
lastDept = 'AAAAA'

<u>ProcessEmployee</u>
READ name, department, salary
IF department < > lastDept
    DO DeptBreak
ELSE
    IF lineCnt > = 60
        DO Heads
    ENDIF
ENDIF
WRITE name, salary
ADD 1 to lineCnt
ADD 1 to emplCnt

<u>DeptBreak</u>
WRITE emplCnt
emplCnt = 0
DO Heads
lastDept = department

209

```
Heads
EJECT page
ADD 1 to pageCnt
SKIP 6 lines
WRITE page heading, department, pageCnt
WRITE column heading (dbl spc)
SKIP 1 line
lineCnt = 10
```

Why won't this design work? Remember that we said we need to pay particular attention to the first record and the last record? What happens here on the first record? It creates a false control break (because we initialized the compare field to 'AAAAA') and tries to write a total line before any records have been processed at all! And what happens to the last record? We should have a count written after it since the last record must be the end of the last department. But we don't write the count value for the last department because we write the count only when we are in the loop and read a *new* department value.

The design that follows corrects both of these problems. We are still forcing a false control break on the first record by initializing the compare field to 'AAAAA,' but we avoid writing the total line on the false break by using a flag (firstRecord). We get our headings on the first page because they are called from our break module. After the loop we write out the count for the last department.

```
Mainline
DO StartUp
WHILE there are data
    DO ProcessEmployee
ENDWHILE
WRITE emplCnt
CLOSE files

StartUp
OPEN files
lastDept = 'AAAAA'
firstRecord = 'yes'
pageCnt = 0
```

```
ProcessEmployee
READ name, department, salary
IF department < > lastDept
    DO DeptBreak
ELSE
    IF lineCnt > = 60
        DO Heads
    ENDIF
ENDIF
WRITE name, salary
ADD 1 to lineCnt
ADD 1 to emplCnt


DeptBreak
IF firstRecord = 'yes'
    firstRecord = 'no'
ELSE
    WRITE emplCnt
ENDIF
emplCnt = 0
DO Heads
lastDept = department


HEADS
EJECT page
ADD 1 to pageCnt
SKIP 6 lines
WRITE page heading, department, pageCnt
WRITE column heading (dbl spc)
SKIP 1 line
lineCnt = 10
```

We can improve this a bit by making better use of modules. We won't really change anything except where steps get done. It is very common to write the detail line in a separate module. That makes modification of the design/program easier because the output sections are easily identified, and it pulls together all the tasks that are closely related to writing the line (like checking for a full page and adding to the line counter). We will add a WriteDetailLine module as well as a module to write the employee count for the departments. Because we write the count in two different places in the design, it is clearer to do the actual writing from a separate module.

```
Mainline
DO StartUp
WHILE there are data
    DO ProcessEmployee
ENDWHILE
DO Finish
```

211

```
StartUp
OPEN files
lastDept = 'AAAAA'
firstRecord = 'yes'
pageCnt = 0
emplCnt = 0

ProcessEmployee
READ name, department, salary
IF department < > lastDept
    DO DeptBreak
ENDIF
DO WriteDetailLine
ADD 1 to emplCnt

FINISH
DO WriteCount
CLOSE files

DeptBreak
IF firstRecord = 'yes'
    firstRecord = 'no'
ELSE
    DO WriteCount
ENDIF
DO Heads
lastDept = department

Heads
EJECT page
ADD 1 to pageCnt
SKIP 6 lines
WRITE page heading, department, pageCnt
WRITE column heading (dbl spc)
SKIP 1 line
lineCnt = 10

WriteDetailLine
IF lineCnt > = 60
    DO Heads
ENDIF
WRITE name, salary
ADD 1 to lineCnt

WriteCount
WRITE emplCnt
emplCnt = 0
```

If are we using a priming read, we can come up with an easier solution. Logically, we know that we will never have a control break on the first record. (How could it be different from the previous record if there is no previous record?) We also know that we will need to process a total line *after* the last record even though we don't read a different value.

```
Mainline
DO StartUp
WHILE moreData = 'yes'
    DO ProcessEmployee
ENDWHILE
CLOSE files

StartUp
OPEN files
moreData = 'yes'
DO Read
lastDept = department
lineCnt = 60
emplCnt = 0
pageCnt = 0

ProcessEmployee
DO WriteDetailLine
ADD 1 to emplCnt
DO Read
IF department < > lastDept
    DO DeptBreak
ENDIF

Read
IF there are data
    READ name, department, salary
ELSE
    moreData = 'no'
    department = 'ZZZZZ'
ENDIF

DeptBreak
WRITE emplCnt
emplCnt = 0
lineCnt = 60
lastDept = department
```

```
WriteDetailLine
IF lineCnt > = 60
    DO Heads
ENDIF
WRITE name, salary
ADD 1 to lineCnt


Heads
EJECT page
ADD 1 to pageCnt
SKIP 6 lines
WRITE page heading, department, pageCnt
WRITE column heading (dbl spc)
SKIP 1 line
lineCnt = 10
```

This design may look a little confusing at first but try to follow it through. We have moved the test for the control break to the end of the loop after the call to the Read module. We will not make the test between the first read (the priming read in StartUp) and the first write (we know we can't have a control break then). We still get our headings because we initialized lineCnt to 60 and we avoid the problem of writing the counter prior to the first page. For all subsequent records, we read the record at the end of the loop and immediately check to see if the department field has changed. If there is a change, we process the break. The order looks different, but we are still performing the same tasks. Our task order in the earlier loop was read, check for break, write. We keep the check for break between the read and the write, but the loop now begins with the write so the task order is write, read, check for break. The next important change is the processing of the final record and counter. Look at the Read module again. If there are no more records, we arbitrarily move the value 'ZZZZZ' into the department field. Immediately after the read, we check to see if the department field is different from the previous record. If we have just found that there are no more records, the department field *will* be different because we made it 'ZZZZZ,' so we write the last counter while still in the loop. Now we don't have to worry about writing the last counter after we exit the loop module. One more point: we reset lineCnt to 60 in the break module rather than call the heads module. That's because we know that we will get to the break module after the last record, when we really don't want to go to a new page and write headings. By setting lineCnt to 60, we make sure that we will get headings if we enter the ProcessEmployee module again but avoid headings if this is the last record.

Since we now write the employee count in only one place (the DeptBreak module), this design no longer uses the WriteCount module.

Desk check the program with the following data:

Smith	Management	42500
Franklin	Management	51750
Davidson	New Car Sales	38500
Lewis	New Car Sales	51000
Jones	Service	35500
Thomas	Service	42510
Moore	Used Car Sales	41250
(end-of-file)		

The chart on the following page "traces" the memory variables through the first three input records and creates the output report through the desk checking. You should complete the chart. Be sure you work through the design line by line.

The Last Revision: Subtotals and Final Totals

Still with us? Let's add the final option for this chapter. We have included a total line for each control break. Frequently we want a subtotal or equivalent with each control break segment but also want a final total at the end of the report. The design below and continuing on page 217 includes salary subtotals by department and a final total for the whole company. Notice that we now need two accumulators: one to use over and over for the department totals and one to keep the final, company total.

```
Mainline
DO StartUp
WHILE moreData = 'yes'
     DO ProcessEmployee
ENDWHILE
DO Finish


StartUp
OPEN files
moreData = 'yes'
DO Read
lastDept = department
lineCnt = 60
pageCnt = 0
deptTot = 0
compTot = 0
```

MEMORY								OUTPUT
moreData	lastDept	lineCnt	pageCnt	emplCnt	name	department	salary	

Beginning of program—StartUp

moreData	lastDept	lineCnt	pageCnt	emplCnt	name	department	salary	OUTPUT
yes	Management	60	1	0	Smith	Management	42500	Mgmt Dept Listing Page 1
								Name Dept Salary
								Smith Mgmt 42500

Entering Process module the first time—Write first record, Read second record

| | Management | | | 1 | Franklin | Management | 51750 | Franklin   Mgmt   51750 |

Second Loop through Process—Write second record, Read third record

	Management			2	Davidson	NewCarSales		Employee count = 2
								————————
								NewCar Dept Listing Page 2

Control break because department has changed

| | New Car Sales | | | 0 | Davidson | NewCarSales | 38500 | Name   Dept   Salary |
| | | | | | | | | Davidson   NewCar   38500 |

216

<u>ProcessEmployee</u>
DO WriteDetailLine
ADD salary to deptTot
DO Read
IF department < > lastDept
    DO DeptBreak
ENDIF

<u>Finish</u>
WRITE compTot
CLOSE files

<u>Read</u>
IF there are data
    READ name, department, salary
ELSE
    moreData = 'no'
    department = 'ZZZZZ'
ENDIF

<u>WriteDetailLine</u>
IF lineCnt > = 60
    DO Heads
ENDIF
WRITE name, salary
ADD 1 to lineCnt

<u>DeptBreak</u>
WRITE deptTot
ADD deptTot to compTot
deptTot = 0
lineCnt = 60
lastDept = department

<u>Heads</u>
EJECT page
ADD 1 to pageCnt
SKIP 6 lines
WRITE page heading, department, pageCnt
WRITE column heading (dbl spc)
SKIP 1 line
lineCnt = 10

Notice that we add to the deptTot in the ProcessEmployee module but not to the compTot. When we have a change in department, we write the deptTot and add that value to the compTot before we set deptTot back to 0. Why do it that way? It's more efficient and no more confusing. If we have 3000 employees in 10 departments, we will add to the deptTot 3000 times, once for each employee. But we will only have 10 adds to the compTot, once for each department. If we added the salary to deptTot and to compTot in the Process module, we would have 6000 adds, two for each employee. We've saved 2990 adds!

To summarize, when we know we are designing a control break program, we should start by identifying the normal sequential processing, the break test field, and the special processing. In designing the break module, we should mentally review the following list as a reminder of steps we may have to take:

- Write any footer, subtotal, or message line needed
- Add any subtotal value to final total
- Reset subtotal field to 0
- Reset compare field to value in current record
- Prepare for any other necessary processing (headings, etc.)

A FINAL EXAMPLE

One more variation on this department listing. For this example, we will write the average salary for each department as well as the average salary for the company as a whole. Remember that for the average we must have both the total salary and the count. We will calculate the average just before we write it. We'll do this one without a priming read, so we need to be sure we are processing our first and last records correctly. We will also *not* go to a new page every time the department changes. We will skip five lines after the average for the previous department, then write a subheading for the new department.

```
Mainline
DO StartUp
WHILE there are data
    DO ProcessEmployee
ENDWHILE
DO Finish

StartUp
OPEN files
firstRecord = 'yes'
deptTot = 0
deptCnt = 0
compTot = 0
compCnt = 0
lastDept = 'AAAAA'
newDept = 'yes'
```

ProcessEmployee
READ name, department, salary
IF department < > lastDept
    DO DeptBreak
ENDIF
DO WriteDetailLine
ADD 1 to deptCnt
ADD salary to deptTot

Finish
DO ProcessSubTotal
compAvg = compTot / compCnt
WRITE compAvg (dbl sp)
CLOSE files

DeptBreak
IF firstRecord = 'yes'
    firstRecord = 'no'
ELSE
    DO ProcessSubTotal
ENDIF
SKIP 5 lines
ADD 5 to lineCnt
lastDept = department
newDept = 'yes'

WriteDetailLine
IF lineCnt > = 59
    DO Heads
ENDIF
IF newDept = 'yes'
    newDept = 'no'
    WRITE 'Listing for department: ', department
    ADD 1 to lineCnt
ENDIF
WRITE name, salary
ADD 1 to lineCnt

Heads
EJECT page
ADD 1 to pageCnt
SKIP 6 lines
WRITE page heading, pageCnt
WRITE column heading (dbl spc)
SKIP 1 line
lineCnt = 10

```
ProcessSubTotal
deptAvg = deptTot / deptCnt
WRITE deptAvg (dbl spc)
ADD deptCnt to compCnt
ADD deptTot to compTot
deptCnt = 0
deptTot = 0
ADD 2 to lineCnt
```

We use two flags here to help control the processing. The firstRecord flag you have seen before. We use it to avoid the false control break on the first record. The newDept flag is used to control the writing of the subheading for the department. You might be tempted to write the subheading in the DeptBreak module right after you skip the five lines. But what if the page is full? You would either need to check lineCnt in the DeptBreak module (and call Heads if the page is full) or write the subheading when needed from within the WriteDetailLine module. The flag newDept lets us know when the subheading is needed once we get into the WriteDetailLine module. Notice also that we skip the five lines between departments in the DeptBreak module, not in the ProcessSubTotal module. That way we don't skip the lines after the average for the last department, immediately before the final, company average.

EXERCISES

Each of the following exercises assumes an input file of dogs entered in the Old Dominion Obedience Match. Each record contains the owner's name, dog's name, entry class (subnovice, novice, open, utility), entry number, and score. The file is in order by entry class and within entry class alphabetically by owner's name.

1. Design a program that will create a listing of all entries with each entry class beginning on a new page. Include appropriate headings.

2. Modify design #1 so that the listings for each class start with page 1 (so the report can be separated into four sections, each beginning with page 1).

3. Design a program that will list all entries by class, and at the end of each class give the highest score along with the name of the owner whose dog earned it. All pages should be numbered consecutively, but each class should begin on a new page.

4. Modify design #3 so that a new class does not begin on a new page (unless the previous page is full). Skip five lines between classes and write a subheading for each class.

5. Design a program that lists the average score, the highest score, and high score owner for each entry class but does not include the names of all entries in the class. (Don't get confused, it is still a control break program—what is the normal processing?)

6. Design a program that will begin the listing for each entry class on a new page and will give the average score for all classes (appropriately identified) on a separate page at the end of the report. (HINT: use parallel arrays.)

Chapter 13
Multi-Level Control Breaks

Objectives

After completing this chapter, you should be able to:

1. Provide a sequenced list of the tasks to be performed in a multi-level control break.
2. Identify the order in which the various break levels should be tested.
3. Identify the order in which the various break levels should be processed.
4. Design a multi-level control break program that uses a priming read.
5. Design a multi-level control break program that does not use a priming read.
6. Calculate the correct value for a line count check to ensure that no total will be printed at the top of a page or in the bottom margin.
7. Design a multi-level control break program that includes the values from the compare fields in heading and total lines and uses group indication in writing the detail lines.

INTRODUCTION

In the previous chapter we designed a variety of control break programs based on an input file containing each employee's name, department, and salary. Most of the designs provided some form of summary information about each department: number of employees, average salary, and so on. Our design was able to take an input file that on the surface had only individual information and combine the information to tell something about the department groups.

Suppose we vary our input file slightly. Our new file represents all of the employees in a conglomerate including multiple companies, with each company having multiple departments. We want to use that file to create a printed report giving the individual employee information as well as the total salary for each company and each department within each company.

What must our design include to accomplish those tasks? We know that to have department totals, we needed a single accumulator that could be reused for each department. Once we wrote the total for a given department, we set the accumulator back to 0 in preparation for accumulating salaries from the next department. If we are to write department and company totals, we will need two accumulators: one that can be used and reused for each company and a second that can be used and reused for each department. We also know that when we were doing totals for just the department, we needed a compare field to detect when the department value had changed. Since we now need to know both when the department changes and when the company changes, we will need two compare fields. By adding the extra layer of subtotals, we really haven't added that much complexity: one more accumulator and one more compare field.

What requirements does this new design impose on the nature of our input file? Again, when we were designing a program that performed special break processing when the department changed, we had to be able to assume that our input file was in order by department; that is, all of the Accounting employees were together, all of the Sales employees were together, and so forth for each department. Now we have two layers of special break processing. What must the order be of the input file? If we put *all* the accounting employees together, we will be grouping employees from different companies just because they happen to work in similar departments. We certainly don't gain much information from that kind of grouping. Our first grouping should be by company, and then within a given company we can divide the employees by department. So our input file must have all the employees from one company together and within that group have all the employees from a given department together. Another way of saying that is to say the file is *sorted* by company and within company, sorted by department. A portion of the input file is shown below. (The field order is name, company, department, salary.)

Sample Input File:

Marvin Martin	Tri-State	Accounting	33450
Opal Overtime	Tri-State	Accounting	31900
Henry Higgenbothem	Tri-State	Marketing	41350
Susan Supperly	Tri-State	Marketing	44000
Jake Jacobs	Tri-State	Marketing	25750
Adam Appleby	Tri-State	Personnel	30500
Wallace Wilson	Tri-State	Personnel	39125
Beulah Betters	First Choice	Accounting	35880
Carmen Carruthers	First Choice	Marketing	39500
Thom Tompkins	First Choice	Marketing	51000
Ursala Upham	First Choice	Personnel	33000

SAMPLE: A TWO-LEVEL BREAK WITH SUBTOTALS

We'll assume that for this design we want a printed report including department and company totals (but no final total) and that we want each new company to begin on a new page but departments may be continued on the same page. A sample design solution follows.

```
Mainline
DO StartUp
WHILE there are data
    DO ProcessEmployee
ENDWHILE
DO Finish

StartUp
OPEN files
firstCheck = 'yes'
deptTot = 0
compTot = 0
lineCnt = 60
```

ProcessEmployee
READ name, company, department, salary
IF firstCheck = 'yes'
    firstCheck = 'no'
    lastDept = department
    lastComp = company
ELSE
    IF company < > lastComp
        DO CompanyBreak
    ELSE
        IF department < > lastDept
            DO DeptBreak
        ENDIF
    ENDIF
ENDIF
DO WriteDetailLine
ADD salary to deptTot

Finish
DO CompanyBreak
CLOSE files

CompanyBreak
DO DeptBreak
WRITE compTot (dbl spc)
compTot = 0
lastComp = company
lineCnt = 60

DeptBreak
WRITE deptTot (dbl spc)
ADD 2 to lineCnt
ADD deptTot to compTot
deptTot = 0
lastDept = department

WriteDetailLine
IF lineCnt > = 60
    DO Heads
ENDIF
WRITE company, department, name, salary
ADD 1 to lineCnt

Heads
EJECT page
SKIP 6 lines
WRITE page headings
WRITE column headings (dbl spc)
SKIP 1 line
lineCnt = 10

Notice that we have again used a flag to identify the first record in the loop. Our first record is treated differently because we must initialize the department and company compare fields. If firstCheck has a value of 'no,' we know that this is not the first time through the loop, and we must then check to see if our record has a new value in department or company (we are using "new" to mean a value different from the value in the compare fields). We check the company field first. Why? If the company has changed, we *know* that the department has also changed. Even if the current record includes the same department value as that of the compare field, it is a *different* department of the same name. Many companies have an accounting department, but they are all different departments because they are in different companies. So we check the company first; if it is different, we know we have a new department and a new company. If the company has not changed, it is still possible that the department has changed, so we must do a second check comparing the current department to the lastDept. We have nested the IFs because there is no need to check for any break if this is our first record (firstCheck = 'yes'), and there is no need to check the department if we have a change in company.

When we actually processed the break, however, we switched the order around. The first step in the CompanyBreak module is to perform the DeptBreak. We know that when we have a change in company we will write a subtotal for the company and for the department. Which do we want to write first? The department. So we must *process* the department break before the company break. It is also true that if we don't process the department break first, the company subtotal will be wrong since the values from the last department will not yet have been added in. Our generalized rule is: **Check the fields from *most* global to least global. *Process* the breaks from *least* global to most global.**

In our ProcessEmployee module we added the current record's salary to the deptTot accumulator, but we do not add the salary to the compTot accumulator. When we have a change in department, we can add the deptTot value to the compTot accumulator before we set the deptTot back to 0.

We have made sure that a new company will begin on a new page by setting the line count to 60 in the CompanyBreak module. We don't call Heads from the module because we know we will also call CompanyBreak from Finish to get the last subtotal, and we don't want to call Heads after writing the last company subtotal.

We have essentially done the same list of steps twice. A two-level break is no harder than a single-level break as long as you know the steps to be followed. Naturally some steps may not be relevant to every program, but, in general, for each level in a control break design, we should consider the following steps.

> Perform the next lower level break.
> Write the subtotal for the current break level.
> Add the subtotal to the next higher level accumulator.
> Reset the subtotal accumulator to 0.
> Reset the current level compare field to the current record.
> Prepare for any other necessary processing.

ANOTHER SAMPLE: A THREE-LEVEL BREAK WITH SUBTOTALS AND FINAL TOTAL

Suppose that in our conglomerate, our companies are grouped by region. We have a Northeast region, a Southern region, Midwest region, and so forth. If our input file also includes the name of the region and is sorted by region first, then within region sorted by company, and within company sorted by department, we can do a three-level break. We will modify our design so that it includes salary subtotals for each region, each company, and each department within a company. Remembering our rule we will *check* the fields for changes from most global (region) to least global (department), and we will *process* the breaks from least global to most global. We will also add a final total to this design (the total salary for the conglomerate), so we now need four accumulators, one each for the conglomerate, the regions, the companies, and the departments. We need three compare fields: region, company, and department. We will again assume that we want a new page for each company (that will of course get us a new page for each region also) and a five-line gap between departments.

```
Mainline
DO StartUp
WHILE there are data
    DO ProcessEmployee
ENDWHILE
DO Finish
```

StartUp
OPEN files
firstCheck = 'yes'
deptTot = 0
compTot = 0
regionTot = 0
finalTot = 0
lineCnt = 60

ProcessEmployee
READ name, region, company, department, salary
IF firstCheck = 'yes'
    firstCheck = 'no'
    lastDept = department
    lastComp = company
    lastRegion = region
ELSE
    IF region < > lastRegion
        DO RegionBreak
    ELSE
        IF company < > lastComp
            DO CompanyBreak
        ELSE
            IF department < > lastDept
                DO DeptBreak
                SKIP 5 lines
                ADD 5 to lineCnt
            ENDIF
        ENDIF
    ENDIF
ENDIF
DO WriteDetailLine
ADD salary to deptTot

Finish
DO RegionBreak
WRITE finalTot (dbl spc)
CLOSE files

RegionBreak
DO CompanyBreak
WRITE regionTot (dbl spc)
ADD regionTot to finalTot
regionTot = 0
lastRegion = region

```
CompanyBreak
DO DeptBreak
WRITE compTot (dbl spc)
ADD compTot to regionTot
compTot = 0
lastComp = company
lineCnt = 60


DeptBreak
WRITE deptTot (dbl spc)
ADD 2 to lineCnt
ADD deptTot to compTot
deptTot = 0
lastDept = department


WriteDetailLine
IF lineCnt > = 60
    DO Heads
ENDIF
WRITE region, company, department, name, salary
ADD 1 to lineCnt


Heads
EJECT page
SKIP 6 lines
WRITE page headings
WRITE column headings (dbl spc)
SKIP 1 line
lineCnt = 10
```

There really aren't a whole lot of changes in this design. We have the new RegionBreak module, and there is the necessary editing in ProcessEmployee, Finish, and CompanyBreak, but no major logic changes. All three break modules are essentially the same; you just need to be clear about which is the lower level and which is the higher level. DeptBreak doesn't have a lower level module to call. Once you are sure you understand your list of steps in a control break, you can impress the world by designing programs with subtotals at 10 levels. Only you and your classmates need to know that it's almost as easy as a block copy on your word processor.

Our final total didn't add too much complexity either. We now have a higher or more global level to add the region total to before we set it back to 0, and we have totals to write in Finish.

Notice that for the five-line gap between departments, we did not skip the five lines in the DeptBreak module. That would have given us the same five-line gap between the department total and the company total when we had a change in company. Instead, we skipped the lines after returning from the DeptBreak module at the call location indicating a change in department without a change in company or region.

Try desk checking this design with the data from page 225. (You will have to add the region field.)

THE SAME SAMPLE WITH A PRIMING READ

Let's look at the same design again, but this time with a priming read. Remember that the priming read gives us the advantage of knowing the first field values before we go into our ProcessEmployee module, so we can initialize our compare fields in StartUp. It also gives us the possibility of recognizing the end of our input file before we actually exit the loop. When we have no more input data, we can then "arrange" our logic so that our last subtotals are written while still in the loop instead of having to call them from the Finish module.

```
Mainline
DO StartUp
WHILE moreData = 'yes'
     DO ProcessEmployee
ENDWHILE
DO Finish

StartUp
OPEN files
moreData = 'yes'
DO ReadRecord
lastDept =department
lastComp = company
lastRegion = region
deptTot = 0
compTot = 0
regionTot = 0
finalTot = 0
lineCnt = 60
```

<u>ProcessEmployee</u>
DO WriteDetailLine
ADD salary to deptTot
DO ReadRecord
IF region < > lastRegion
    DO RegionBreak
ELSE
    IF company < > lastComp
        DO CompanyBreak
    ELSE
        IF department < > lastDept
            DO DeptBreak
            SKIP 5 lines
            ADD 5 to lineCnt
        ENDIF
    ENDIF
ENDIF

<u>Finish</u>
WRITE finalTot (dbl spc)
CLOSE files

<u>ReadRecord</u>
IF there are data
    READ name, region, company, department, salary
ELSE
    moreData = 'no'
    region = 'ZZZZZ'
ENDIF

<u>RegionBreak</u>
DO CompanyBreak
WRITE regionTot (dbl spc)
ADD regionTot to finalTot
regionTot = 0
lastRegion = region

<u>CompanyBreak</u>
DO DeptBreak
WRITE compTot (dbl spc)
ADD compTot to regionTot
compTot = 0
lastComp = company
lineCnt = 60

```
DeptBreak
WRITE deptTot (dbl spc)
ADD 2 to lineCnt
ADD deptTot to compTot
deptTot = 0
lastDept = department

WriteDetailLine
IF lineCnt > = 52
    DO Heads
ENDIF
WRITE region, company, department, name, salary
ADD 1 to lineCnt

Heads
EJECT page
SKIP 6 lines
WRITE page headings
WRITE column headings (dbl spc)
SKIP 1 line
lineCnt = 10
```

A FEW OTHER TOPICS OF INTEREST IN CONTROL BREAKS

There are several other minor concerns that need to be mentioned. We have made some assumptions in our designs so far about where we would do a check on the line counter. Notice, that we check it *only* when we write the detail line. We don't check to make sure there is room to write any one of the total lines. We are assuming that there will *always* be room for any and all total lines that may need to be written. In the previous example, we went to a new page if the lineCnt was greater than or equal to 52 so that if by chance the current detail, employee line being written turned out to be the last detail line, we would then be sure there was space for four double spaced total lines. If we want to be sure that our totals will always be on the same page with at least one detail line, our solution works. If we want to put as many lines as possible on a given page even if that means having department and company totals at the bottom of one page and the region total at the top of the next page, we must change our design a bit. For the latter situation, we must know the last line that can be used for writing. Every time we write a line (detail and/or total), we must do two additional steps. Before we write, we must first check to be sure there is room to write that particular line. After writing the line, we must add the appropriate value to the line counter.

Second, we frequently want to modify our headings to reflect the current group being written. If we are writing the employees for the Tri-State Company in the Northeast region, we might want the page headings to include the company and region names. We might also want to include similar identifiers in the total lines. Neither of these steps is difficult; just keep track of what you are writing. When writing the total line, you are writing a total for the previous group, not the group represented by the current record. (Remember, the change in the current record prompted you to write the total for the previous group.) So if this is a department total line, you would identify it using the lastDept compare field, not the department field of the current record. When you write the headings, on the other hand, the compare field and the current record field will have the same values so it doesn't matter which you write.

Finally, we frequently want to make our printed report easier to read by not repeating unchanged fields. For example, once we have written the first record from the Tri-State Company, there is no need to repeat the company name for each subsequent record. We might want to write the department, company, or region only with the first record in that group and leave the column blank in subsequent records. As we have been writing our output, a segment of our report might look like the sample on the next page. (I've added the kind of total line identifiers mentioned above and included more records than we had in the input sample shown previously.)

Northeast	Tri-State	Accounting	Marvin Martin	33,450
Northeast	Tri-State	Accounting	Opal Overtime	31,900
Northeast	Tri-State	Accounting	Trevor Richards	29,455
Northeast	Tri-State	Accounting	Cynthia Collins	35,950

Total Salary for Accounting Department 128,755

Northeast	Tri-State	Marketing	Henry Higgenbothem	41,350
Northeast	Tri-State	Marketing	Susan Supperly	44,000
Northeast	Tri-State	Marketing	Jake Jacobs	25,750
Northeast	Tri-State	Marketing	Suzanne Thomas	37,500
Northeast	Tri-State	Marketing	Wally Westerly	25,500

Total Salary for Marketing Department 174,100

Northeast	Tri-State	Personnel	Adam Appleby	30,500
Northeast	Tri-State	Personnel	Wallace Wilson	39,125
Northeast	Tri-State	Personnel	Gretchen Garbo	41,250

Total Salary for Personnel Department 110,875

Total Salary for Tri-State Company 413,730

Northeast	First Choice	Accounting	Beulah Betters	35,880
Northeast	First Choice	Accounting	David Douglas	31,250
Northeast	First Choice	Accounting	Evan Evinrude	29,755

Total Salary for Accounting Department 96,885

Northeast	First Choice	Marketing	Carmen Carruthers	39,500
Northeast	Firsh Choice	Marketing	Thom Thompkins	51,000
Northeast	First Choice	Marketing	Ursala Upham	33,300
Northeast	First Choice	Marketing	Penelope Peters	44,000
Northeast	First Choice	Marketing	Lester Richards	36,777

Total Salary for Marketing Department 204,577

Total Salary for First Choice Company 159,380

Total Salary for Northeast Region 405,455

If we write our output so that we don't repeat the region, company, and department fields, our output will be easier to read, and the new fields will be highlighted. This process is called "Group Indication" because we are indicating the groups by the outline type style.

The output segment might then look like the sample that follows. I've also changed the total identifiers to demonstrate a different method.

Northeast	Tri-State	Accounting	Marvin Martin	33,450	
			Opal Overtime	31,900	
			Trevor Richards	29,455	
			Cynthia Collins	35,950	
			Dept TOTAL	128,755	**Accounting**
		Marketing	Henry Higgenbothem	41,350	
			Susan Supperly	44,000	
			Jake Jacobs	25,750	
			Suzanne Thomas	37,500	
			Wally Westerly	25,500	
			Dept TOTAL	174,100	**Marketing**
		Personnel	Adam Appleby	30,500	
			Wallace Wilson	39,125	
			Gretchen Garbo	41,250	
			Dept TOTAL	110,875	**Personnel**
			Comp TOTAL	413,730	**Tri-State**
	First Choice	Accounting	Beulah Betters	35,880	
			David Douglas	31,250	
			Evan Evinrude	29,755	
			Dept TOTAL	96,885	**Accounting**
		Marketing	Carmen Carruthers	39,500	
			Thom Thompkins	51,000	
			Ursala Upham	33,300	
			Penelope Peters	44,000	
			Lester Richards	36,777	
			Dept TOTAL	204,577	**Marketing**
			Comp TOTAL	159,380	**First Choice**
			Region TOTAL	405,455	**Northeast**

How do we do it? By the time we are ready to write the detail line we don't know if we had a control break or not, so we must use some means to "remember" what needs to be written. One solution is to use a series of flags indicating if a break occurred. Unfortunately, with a three-level break design, we would need three different flags, one for each level. The module writing the detail line gets a bit cumbersome but is doable. Assuming that we have set the appropriate flags to 'yes' in the related break modules (that is in DeptBreak we would set newDept to 'yes', in CompanyBreak we would set newComp to 'yes', etc.), our module might look like this.

```
WriteDetailLine
IF lineCnt > = 52
    DO Heads
ENDIF
IF newRegion = 'yes'
    WRITE region, company, department, name, salary
    newRegion = 'no'
    newComp = 'no'
    newDept = 'no'
ELSE
    IF newComp = 'yes'
        WRITE spaces, company, department, name, salary
        newComp = 'no'
        newDept = 'no'
    ELSE
        IF newDept = 'yes'
            WRITE spaces, spaces, department, name, salary
            newDept = 'no'
        ELSE
            WRITE spaces, spaces, spaces, name, salary
        ENDIF
    ENDIF
ENDIF
ADD 1 to lineCnt
```

Notice the importance of resetting the flags. Once we have used the information, we set the flag or flags back to 'no' in preparation for the next break. If we have a region break, we must set all three flags back because we would have changed each of the flags to 'yes' in the three break modules.

Another solution to the problem is to assume that we will write a different field than the input field. Let's say our input fields are region, company, department, name, and salary. If our write calls for us to write the fields regionOut, compOut, deptOut, we have complete control over what is moved into these output fields. Our write module might look like the one shown on the next page.

```
WriteDetailLine
IF lineCnt > = 52
    DO Heads
ENDIF
WRITE regionOut, compOut, deptOut, name, salary
ADD 1 to lineCnt
regionOut = spaces
compOut = spaces
deptOut = spaces
```

Because we set the three break-dependent fields to spaces, we will write spaces unless we specifically move a value into the fields. In each of the break modules, we could move the current record's value into the output field (that is, in the DeptBreak module include deptOut = department, in CompanyBreak include compOut = company, etc.). If we just had a control break on that field, the output field will have the input field value and otherwise will have spaces. When we write the output field in the write module, we will get spaces or the field value.

With group indication we must also account for continuation to a new page because the previous page was full. If we are in the same region, same company, and same department, we would not ordinarily repeat these field values in the detail line. But, since the reader can't easily glance up to a previous line to check a value, we probably want to write all fields for the first record on a page whether or not the fields have changed. How? If we're using the flag method, we could set the newRegion flag to 'yes' in the Heads module. If we're using separate output fields, we would need to move the needed values into the output fields in the Heads module.

A FINAL EXAMPLE

For this final example, we will assume that we want a three-level break, including region, company, and department salary subtotals and a final total. The detail record fields should be group indicated, but if a group is continued to a new page all fields should be repeated. Each new department, company, and region should begin on a new page. Headings and total lines should reflect the appropriate grouping. Headings should include a one-inch top margin, report headings, page headings, and double-spaced column headings. The first detail line should be double-spaced from the column headings. Subtotal and total lines should be double-spaced. The minimum bottom margin is one inch. No total lines should be written at the top of a page.

With a one-inch bottom margin, we would ordinarily print the last line on any given page on line 60, and our check for a full page would therefore be IF lineCnt > = 60. We have four possible total lines that could be written after any detail line (since we don't know when we write a detail line if it is the last detail line). Each total line is double-spaced so a total of 8 lines could be used with total lines. That means when we do our line check in the write module, we need to be sure we have room to write 9 lines (1 detail line plus the 4 total lines each preceded by a blank line). If we have already used 52 lines, we must go to a new page.

```
Mainline
DO StartUp
WHILE there are data
    DO ProcessEmployee
ENDWHILE
DO Finish


StartUp
OPEN files
firstCheck = 'yes'
deptTot = 0
compTot = 0
regionTot = 0
finalTot = 0
lineCnt = 52
pageCnt = 0


ProcessEmployee
READ name, region, company, department, salary
IF firstCheck = 'yes'
    firstCheck = 'no'
    lastDept =department
    lastComp = company
    lastRegion = region
ELSE
    IF region < > lastRegion
        DO RegionBreak
    ELSE
        IF company < > lastComp
            DO CompanyBreak
        ELSE
            IF department < > lastDept
                DO DeptBreak
            ENDIF
        ENDIF
    ENDIF
ENDIF
DO WriteDetailLine
ADD salary to deptTot
```

<u>Finish</u>
DO RegionBreak
WRITE 'Total Salary for Conglomerate = ', finalTot (dbl spc)
CLOSE files

<u>RregionBreak</u>
DO CompanyBreak
WRITE 'Total Salary for ', lastRegion, ' = ', regionTot (dbl spc)
ADD regionTot to finalTot
lastRegion = region
regionTot = 0
regionOut = region

<u>CompanyBreak</u>
DO DeptBreak
WRITE 'Total Salary for ', lastComp, ',= ', compTot (dbl spc)
ADD compTot to regionTot
compTot = 0
lastComp = company
compOut = company

<u>DeptBreak</u>
WRITE 'Total Salary for ', lastDept, ' = ', deptTot (dbl spc)
ADD deptTot to compTot
deptTot = 0
lastDept = department
deptOut = department
lineCnt = 52

<u>WriteDetailLine</u>
IF lineCnt > = 52
    DO Heads
ENDIF
WRITE regionOut, compOut, deptOut, name, salary
ADD 1 to lineCnt
regionOut = spaces
compOut = spaces
deptOut = spaces

<u>Heads</u>
EJECT page
SKIP 6 lines
IF pageCnt = 0
    WRITE report heading
    SKIP 1 line
    lineCnt = 8
ELSE
    lineCnt = 6
ENDIF
ADD 1 to pageCnt
WRITE 'Employee Listing For ', region, company, department, 'Page ', pageCnt
WRITE column headings (dbl spc)
SKIP 1 line
ADD 4 to lineCnt
regionOut = region
compOut = company
deptOut = department

EXERCISES

The following exercises all use as input a file containing the top 1000 recordings for 1995. For each recording the file includes a musical classification, the recording company, the label number, the performer(s), and the number sold. The file is in order by musical classification, within classification by company, and within company by performer.

1. Design a program to produce a listing of all recordings that gives the average number of recordings sold for each musical classification and each company. The lines giving the averages should be written double-spaced after the last detail line for that category. No average line should be written on the top of a new page. Begin a new page only when a page is full (i.e., not for new company or new classification). Skip five lines before beginning a new classification and three lines before beginning a new company within the same classification.

2. Modify design #1 so that it includes the average number of recordings sold of all records in the file and so that it writes the report using group indication. Each new classification should begin on a new page.

3. Modify design #2 so that only the averages are written. Do not include any detail lines. The entire report will now fit on one page.

4. Design a program that will create a report listing all fields for all recordings plus give the average number of recording *companies* in a musical classification and the average number of *performers* in a musical classification.

5. Design a program that creates a report listing the classification, company, label number, and performer for each recording and the count of the number of performers in each company group. At the end of the report include a count of the number of classifications included.

6. Design a program to create a listing of all the top recordings. In addition, for each classification and for each company within a classification, give the performer(s) and the label number for the recording that has sold the most copies. Use group indication in the report.

Chapter 14

Two-Dimension Arrays

Objectives

After completing this chapter, you should be able to:

1. Describe the differences between column major and row major loading order.
2. Design modules to load a two-dimension array using both column major and row major order.
3. Describe the limitations in loading a two-dimension array of unknown size.
4. Design a module to search a two-dimension array using "headers" within the two-dimension array.
5. Design a module to search a two-dimension array using "headers" in separate one-dimension arrays.
6. Design a module to search a two-dimension array that has headers representing range limits.
7. Design a module to search an entire two-dimension array for a specific element.

INTRODUCTION

We have used single dimension arrays (and done a lot with them). We know that a single dimension array requires a single subscript (we frequently called it ptr) to point to the particular position in the array that is of interest. We also know that by varying the subscript's value in a loop we can eventually point to each element in the array, a useful ability for loading an array, searching an array, or writing an array.

We have been limited, however, in the kinds of data we could represent in our array. Anything that required a simple list, what we would probably picture as similar items listed one under another, could easily be handled in our design as an array. In addition, a combination of related lists could be represented as parallel arrays. But frequently, we must deal with data that are more complex than a single list of elements. We often need two "points of reference" to identify the information we need.

Picture a typical road map. If we are looking for Dodge City, we might check the index and find the "coordinates" for the town. The index could tell us that Dodge City will be found at the intersection of "I" and "3." By moving one finger across the map from position "I" and another finger down the map from position "3," we can expect to find Dodge City where our two fingers meet. But if the index had given us only one of the coordinates, we would have had a much more difficult time. The map is a two-dimension area, and we need to define both dimensions to find the town.

A two-dimension array is the same kind of two-dimension area, and we need to identify the positions in both dimensions to define a given point. Look at the representation of the familiar federal income tax table.

| | | Filing Status | | |
Taxable Income	Single	Married Filing Jointly	Married Filing Separately	Head of Household
20000-20049	3196	3004	3595	3004
20050-20099	3210	3011	3609	3011
20100-20149	3224	3019	3623	3019
20150-20199	3238	3026	3637	3026
20200-20249	3252	3034	3651	3034
20250-20299	3266	3041	3665	3041
20300-20349	3280	3049	3679	3049
20350-20399	3294	3056	3693	3056

In order to find your tax amount you need two pieces of information. You need to know the proper range in which your adjusted gross income falls, and you need your filing status. If you have only the adjusted gross income, you can identify the row that contains your tax amount, but you still don't know which of the several values in that row will be your tax. Once you identify the proper row and column, you can do the same thing you could do on the map to find Dodge City: run one finger horizontally across the proper row and another finger vertically down the proper column until your fingers meet. (If you're like many of us you then groan loudly, and not because of the impact of one finger against the other.)

This is a two-dimension array (actually the term "table" can also be properly used now). With a two-dimension array we need two subscripts, one for the row and one for the column. We still give the subscripts within parentheses after the array name, and now we will separate the two subscripts with a comma as in Taxes(4,2). Commonly the subscript for the row is given first, followed by the subscript for the column.

A POSITIONAL EXAMPLE

Let's look at one more example. Many businesses have salary schedules that are divided into major levels with each level further divided into steps. A salary schedule might look like the following.

Salary Schedule for XYZ Corporation

Level	Step 1	2	3	4	5
1	20000	20500	21000	21500	22000
2	23000	23500	24000	24500	25000
3	26000	26500	27000	27500	28000
4	29000	29500	30000	30500	31000
5	33000	33500	34000	34500	35000

If you have just been hired by XYZ Corporation and want to learn your starting salary, you must know your salary level and salary step. This is a positional table. Only the salaries would be stored, but they would be stored positionally within the two-dimension array. All of the level 1 salaries would be in row 1 with the step 1 salary in column 1 of that row, the step 2 salary in column 2 of that row, and so on through level 5. You don't have to search the array because you automatically know the correct row and column when you know the level and step. If we were writing a short design segment to read in a level number and a step number and then write out the salary, it would take only two lines (assuming the array had already been loaded).

```
READ level, step
WRITE salary(level,step)
```

We are using level as the subscript for the row and step as the subscript for the column to access the needed salary.

Another approach, however, would be to start with the salary and try to find the appropriate level for that salary. Suppose you wanted to know what level and step you would need to reach to earn a salary of 30,000. You would start searching at level 1, check all the salaries in that level, and if you didn't find a value greater than or equal to 30,000, you would go to level 2 and check all the salaries there, and continue until you found a salary $>= 30,000$ or had searched the entire array.

```
search = 'yes'
row = 0
WHILE row < 5 AND search = 'yes'
    ADD 1 to row
    col = 0
    WHILE col < 5 AND search = 'yes'
        ADD 1 to col
        IF salary(row,col) >= 30,000
            search = 'found'
        ENDIF
    ENDWHILE
ENDWHILE
IF search = 'found'
    WRITE 'You can earn $30,000 at level ', row, ' step ', col
ELSE
    WRITE 'You'll never get up to $30,000 with this company!'
ENDIF
```

This design segment does exactly what was described in the paragraph above. The subscript row is set to 1, and the subscript col is changed in the nested loop to check all of the first row. Then the row subscript is incremented to check the second row. This process continues until a salary $>= 30,000$ is found or the entire array is searched. We'll get back to searches later in this chapter.

LOADING TWO-DIMENSION ARRAYS

When we loaded our one-dimension arrays, we took the first value and put it in the first position of the array, put the second value in the second position, and continued until we had filled the array or used up all the input values. With a two-dimension array, we have an interesting question to resolve first. We can easily get the first value and put it in the first position (row 1, column 1); but what is the second position? Is our second position the same row but over one column (1,2) or the same column but down one row (2,1)? There is no firm answer to the question. We must know in what order the data will be provided before we can load the array.

If we were loading the salary schedule array shown earlier, the input data file could begin like this:

```
20000
20500
21000
21500
22000
23000
etc.
```

In this case, we would need to know that we should load all of row 1, then load all of row 2, and so forth to row 5. Because we have two dimensions, we will need to have two loops in the loading process. One loop will vary the row subscript, and for each iteration of that loop, we will be loading a separate row. But within one row, we need to load multiple columns, so we will have a second, nested loop that varies the column subscript. To load the salary schedule with five rows and five columns from the input file just described, our loading loops could look like the load below.

```
row = 0
WHILE row < 5
    ADD 1 to row
    col = 0
    WHILE col < 5
        ADD 1 to col
        READ salary(row,col)
    ENDWHILE
ENDWHILE
```

We have two subscripts: Row is used as the subscript to point to the correct row, and col is used as the subscript to point to the correct column. We could have used ptr1 and ptr2 as the variable names (or any other two names), but using row and col helps to make the design readable and helps us keep track of what we are doing in the design. This load is called *row major* loading because we do the loading in row-level groups, all of row 1, then all of row 2, and so forth.

This isn't the only kind of loading we could do, however. Remember, we said we needed to know the order of the input data file. The first example assumes row major order in the input file, that is the input file has the data one row at a time. But the data could have been in a different order. Suppose our input data file was in the following order.

```
20000
23000
26000
29000
33000
20500
23500
etc.
```

This time we have *column major* order, all of column 1, then all of column 2, and so on. Obviously we have to change our loading design if the input file presents column major order, or the salary schedule array will be a mess. With column major order, we still need nested loops, but now the loop that controls the column is the outer loop.

```
col = 0
WHILE col < 5
    ADD 1 to col
    row = 0
    WHILE row < 5
        ADD 1 to row
        READ salary(row,col)
    ENDWHILE
ENDWHILE
```

This time our column subscript will stay at 1 while the inner loop varies the row subscript from 1 to 5, so we read all 5 values in column 1. Then the column subscript will be incremented to 2, and the row subscript will be varied again from 1 to 5 to read the second column.

These loads have used count-controlled loops because we knew how many salary levels and steps we had to load. With single dimension arrays, we also looked at event-controlled loops when the number of array items was unknown at the time of the load. Could we do the same with a two-dimension array? Yes, but we need to work a bit more. Remember, we are going to load all of the first row or all of the first column, then go to the second row or column. If we don't know how many values go in the first row, how do we know when to stop putting values in row 1 and put the next value in row 2, column 1? We need to know the number of values to load, or we need to have a sentinel value marking the end of the first row or column. It would be very unusual to have a two-dimension array in which we didn't know the number of values for either the row or the column. More likely we know one of the dimensions, but may not know the other. If we know one dimension but don't know the other and don't have a sentinel value, we must load the array with the known dimension as the inner loop and the unknown dimension as an EOF controlled outer loop. If we know the size of one dimension and have sentinel values marking the end of the other dimension (or if we have sentinel values marking the end of both dimensions), we can load the array in row major or column major order. Remember, though, that a sentinel value always requires a priming read.

In the load below, we load a full row, then check to see if there are more data. While there are data, we continue to load the array, one row at a time. Notice that this load assumes that the data will come in full-row sets—we don't check for end of file within a row. We could just as easily have had a sentinel controlled outer loop (with a priming read of course).

```
row = 0
WHILE there are data
    ADD 1 to row
    col = 0
    WHILE col < 5
        ADD 1 to col
        READ salary(row,col)
    ENDWHILE
ENDWHILE
numRow = row
```

We will assume that one of our dimensions is always known.

USING A TWO-DIMENSION ARRAY

Once we get our array loaded, we can do all kinds of things with it. In a business setting, we will probably be searching the array more than anything else. But let's look first at a few other kinds of operations we could perform. Arrays are frequently used for graphic representations for which we need to be able to access particular segments of the array.

Assume we have a 10 x 10 array named BOX and we want the entire array initialized to the "=" character. That's just like loading the array except we don't have to worry about row major or column major order.

```
row = 0
WHILE row < 10
    ADD 1 to row
    col = 0
    WHILE col < 10
        ADD 1 to col
        box(row, col) = "="
    ENDWHILE
ENDWHILE
```

```
     1 2 3 4 5 6 7 8 9 0
  1  = = = = = = = = = =
  2  = = = = = = = = = =
  3  = = = = = = = = = =
  4  = = = = = = = = = =
  5  = = = = = = = = = =
  6  = = = = = = = = = =
  7  = = = = = = = = = =
  8  = = = = = = = = = =
  9  = = = = = = = = = =
  0  = = = = = = = = = =
```

Let's get a bit fancier. We want the perimeter initialized to the "|" character. In other words, row 1 and row 10, col 1 and col 10 will all be changed to the new character, but the inside of the array will not be changed. My solution will initialize the corner cells twice, but that's more efficient than checking them. It also uses a "generic" subscript that is sometimes the row and sometimes the column. (This works because our array is square, the same number of rows and columns.) Each of the four assignment statements in the loop changes one of the four sides of the array, one element at a time.

```
ptr = 0
WHILE ptr < 10
    ADD 1 to ptr
    box(ptr,1) = "|"
    box(ptr,10) = "|"
    box(1,ptr) = "|"
    box(10,ptr) = "|"
ENDWHILE
```

```
     1 2 3 4 5 6 7 8 9 0
  1  | | | | | | | | | |
  2  | = = = = = = = = |
  3  | = = = = = = = = |
  4  | = = = = = = = = |
  5  | = = = = = = = = |
  6  | = = = = = = = = |
  7  | = = = = = = = = |
  8  | = = = = = = = = |
  9  | = = = = = = = = |
  0  | | | | | | | | | |
```

One last operation. We want the diagonals initialized to the "#" character. The top left to bottom right diagonal is fairly easy because its row and column subscripts are always the same (1,1; 2,2; 3,3; etc.). The top right to bottom left diagonal is not so obvious since its row and column subscripts vary in different patterns; one goes down as the other goes up (1,10; 2,9; 3,8; 4,7; etc.). If we study those subscripts, we may eventually realize that they always sum to one more than the number of rows or columns. We use that observation in the solution.

Chapter 14 *Two-Dimension Arrays*

```
ptr = 0
WHILE ptr < 10
    ADD 1 to ptr
    box(ptr,ptr) = "#"
    box(ptr, 11-ptr) = "#"
ENDWHILE
```

```
     1  2  3  4  5  6  7  8  9  0
  1  #  |  |  |  |  |  |  |  |  #
  2  |  #  =  =  =  =  =  =  #  |
  3  |  =  #  =  =  =  =  #  =  |
  4  |  =  =  #  =  =  #  =  =  |
  5  |  =  =  =  #  #  =  =  =  |
  6  |  =  =  =  #  #  =  =  =  |
  7  |  =  =  #  =  =  #  =  =  |
  8  |  =  #  =  =  =  =  #  =  |
  9  |  #  =  =  =  =  =  =  #  |
  0  #  |  |  |  |  |  |  |  |  #
```

The first assignment refers to box (ptr,ptr) and gives us the top left to bottom right diagonal. The second assignment gives us the top right to bottom left diagonal by calculating the column subscript as 11 minus the current value of the row subscript. Try it, it works!

SEARCHING TWO-DIMENSION ARRAYS

Any use of arrays will almost certainly include searching since that is one of the primary reasons for storing data in an array initially. Our search methodology will again depend on the order of the array data. We already know that if our data are ordered and stored positionally, we will not have to do a search at all. If our data are not ordered, we will have to do a sequential search. If our data are in ascending or descending order, we can do a sequential search with early exit or a binary search.

But there is another question that must be considered. Let's look at another array to see the problem. This array provides the percentage of nitrogen (N), phosphorus pentoxide (P_2O_5), and potassium oxide (K_2O) available in various animal manures (information of great interest to gardeners).

Animal Manure	N	Percent P$_2$O$_5$	K$_2$O
Cattle, dried	1.5	2.0	2.3
Cattle, fresh	0.5	0.2	0.5
Chicken, dried	4.5	3.5	2.0
Chicken, fresh	1.5	1.0	0.5
Goat, dried	1.4	1.0	3.0
Horse, fresh	0.7	0.3	0.5
Swine, fresh	0.7	0.6	0.7
Sheep, dried	4.2	2.5	6.0
Sheep, fresh	1.4	0.7	1.5

(Source: Splittstoesser, Walter, *Vegetable Growing Handbook*, AVI Publishing, 1979, p. 88.)

The question to be considered is: How much of the above table actually goes in the array? We could probably agree that the labels "Animal Manure" and "Percent" should not be included. But what about the chemical column labels and the animal row labels? If we store just the numbers, will we be able to interpret the array? Even if we want to store the labels, can we? Remember that our array must have like items; all the elements stored in the array will be stored under the same name and must be the same type (all numeric, all alphabetic, etc.). In the above array, the labels are alphanumeric and the other values are numeric. They can't both go in the same array. In other arrays, the labels and other values may be of the same type, but we still may not want to put the labels in the array since they represent different kinds of data even when they are the same data type. If we can't put the labels in the array, what do we do with them? Put them in single-dimension parallel arrays. In our example above, we would have three arrays: two single-dimension arrays holding the labels and one two-dimension array holding the percentage values. Something like the arrays shown on the next page.

Colheads

Nitrogen	Phosphorus	Potassium

Rowheads

Percents

Rowheads	Nitrogen	Phosphorus	Potassium
Cattle, dried	1.5	2.0	2.3
Cattle, fresh	0.5	0.2	0.5
Chicken, dried	4.5	3.5	2.0
Chicken, fresh	1.5	1.0	0.5
Goat, dried	1.4	1.0	3.0
Horse, fresh	0.7	0.3	0.5
Swine, fresh	0.7	0.6	0.7
Sheep, dried	4.2	2.5	6.0
Sheep, fresh	1.4	0.7	1.5

In many ways, this makes our job easier. We now just have to search the single dimension arrays for a match and save the subscript for use in the "parallel" two-dimension array. If we want to know the percentage of potassium from goat manure, we would search the rowHeads array for "Goat, dried" and save the subscript. Then we would search the colHeads array for Potassium and again save the subscript. The desired percentage is then accessed in the percents array by using the two saved subscripts.

A sample design solution is on the next page.

```
        search = 'yes'
        ptr = 0
        WHILE search = 'yes' AND ptr < 9
            ADD 1 to ptr
            IF rowHeads(ptr) = 'Goat, dried'
                search = 'found'
                row = ptr
            ENDIF
        ENDWHILE
        IF search = 'yes'
            WRITE 'Sorry, that manure is not included in array'
        ELSE
            search = 'yes'
            ptr = 0
            WHILE search = 'yes' AND ptr < 3
                ADD 1 to ptr
                IF colHeads(ptr) = 'Potassium'
                    search = 'found'
                    col = ptr
                ENDIF
            ENDWHILE
            IF search = 'yes'
                WRITE 'Sorry, that nutrient is not included in array'
            ELSE
                WRITE 'The percentage is ', Percents(row,col)
            ENDIF
        ENDIF
```

How would this change if the labels had been stored in the array? Let's rewrite our array using arbitrary (but not positional) numeric codes for the animals and nutrients so that they can be included in the two-dimension array. Our array might then look like the representation on the next page.

Percents

	99	105	121
34	1.5	2.0	2.3
39	0.5	0.2	0.5
41	4.5	3.5	2.0
47	1.5	1.0	0.5
49	1.4	1.0	3.0
52	0.7	0.3	0.5
55	0.7	0.6	0.7
58	4.2	2.5	6.0
60	1.4	0.7	1.5

Our array now has 10 rows and four columns. Row 1 (columns 2, 3, and 4) holds the column labels. Column 1 (rows two through 10) holds the row labels. Notice that there is nothing in row 1, column 1. (We should note as an aside that although we now have a "legal" array with all values of numeric data type, we don't have a "good" array. Our numeric values still represent two different things: numeric codes and percentage values. A well-designed array should include only one type of value. We will continue with the example, but you should recognize that we are stretching our design principles here.) Now when we search for the correct row and column, we are searching within the two-dimension array, but we're still searching just one dimension at a time. First we find the correct row and then the correct column (or vice versa). The numeric code for goat manure is 49, so we'll search column 1 for a 49. The code for potassium is 121, so we'll search row 1 for a 121.

```
        search = 'yes'
        ptr = 1
        WHILE search = 'yes' AND ptr < 10
            ADD 1 to ptr
            IF percents(ptr,1) = 49
                search = 'found'
                row = ptr
            ENDIF
        ENDWHILE
        IF search = 'yes'
            WRITE 'Sorry, that manure is not included in array'
        ELSE
            search = 'yes'
            ptr = 1
            WHILE search = 'yes' AND ptr < 4
                ADD 1 to ptr
                IF percents(1,ptr) = 121
                    search = 'found'
                    col = ptr
                ENDIF
            ENDWHILE
            IF search = 'yes'
                WRITE 'Sorry, that nutrient is not included in array'
            ELSE
                WRITE 'The percentage is ', percents(row,col)
            ENDIF
        ENDIF
```

There are several differences, all minor but important. We have changed the name of the arrays being searched, of course. We have also changed the *range* of the array to be searched. When searching for the proper row, we must compare our desired numeric code with the code stored in rows two through 10 (instead of one through nine before). And when searching for the proper column, we check columns two through four. In each case the first row or column is skipped by initializing ptr to 1 and then adding to it before we do any comparison.

SEARCHING WITH RANGE HEADINGS

Frequently one or both of the dimension headings will be a range of numbers, not a single number or label. The tax table that we looked at in the beginning of the chapter used ranges for the row labels. To find the proper row, the user needed to find the range within which his or her taxable income would fall. When we implement an array like that in a design, we need to change it somewhat. We don't need to include both limits of each range. We will only include the minimum or maximum (usually minimum) as the label.

The following sample is a simplified pricing chart for mailing packages. The cost depends on both the zone to which you are mailing and the weight range into which the package falls.

to zone	Weight in Pounds			
	0 to 1.5	1.6 to 3	3.1 to 4.9	5 or over
2	2.10	4.70	6.90	10.00
4	2.70	5.25	8.50	14.80
6	3.30	6.70	11.00	17.90
7	4.20	7.90	13.10	20.50
9	5.80	9.90	16.60	29.00

When we store this in an array, we need a way to represent the ranges that will still preserve the needed information but make our comparisons clearer. A solution is to store only the minimum value for that column. Our stored array then looks like this.

	0.0	1.6	3.1	5.0
2	2.10	4.70	6.90	10.00
4	2.70	5.25	8.50	14.80
6	3.30	6.70	11.00	17.90
7	4.20	7.90	13.10	20.50
9	5.80	9.90	16.60	29.00

Our search for the proper row would be exactly the same as usual. Our search for the proper column would check to see if the weight is within the allowed range for that column. If we started at the lowest number and worked up, we wouldn't be able to tell if the column is correct. For example, if we're looking for the proper column for a package weighing 2.3 pounds and check to see if the weight is greater than or equal to the first range value, the answer would be yes! Since 2.3 is $>= 0.0$, it would appear that we have found the proper column but of course we haven't. An easier solution is to start at the opposite end and work right to left. Since 2.3 is not greater than or equal to 5.0, we know that the last column is not correct. Then we can see if 2.3 is greater than or equal to 3.1, and continue checking the minimum entries until we identify the proper column. A design solution for a package weighing 2.3 pounds and going to zone 7 follows. Our array is named Mailing.

```
ptr = 1
search = 'yes'
WHILE ptr < 6 AND search = 'yes'
    ADD 1 to ptr
    IF mailing(ptr,1) = 7
        search = 'found'
        row = ptr
    ENDIF
ENDWHILE
IF search = 'found'
    ptr = 6
    search = 'yes'
    WHILE ptr > 2 AND search = 'yes'
        SUBTRACT 1 from ptr
        IF weight > = mailing(1,ptr)
            search = 'found'
            col = ptr
        ENDIF
    ENDWHILE
    IF search = 'found'
        WRITE 'The cost is ', mailing(row, col)
    ELSE
        WRITE 'ERROR, you must have entered a negative weight'
    ENDIF
ELSE
    WRITE 'ERROR, invalid zone entered'
ENDIF
```

Note that on the inner search (for the proper weight column), we have initialized ptr to 6 and then subtracted 1 from it before we use it. That means the first column we check will be the fifth column (in this case, we have five columns). We continue that loop while the ptr is *greater than* 2 so that we do not check the first column. If we entered when ptr = 2 and then subtracted 1, we would be checking position (1,1) which should be empty.

We could also have defined the ranges by storing the maximum value for the column. In that case we would need to have a maximum value for the fifth column. In some cases a maximum is available (for mailing packages, for example, there probably is a maximum weight that will be accepted), but other uses may not have a maximum (a store is probably willing to sell you as many widgits as you are willing to buy). The nature of the data will dictate whether you use a maximum or a minimum. For maximums, compare the ranges left to right (starting with the smallest value and working up). For minimums, compare the ranges right to left (starting with the largest value and working down).

LOADING, AGAIN

We have already mastered row-major and column-major loading, but what if the headings for the arrays data are stored in the same data file? It is not unusual to have the heading (label) data interspersed with the array data so that we are loading multiple arrays at once. For example, let's load the arrays shown on page 253. We'll assume the data are in row-major order, preceded by the data for the colHeads array, as in:

Input data:	Nitrogen
	Phosphorus
	Potassium
	Cattle, dried
	1.5
	2.0
	2.3
	Cattle, fresh
	0.5
	0.2
	0.5
	etc.

When we load, we load the colHeads array first, then load the rowHeads as a part of the loop loading percents.

```
col = 0
WHILE col < 3
    ADD 1 to col
    READ colHeads(col)
ENDWHILE
row = 0
WHILE row < 9
    ADD 1 to row
    READ rowHeads(row)
    col = 0
    WHILE col < 3
        ADD 1 to col
        READ percents(row,col)
    ENDWHILE
ENDWHILE
```

If our data were in column-major order, we would just switch the order of the loading so that the rowHeads array was loaded first and the colHeads array was loaded in the Percents loading loop.

When we load the row and column labels within the same array as the array data, we have another variation. We must remember now to skip the column 1, row 1 position. As an example, let's load the mailing cost array from page 257, assuming row-major data.

```
row = 0
WHILE row < 6
    ADD 1 to row
    col = 0
    WHILE col < 5
        ADD 1 to col
        IF row > 1 OR col > 1
            READ mailing(row,col)
        ENDIF
    ENDWHILE
ENDWHILE
```

There are many ways we could have controlled the READ. Basically, we want read in each iteration of the inner loop except when row = 1 and col = 1.

BEYOND THE SECOND DIMENSION

Much like control breaks, once you get accustomed to one level, you can add levels without too much stress or panic. A two-dimension array is just a single dimension array in which each element in that array is itself another array—each row has multiple elements, so it is an array. Adding more dimensions, then, simply means that we are adding another outside layer. A three-dimension array is an array in which each element is itself a two-dimension array. They aren't any more difficult to handle; there is just a third subscript to keep track of and perhaps a third layer for a search. Some people find it easiest to picture a three-dimension array as a cube. Others prefer to picture the three-dimension array as multiple layers of two-dimension arrays stacked one on top of the other. (A book is a good analogy in which each page is a two-dimension figure and the multiple pages add the third dimension.) Beyond the third dimension, it gets harder to visualize but no harder to process. Try imagining each book as the three-dimension array and multiple volumes as the fourth dimension.

Although the programming language being used may set limits on the number of dimensions allowed in an array, the computer's ability to handle arrays is really limited only by its memory. Memory is an important factor, though, as the number of dimensions increases. A 10x10 array has 100 elements. If we add a third dimension to it, ten 10x10 arrays, or one 10x10x10 array, we have 1000 elements. We may have a simple two-dimension array to hold the grades for a class of students. If the class has 30 students and each student has 20 possible grades, we have a total of 600 elements in the array. If we make that a three-dimension array to hold grades for the teacher's five classes (a 5x30x20 array) we have 3000 elements. And if we make it a four-dimension array holding grades for all 50 of the teachers in the school (50x5x30x20) we are now using 150,000 elements! Memory can start to become a precious resource.

EXERCISES

1. Design a program segment that will declare and load an array(s) to hold the grades for the ENG 101 class. Assume there are exactly 30 students and that each student has exactly 10 numeric grades. The input file has the student's name and then the 10 grades for that student.

2. Modify the loading segment from design # 1 so that we can load grades until end of file (that is, we don't know if we have a full class of 30 students). You may assume that each student included has a complete set of grades.

3. Design a program segment to calculate the average grade for each student and write each student's name and average using the array(s) loaded in design # 2.

4. Design a program segment to calculate the average grade for each test/assignment and write out the assignment number (1 through 10) and the average grade using the array(s) loaded in design # 2.

5. Assume that the array data file begins with identifiers for the 10 grades. Modify the declaration and loading from design # 1 so that you also store the grade identifiers.

6. Design a program to read in (interactively) a student's name and write out that student's 10 grades using the array(s) loaded in # 2.

7. Modify design # 6 so that you also read in (interactively) a grade identifier and then write out the one requested grade for the identified student.

8. Design a program that inarticulate weather persons can use to identify the proper adjective to describe the next day's weather. The program will read in the season and the temperature, consult an array to find the proper adjective, and write out the adjective. That process will continue in a loop until the end-of-file. The array data will come from a second file described on the next page. Your program will, of course, need to declare and load any necessary arrays. No headings or page control are necessary.

Array data input file: (starts with the minimum temperature for each of 9 temperature ranges, then the season and the nine adjectives for each season)

-70
 0
15
32
45
60
75
85
99
Winter
bitter
very cold
below freezing
seasonable
beautiful
unseasonably warm
unbelievably hot
ozone trauma
a record record
Spring
beyond cold
freak cold
frosty nights
etc.

Detail input file: (Season, temp)
Winter, 44
Winter, 73
Spring, 34
Spring, 89
etc.

REVIEW D: Review Exercises for Chapters 12 through 14

1. Design a program that creates an inventory listing for the Video HideAway store. All videotapes are categorized by the rating system: 1(out of date), 2(recent but lousy), 3(recent and good), and 4(never available). They are also grouped by type: V(VHS), B(Beta), and D(Disk). The input file is ordered by the 1–4 rating levels. Your program's output should start each new 1–4 rating level on a new page and should include a line at the end of each group indicating how many tapes there are in that rating level. Do not write detail lines below the 55th line on the page (that allows space for the total line if needed).

2. Revise design # 1 so that it does a two-level break. Assume now that the file is in order by the type of the tape (V,B,D) groupings and within each tape-type group in order by the numeric rating level. Each new tape-type should begin on a new page, and each rating level within the tape-type should be preceded by five blank lines. Write the count of tapes for each subgroup (rating level) and each type group. Do not print beyond the 55th line except for totals.

3. Design a program that will be used on a computer connected to chemical analysis equipment in the lab. One piece of equipment takes a temperature reading of the outdoor temperature every five minutes and returns the first two digits of the three digit temperature reading (e.g., for a temp of 78 would return 07). Those two digits are passed on to the computer. When the digits have changed, the computer should write out the message "Temperature has significant change" and pass a message to the mechanical arm to hold out either a sweater (for a decrease) or a swimsuit (for an increase). Program loop should stop when there is no change over 20 readings.

4. Modify design # 3 to make it a bit more realistic. (After all, a swimsuit is not really called for just because the temperature goes from –5° to +5°.) Assume you have access to a data file that holds 17 brief descriptions of appropriate clothing, one for each temperature level from –40° to 120° (in 10°increments), beginning with the description for –40° ('Your heaviest coat and hat') up to the description for 120° ('The least you can decently wear'). Instead of passing the message to the mechanical arm, display two messages to the user: the first to remove the clothing from the previous temperature and the second to put on the clothing for the new temperature. Loop control is unchanged. HINT: The temperature sensor will return values that range from –04 (for -40°) to 12 (for 120°). The description for –40° (–04 value) will be stored in position 1 if you store them in an array. The description for 20° (02) will be stored in position 7. There's a pattern here.

5. We're working for the IRS. They have a new system that uses only the gross household income and the number of dependents to calculate the tax due. Gross income is divided into 20 income levels. The new tax code uses a maximum of 6 dependents (anyone with more than 6 dependents still has his or her tax calculated using the value 6). We need to design

the program that will load a tax table using the tax level (1 – 20) and number of dependents (1 – 6) as the subscripts (a positional, two-dimension table). After loading the table (data are in row major order in their own file), use the table until the end of the input file. (Read in tax level and # of dependents and write out the tax amount.)

6. The new tax program is inadequate because it assumes the user knows her or his current tax level. The file holding the tax array data has been rewritten so that it begins with the 20 minimum income amounts for the 20 income levels, beginning with level 1. Modify design # 5 so that you use this new and improved file. The user will now enter his or her gross income and number of dependents, and your design will write out the tax amount.

7. Now we're working for a wholesale supply store. We need a program that will give the per unit price for our inventory items. Prices differ for various items (we sell just under 500 items) and by the quantity purchased since customers get a discount for bulk purchases. We have two input files. The first holds the day's sales: customer number, inventory item ID purchased, and quantity purchased. The second file holds our inventory pricing information. It begins with the minimum quantity for the six pricing groups; then it holds the prices for all inventory items, beginning with the inventory item ID; then the six per unit prices for that item. Write out the cost for each sale in the sales file.

Chapter 15
Sorting

Objectives

After completing this chapter, you should be able to:

1. Describe the purpose of a sorting operation.
2. Define the meaning of primary and secondary sort (key) fields.
3. Describe the differences between an external (library) sort, a language (code-dependent) sort, and a designed/coded sort.
4. Design a bubble sort for an array.
5. Design an insertion sort for an array.
6. Design a program to sort an array as it is being loaded.

INTRODUCTION

Sorting, whether files or arrays, is a major operation in almost any computer application. Many uses of data require that the data are already in a sorted order, as we have seen with our control break programs. Furthermore, many applications are more useful or meaningful when the input data are sorted. A simple read/write report does not require that the input data be sorted. But if the report is a list of the finishers of the Boston Marathon, it will be much more useful if it is in sorted order.

Sorting requires arranging the individual elements of an array or file in order based on a specified field. If our list of Boston Marathon finishers is in order by their finishing time, we would say that time is the sort field, or key field. Some sorts use two or more key fields. The telephone book is sorted on last name. But when two or more people have the same last name, those people are sorted on first name. We would say that last name is the primary sort (or key) field and first name is the secondary sort field.

We will look at *array* sorting in this chapter because we have already discussed the means to manipulate array elements. Sorting records within a file uses similar algorithms, but the algorithms are applied to file manipulation techniques that we have not (and will not) cover in this text. Once you have a few sorts under your belt, it will not be difficult for you to apply them to any needed situation, including file sorts.

Because sorting is such a common and necessary application, there are many sort algorithms available and many means of accessing those algorithms. Sort utilities are frequently provided along with the operating system as part of a lease or purchase package. Some programming languages provide a sort command. And of course, we can design and code our own sort.

SORT UTILITIES

No matter what operating system you are using on a microcomputer, a mainframe, or anything in between, there is most likely at least one sort utility provided for your use. Exactly how you invoke that utility, what preparatory steps must be taken (i.e., the form the data must be in), and what sort algorithm will be used all depend on the utility. As a general rule, you will need to provide the utility with the name of the file to be sorted, the key field or fields on which it should be sorted, whether you want an ascending or descending sort, and where the result should go. Not all utilities will require each of these. Some utilities may assume an ascending sort, some may assume a standard output file, and some make make other assumptions.

Additional sort utilities may have been written "in house" or purchased separately from the operating system. Since some sort algorithms are more efficient on different kinds of data or different size lists or lists that begin in some partial order, it is reasonable to have multiple sort utilities. Each of these would be stored in the "library" of utilities available to programs. Much as you check a book out of a library for temporary use, you can *call* a sort utility from the subroutine library for temporary use by your program.

When we defined our flowchart symbols (light years ago), we defined a symbol called the External Process symbol. It is this symbol that we would use in a flowchart when calling a sort utility. In pseudocode we would continue to use the command DO but specify that it is an external module. External modules are not further defined within the design because the coder will not have to write them out.

The advantage of the utility is that it is already written, and we know it works so we don't have to worry about testing the sort. The disadvantage is that an all-purpose sort may not be the best sort for our particular data. One-size-fits-all often means no one is fitted well.

From a design perspective there is not much to *using* a utility sort. You do need to know the requirements and limitations of the particular utility available. But you don't have to design the sort.

LANGUAGE SORTS

Some programming languages, in recognition of the importance of the sorting operation, include a sort command within the language. From a design perspective a SORT command can be treated much like a sort utility. We don't have to design the sort, but we do need to work within the requirements and limitations of the command. The languages that provide a sort command are primarily business, report-oriented languages like COBOL.

CODED SORTS

Because we're interested in designing algorithmic solutions, we are more interested in our own coded sorts than in predefined solutions like utility sorts or sort commands. You are probably asking yourself, "If I have a sort utility available, why would I *ever* want to go through the work of designing my own sort?" It's a reasonable question. It is possible, of course, that you won't have a sort utility available. But it is also possible that the utility available is not the best one for the nature of your data. There are many, many algorithms available. Some sorts work best with small lists of data, some with very long lists. Some work best with data that are truly random; some are best with data that are skewed toward one extreme or the other; some are best with data that are already partially sorted. If you know something about your data and you also have a few sorts in your repertoire, you can probably design a more efficient sort for your particular need. If your program is going to be used repeatedly over a long period of time, the efficiency of the sort is important. If the program is going to be run once and then junked, it may not be worth the design and coding time required to include a custom sort, and the utility sort is a good compromise.

We will look at only two sorts, both of which are fairly simple (by comparison to other sort algorithms). Many of the sort algorithms, particularly those that work best for large files or for very skewed files, require a knowledge of other processing techniques or other ways to manipulate and store data that we have not discussed.

BUBBLE SORT

The bubble sort is frequently one of the first sorts taught to programming students. It requires repeated "passes" over the unsorted portion of the array. In each pass *each* adjoining pair of values is compared and switched if they are out of order. This process has the effect of moving the largest value in the array (or a portion of the array) to its appropriate position and "bubbling" the smaller values slowly up to the top. Since each pass puts one value (the largest value found) in its correct position, the unsorted portion of the array gets smaller by one element after each pass.

In the following algorithm *len* is the length of the array and *list* is the array itself. The flag *hadSwitch* is used to check if any pairs were out of order on the previous pass. If all the pairs were in order, then the array must be sorted and we can stop the sort. *PassCnt* is used to count the number of passes we make over the array checking for out of order pairs. At the most we will need *len-1* passes. *StopPt* marks the point in the array to stop checking the pairs during a given pass. Since the unsorted portion of the array keeps getting smaller, *stopPt* will keep moving up.

```
BubbleSort
stopPt = len
hadSwitch = 'yes'
passCnt = 1
WHILE passCnt < len AND hadSwitch = 'yes'
    hadSwitch = 'no'
    ptr = 1
    WHILE ptr < stopPt
        IF list(ptr) > list(ptr + 1)
            DO Switch
        ENDIF
        ADD 1 to ptr
    ENDWHILE
    SUBTRACT 1 from stopPt
    ADD 1 to passCnt
ENDWHILE


SWITCH
hold = list(ptr)
list(ptr) = list(ptr + 1)
list(ptr + 1) = hold
hadSwitch = 'yes'
```

Assuming an array of 10 elements, our "worst case" would require nine passes through the array. Each pass gets the largest value of those that remain to be sorted into its correct position. After nine passes, the nine largest values are definitely in their correct positions. If only one value is left and only one position is left, it too must be correct. What follows is a "blow by blow" account of each required pass.

$]$ = comparison (no switch)

χ = comparison and switch

shaded cells = portion of array in order (below stopPt)

unshaded cells = portion of array still being checked

271

First Pass:

10	10	10	10	10	10	10
11	11	11	11	11	11	11
42	3	3	3	3	3	3
3	42	42	42	42	42	42
56	56	18	18	18	18	18
18	18	56	7	7	7	7
7	7	7	56	6	6	6
6	6	6	6	56	37	37
37	37	37	37	37	56	29
29	29	29	29	29	29	56

hadSwitch = 'yes'

Each set of pairs is compared, but not all have to be switched. The first comparison, between 10 and 11, shows that those numbers are in order. The second comparison, 11 and 42, also shows the numbers are in order. But the third comparison, 42 and 3, shows the numbers are out of order and they must be switched. The comparisons continue until the entire array has been checked. Notice that about halfway down, 56 is switched with 18. After that each comparison requires a switch because 56 is the largest number in the array and it is "sinking" to the bottom. At the end of the first pass, 56 is in its correct position; the unsorted portion of the array is positions 1 through 9. StopPt is changed to 9 to reflect that we no longer need to check position 10.

Second Pass:

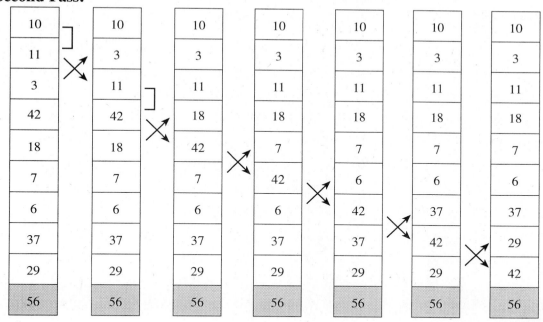

hadSwitch = 'yes'

This time 42 sinks to the bottom. Notice that our smaller numbers like 3, 7, and 6 are slowly bubbling up to the top, moving up one position in each pass through the array.

Third Pass:

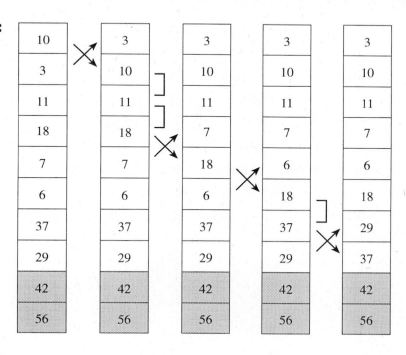

hadSwitch = 'yes'

Fourth Pass:

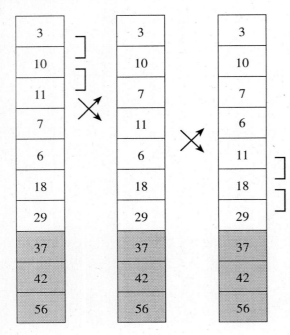

hadSwitch = 'yes'

Fifth Pass:

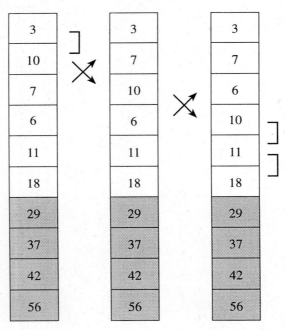

hadSwitch = 'yes'

Sixth Pass:

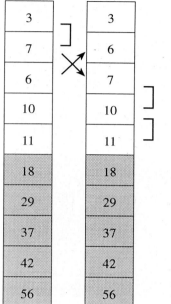

hadSwitch = 'yes'

Notice that at the end of the sixth pass, the array is sorted. But we can't know that by the algorithm. Since at least one switch occurred during the pass, it is possible that the array is not yet in order.

Seventh Pass:

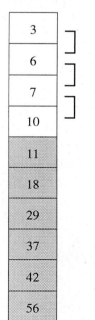

hadSwitch = **'no'**

In the seventh pass, no switches were made, so the hadSwitch flag remains 'no' and we exit from the loop. Because of the nature of the data, our array was sorted in fewer passes than the worst case scenario of nine passes.

The bubble sort is frequently used because it is easier to understand than many of the other possible sorts, but it is not necessarily the most efficient. With a small array, however, it is a reasonable sort algorithm to use.

One of the problems with the bubble sort is that it takes so many passes for a value that is grossly out of order to get to its proper position. As we saw above, it took six passes for the value 6 to bubble slowly up to its correct position. If our array had had 100 elements and the only number out of order was the smallest element which was in the last position, our sort would have required 99 passes just to get that one value in position. The smallest value would move up only one position in each pass. There are many variations on the bubble sort that move the values more than one position in a switch. The basic bubble always compares a value to the value which follows it and switches the two if appropriate. We could vary that by comparing a value to the value 10 positions away, or 20 positions away, and switching if necessary. Using an interval larger than one, say 10 or 20, means that those small values are moving to the top in giant steps instead of baby steps. The interval needs to be changed as we get the array closer to sorted order until we eventually do use an interval of one. The shell sort is one example of this kind of variation of the bubble sort.

INSERTION SORT

The insertion sort is a very different kind of sort. The bubble sort puts the array in sorted order by multiple comparisons and switches within the existing array. The insertion sort creates a *new array* which it builds in sorted order. We'll look at several variations.

First, let's assume that we already have a sorted array but want to add another value to it and maintain the sorted order. We don't want to just add the new value at the end of the array, so we need to find the correct position for the new value, make room there for the value, and then insert it. The following module will do those steps. *List* is the name of the sorted array. *Len* is the current length of the array. *Item* is the value that we want to insert in the array. Our module will start at the end of the array and work up looking for the first value that is less than the value to be inserted. When a lower value is found, we know that we should insert the new value directly after it. As it compares each value to the insertion item, it also moves the array value down one position to make room for the new item. Notice that this algorithm assumes that there is room in the array for an additional item.

276

<u>Insert</u>
```
ptr = len
continue = 'yes'
WHILE ptr > 0 AND continue = 'yes'
    IF list(ptr) > item
        list(ptr + 1) = list(ptr)
        SUBTRACT 1 from ptr
    ELSE
        continue = 'no'
    ENDIF
ENDWHILE
list(ptr + 1) = item
ADD 1 to len
```

The body of this loop copies our current item (the one pointed to by ptr) down to the position below it (ptr + 1) and changes ptr so it is pointing to the previous value in the array. The loop continues until ptr is pointing to a value in the array which is less than or equal to the value to be inserted (or we have checked the entire array and never found a value which was less than or equal). When we exit from the loop, ptr holds the position that should be immediately *before* the inserted item (or to 0 if no value was less than the insert item), so we insert the new item at position ptr+1.

If we have the sorted array shown below of five elements and want to insert the value 16, we will start by comparing 16 to the last value (33) and continue working *up* until we find the proper position for the insertion.

3	3	3	3
8	8	8	8
10	10	10 : 16	10
21	21 : 16		16
33 : 16		21	21
	33	33	33

First we compare 33 to 16 and move the 33 down when we determine that 33 is not less than or equal to 16. The value of ptr is decremented so that we are pointing to the fourth value (21). We compare the 21 to 16 and move the 21 down since it is not less than or equal to 16. Again ptr is decremented. We compare the 10 to 16. Since 10 *is* less than 16, we do not move it down, we do not decrement ptr, and we exit from the loop. Since the 33 and 21 were moved down and the 10 was not, we have a blank space in our array between the 10 and the 21, exactly where the 16 should go!

That works very well if we have a sorted array and just want to insert one item. But what if we want to sort the entire array? If we are just loading the array, we can sort the array as we load it. As each item is added to the array, it is added in the proper position so we are building a sorted array. Our Insert module adds one element to a sorted array. If we call the Insert module for each element to be loaded in the array, we are always adding one element to a sorted array. Our load process (assuming a declared array of 100 elements) could look like this:

```
LoadSort
len = 0
WHILE there are data and len < 100
    READ item
    DO Insert
ENDWHILE
```

With this load module, we begin with an empty array (len = 0). For each element to be loaded, we read the value then insert it in its proper position using the Insert module from the previous page. At the end of the load we have a sorted array.

Assume we have the input file: 21
                                       7
                                      13
                                      30
                                      18

to be loaded into the array list which we have declared with a length of 6. Since we want the list to be in ascending, sorted order, we decide to sort it as we load. After setting len to 0, we enter the loading loop the first time, which reads the first value from the input file and inserts it into the first position of the array. Since len is 0, we don't enter the loop in the Insert module.

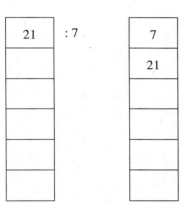

We then continue in the LoadSort loop while there are data to be read from the file and there is space left in the array. Each iteration of the loop will read a value from the input file, then call the Insert module to add the value to the array List.

Second Loop Iteration:
Input value (item) = 7

First we compare the 7 to the 21. Since 21 is larger than 7, it is copied down to the blank space below it. When we subtract 1 from ptr, we get 0 so we exit the loop in the Insert module, put the 7 in the position ptr+1, and add 1 to len.

Third Loop Iteration:
Input value (item) = 13

Fourth Loop Iteration:
Input value (item) = 30

<table>
<tr><td>7</td></tr>
<tr><td>13</td></tr>
<tr><td>21</td></tr>
<tr><td></td></tr>
<tr><td></td></tr>
<tr><td></td></tr>
</table>

: 30

<table>
<tr><td>7</td></tr>
<tr><td>13</td></tr>
<tr><td>21</td></tr>
<tr><td>30</td></tr>
<tr><td></td></tr>
<tr><td></td></tr>
</table>

Fifth Loop Iteration:
Input value (item) = 18

Table 1:
```
7
13
21
30     : 18
```

Table 2:
```
7
13
21     : 18
       
30
```

Table 3:
```
7
13     : 18
       
21
30
```

Table 4:
```
7
13
18
21
30
```

But what if our array is already in memory and now we want to sort it? With the insertion sort we will need to create a second array, and we will copy the existing array to the new array, one element at a time, inserting each element into its proper position. In other words, we're doing it just like the load, but instead of getting the values from the external input file, we get them from the array already in memory. The design looks similar but now we have two arrays, with two pointers to keep track of. *Ptr* was used as the subscript in the Insert Module. *FirstPtr* will be used as the subscript to point to the value to be inserted from the unsorted array, which we will call *firstList*. In order to be able to use the Insert Module without changes, we will take the value from the unsorted array and assign it to the field *item* before calling Insert. *Len* holds the length of the sorted array (which will increase as we insert the items), so we will use *firstLen* for the length of the original, unsorted array.

```
InsertSort
firstPtr = 1
len = 0
WHILE firstPtr < = firstLen
    item = firstList(firstPtr)
    DO Insert
    ADD 1 to firstPtr
ENDWHILE
```

The InsertSort is a good sort for small arrays (less than 25 elements) and is a good sort for larger arrays if they are partially sorted already. For values presented in order, we have very few steps to do (really just one comparison and an assignment).

These two sorts (Bubble and Insertion) are good basic sorts, but you should not limit yourself to them. As you gain more knowledge about ways to store data during processing (an array is one way to structure our data, but there are others), you will be able to work with a greater variety of sorts.

EXERCISES

1. Design a program that will create a list of all finishers of the Boston Marathon from the state of Virginia, in order by their finishing time. The input comes from a file of finishers (name, entry number, state, phone, time) which is in order by their entry number. Use an external sort.

2. Design a program that will create a list of all finishers of the Boston Marathon by state, including a count of the number of finishers from each state. Use the same input file as defined in design #1. Assume that you are using a programming language which includes an appropriate sort command.

3. Design a module that will sort an array of 100 numbers into ascending order using a bubble sort.

4. Careful now: Modify design #3 so that it sorts the array into descending order.

5. Design a module that will load an array of 100 numbers so that the numbers are stored in ascending order using an insertion sort.

6. Design a program that will process applications for the New York City Marathon on a first-come, first-served basis until the race is full (accept 5000 racers). The program should be interactive but will also have a file (which may or may not be sorted) containing all the applications received to date. The runners' names (from this file of applicants) should be loaded into a sorted array. New applications will be keyed in providing name, age, state, and expected finishing time. Each new applicant's name should be inserted in the array of names, maintaining the sorted order. Continue receiving applications until the race (array) is full. Full application data for new applicants should also be appended to the applicant file.

Chapter 16

Merging and Matching Two Input Files

Objectives

After completing this chapter, you should be able to:

1. Distinguish between a file merge design and a file match design.
2. Describe the objectives and assumptions in a merge operation.
3. Design a merge program in which the loop is exited when either file is empty.
4. Design a merge program in which the loop is exited only when both files are empty.
5. Describe the objectives and assumptions in a match operation.
6. Design a match program in which no more than one transaction record will be present for any given master record.
7. Design a match program in which multiple transaction records may be present for any given master record.

INTRODUCTION

In this chapter we will look at programs using two input files. Up to now, any program that used two input files used the first file only in the Start module to load an array or to load needed parameter records. After the initial loading, the first file was no longer needed and the main loop module processed just one file. In the designs in this chapter, we will need data from both files during the primary loop processing.

Having two input files will require some special attention to a few details. When will we exit our Mainline loop? In most of our past designs, we stayed in the loop while we had data to process. That condition was clear enough because we were only processing data from one file. Now we will have to look at the possibility that the two files are of different lengths and are completed at different times in the design. We will also need to define when we *read* from each file.

MERGING TWO FILES

The simplest form of two-input file processing is a merge program which combines two similar sorted files into one sorted file. Usually, our combined file will utilize the same computer "medium" as the two input files. That is, if we're reading two disk files, our output file would also be a disk file. We could just append one file to the end of the other file and then sort the resulting file. That would work, but, since a file sort is a very time-consuming operation and since we already start with sorted files, there is a much more efficient solution. When we start with sorted files, we merely need to pull the records from each file in order and write them to the new file in the appropriate order. Notice that we described our files as "two similar sorted files." We must be able to assume that the files are sorted on the same field. If both files are partial lists of employees, but one is sorted on Social Security Number and the other is sorted on last name, we will not be able to merge them until we resort one of the files.

In general, our system will be to take the "current" record from each of the two files and decide which of the two should go first in the new, combined file. At any given point, we are comparing only two records, one from each file. Our only question is: Of those two records, which one should come first? Once the selected record is written to the new file, we will read the next record from the input file. The key to remember is that we only read another record from a file when we have "processed" the previous record from that file.

Assume we have a file of the members of the Roller Coaster Enthusiasts Club (RCEC) and a second file of the members of the Ferris Wheel Riders of America Club (FWRAC).

The two clubs are joining to form the Supporters of Amusement Parks (SAP), and the membership lists must be merged. If both files are ordered on the same field (for example, name), our merge will be easy. We will take the current record of each file, compare those two records, and write one of them to the new file.

RCEC File

Abernathy, Adam
Carruthers, Carol
Johnson, Jim
Klover, Kenny
Lucketts, Lucy
Masters, Martha
Opperman, Opal

FWRAC File

Bradley, Bertha
Carruthers, Carol
Duddley, David
Frempston, Fred
Ivanoski, Ivan
Lucketts, Lucy
Nestor, Ned
Samuels, Susan

Comparison: Abernathy, Adam   :   Bradley, Bertha

Combined file:

Abernathy, Adam

When the first two records are compared, Abernathy is identified as the record that should come first and Abernathy, Adam is written to the new file. Since a record in the RCEC file has been processed, we read the new current record from that file. What happens to Bradley, Bertha? Nothing yet. That is still the current record in the FWRAC file because it has not yet been processed (written to the new file). Our next comparison will be between

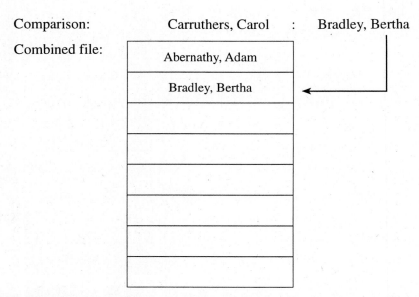

Comparison: Carruthers, Carol   :   Bradley, Bertha

Combined file:

Abernathy, Adam

Bradley, Bertha

After writing Bradley, Bertha's record to the new file, we read the next record from the FWRAC file: Carruthers, Carol.

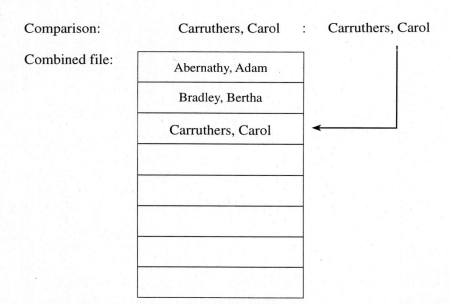

Comparison: Carruthers, Carol   :   Carruthers, Carol

Combined file:

Abernathy, Adam

Bradley, Bertha

Carruthers, Carol

Now we have a very different situation. The two files have the same entry. (Carol is a member of both clubs.) Our design specifications must tell us what action to take if a record occurs in both files. In this case, and in most other cases, we would write the record just once to the new file. But no matter what we do with the new file, we have processed a record from both input files, so we must read the next record from both files:

Comparison: Johnson, Jim   :   Duddley, David

Combined file:

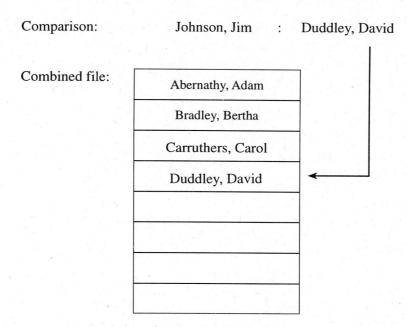

Since we are always comparing just two records, one of three possibilities must be true: RollerName is less than FerrisName, RollerName equals FerrisName, or RollerName is greater than FerrisName. We can define what should be done for each case.

Comparison	Write	Read from
Roller < Ferris	Roller record	Roller file
Roller = Ferris	Either record	Both files
Roller > Ferris	Ferris record	Ferris file

We can summarize the chart by saying that when the compare fields are unequal, we always write the lesser of the two (assuming our files are in ascending sequence) and read from the same file. When the compare fields are equal, our specifications will define the process (usually write either record), and we read from both files.

How do we get Started?

Our loop process must begin with the comparison of two records, so we must have read the records prior to the beginning of the loop. In other words, a merge program will involve a priming read for each input file. We should also test to be sure when we begin that both files have data. We cannot merge two files if one is empty, so if either file is empty we will change the flag to indicate an empty file and write an error message.

```
Start
OPEN files
moreRollers = 'yes'
moreFerris = 'yes'
IF there are data (Roller File)
    READ rollerName, rollerAddr
ELSE
    moreRollers = 'no'
    WRITE 'ERROR -- Roller File is empty!'
ENDIF
IF there are data (Ferris File)
    READ ferrisName, ferrisAddr
ELSE
    moreFerris = 'no'
    WRITE 'ERROR -- Ferris File is empty!'
ENDIF
```

If either file is empty, the appropriate flag will be changed to 'no' and an error message is written. If both files are empty, both flags are changed to 'no' and two error messages are written.

When do we exit the Mainline loop?

The simplest design solution is to exit the loop when either file is completed, in other words, to stay in the loop only while *both* files have data remaining. Our test is then in effect saying, "WHILE we have data in the Roller *file* and we have data in the Ferris file, keep doing this loop." Of course, if we exit when just one file is completed, we presumably still have data in the other file that has not yet been copied to the new file, and our merge is not yet completed. We will have to finish writing the records to the new file in our Finish module. A complete design follows.

<u>Mainline</u>
DO Start
WHILE moreRollers = 'yes' AND moreFerris = 'yes'
    DO MergeRecords
ENDWHILE
DO Finish

<u>Start</u>
OPEN files
moreRollers = 'yes'
moreFerris = 'yes'
DO ReadRoller
IF moreRollers = 'no'
    WRITE 'ERROR -- Roller File is empty!'
ENDIF
DO ReadFerris
IF moreFerris = 'no'
    WRITE 'ERROR -- Ferris File is empty!'
ENDIF

<u>MergeRecords</u>
IF rollerName < ferrisName
    WRITE rollerName, rollerAddr
    DO ReadRoller
ELSE
    IF rollerName > ferrisName
        WRITE ferrisName, ferrisAddr
        DO ReadFerris
    ELSE
        WRITE ferrisName, ferrisAddr
        DO ReadRoller
        DO ReadFerris
    ENDIF
ENDIF

<u>ReadRoller</u>
IF there are data (Roller file)
    READ rollerName, rollerAddr
ELSE
    moreRollers = 'no'
ENDIF

<u>ReadFerris</u>
IF there are data (Ferris file)
    READ ferrisName, ferrisAddr
ELSE
    moreFerris = 'no'
ENDIF

```
Finish
WHILE moreRollers = 'yes'
    WRITE rollerName, rollerAddr
    DO ReadRoller
ENDWHILE
WHILE moreFerris = 'yes'
    WRITE ferrisName, ferrisAddr
    DO ReadFerris
ENDWHILE
CLOSE files
```

The Start module is the same as the one we looked at previously with the exception that it now calls read modules instead of reading directly within the module (a simpler solution since the Reads can also be called from the loop module).

The MergeRecords module is short and follows our earlier chart. Notice that everything is included in an IF. Most of our previous designs either began with a READ or (if they were priming read designs) ended with a READ. With a merge design, we read only within the IF since it is only then that we know from which file we should read.

The Finish module completes the merge. We know that one of the files is empty. (It is also possible that both files are empty if they ended with the same name.) Since a WHILE loop is only entered when the condition is True, we can safely include the two WHILE loops in Finish. IF the tested file is empty, the small loop to "dump" any remaining records will not be entered. But for the file with records not yet included in the new file, the small loops to Write and Read will copy all remaining records.

The above solution "works," but it has some design weaknesses. We are really doing the same kind of processing in two locations. We do our merge/write/read processing in the MergeRecords module, but we also do it in the Finish module. Suppose we remain in the Loop module while *either* of the input files has data? Then all records would be written to the new file from within the loop module. But, I can hear you saying, how can we compare two records after one of the files is empty? Let's look at our processing chart again and try to answer that question.

Comparison	Write	Read from
Roller < Ferris	Roller record	Roller file
Roller = Ferris	Either record	Both files
Roller > Ferris	Ferris record	Ferris file

If the Ferris file is empty, which of the options would we want our processing to follow? The first one! With no records left in the Ferris file, we would want to write and then read the Roller record. If the Roller file is empty, we would want to follow the third line, writing and reading the Ferris record. The next question, of course, is how can we make that happen? How can we make the computer "think" that the rollerName is less than the ferrisName when the Ferris file is empty? We could change our ReadFerris module so that when the file is empty we move a ridiculously "high" value into the ferrisName field. Then when the comparison is made, the rollerName will appear to be less than this "fake" ferrisName. The design that follows shows the necessary changes to the Read modules, the Mainline loop control condition, and the Finish module. The design also adds one more element. It counts the number of records read from each of the input files and the number of records written to the combined output file and writes all three counters in Finish.

```
Mainline
DO Start
WHILE moreRollers = 'yes' OR moreFerris = 'yes'
    DO MergeRecords
ENDWHILE
DO Finish
```

```
START
OPEN files
moreRollers = 'yes'
moreFerris = 'yes'
DO ReadRoller
IF moreRollers = 'no'
    WRITE 'ERROR -- Roller File is empty!'
ENDIF
DO ReadFerris
IF moreFerris = 'no'
    WRITE 'ERROR -- Ferris File is empty!'
ENDIF
IF moreRollers = 'no' OR moreFerris = 'no'
    moreRollers = 'no'
    moreFerris = 'no'
ENDIF
rollerCnt = 0
ferrisCnt = 0
combinedCnt = 0

MergeRecords
IF rollerName < ferrisName
    WRITE rollerName, rollerAddr
DO ReadRoller
    ADD 1 to rollerCnt
ELSE
    IF rollerName > ferrisName
        WRITE ferrisName, ferrisAddr
        DO ReadFerris
        ADD 1 to ferrisCnt
    ELSE
        WRITE ferrisName, ferrisAddr
        DO ReadRoller
        DO ReadFerris
        ADD 1 to rollerCnt
        ADD 1 to ferrisCnt
    ENDIF
ENDIF
ADD 1 to combinedCnt

ReadRoller
IF there are data (Roller file)
    READ rollerName, rollerAddr
ELSE
    moreRollers = 'no'
    rollerName = 'ZZZZZZZ'
ENDIF
```

```
ReadFerris
IF there are data (Ferris file)
    READ ferrisName, ferrisAddr
ELSE
    moreFerris = 'no'
    ferrisName = 'ZZZZZZZ'
ENDIF


Finish
WRITE 'Records read from Roller File = ', rollerCnt
WRITE 'Records read from Ferris File = ', ferrisCnt
WRITE 'Records written to Combined File = ', combinedCnt
CLOSE files
```

This design does not require the extra loops in the Finish module because we know that both input files will have been completely processed by the time the program exits the loop module. The Mainline loop test is now WHILE moreRollers = 'yes' OR moreFerris = 'yes' which in effect is saying while there is data remaining in *either* file stay in the loop. An extra IF statement has been included in the Start module after both of the reads have been completed. Remember that we have changed the loop control to remain in the loop as long as either file has data remaining. But, if either file is *completely* empty (i.e., the read in Start was not successful), we don't want to enter the loop at all since we can't begin a merge operation with just one file. The added IF test checks our two flags and changes both to no, if either is already no, to ensure that we do not enter the loop.

MATCHING TWO INPUT FILES

Matching input files sounds similar to merging two files, but our objective is quite different. With a merge, our only goal was to create the combined file in sorted order. Our "processing" of the input files was limited to checking for order and writing to the new file. With a match program, our objective almost always requires more processing of the data. Furthermore, with a merge program, the two input files contained similar records. With a match program, the two input files will contain different records, although the two files must still have at least one field in common. In general, a match program implies that in processing the records from a given file we need certain data found on matching records from a second file.

For example, we may have a file of all the current students including their student ID number, total past credits, current credits, total GPA, and GPA in the student's major. We want to send out a GPA update letter to each of these students. We have the GPA information that we need, but we cannot address the letter since the file does not contain any names or addresses. We need to match each record with the appropriate record in a second file containing the student ID number, student name, and student address. We must be able to assume that both input files are sorted on the match field (in our example, the student ID number).

With a match program, our expectation is that we will have a match for most records. Our specifications, however, must define what should be done for each possibility in the comparison. In our example, we know that we write the letter when we have a match. What happens if a student is included in the name/addr file but not in the credits file? That probably means that the student isn't enrolled for the current term. We'll assume that our specifications indicate we should not perform any processing for such a condition. What happens if a student is included in the credits file but not in the name/addr file? Now we have a more serious problem. Somehow we have a student who has accumulated credits without ever getting included in our "master" file of student names and addresses. We'll assume that our specifications call for us to write an error message indicating that the student is not included in the name/addr file and not to write the letter. Usually, in a match program we will have one file containing data that does not change often (names and addresses in our example) and a second file containing data that change regularly (credits and GPA). The advantage of keeping the data separate is that the name/addr file is somewhat "protected" and the data are available to a variety of programs without having to make all data about the student available.

A design that implements our example follows. The design refers to the name/addr file as the master or mast file and the credits file as the transaction or trans file.

```
Mainline
DO Start
WHILE moreData = 'yes'
    DO MatchRecords
ENDWHILE
DO Finish
```

```
Start
OPEN files
moreMast = 'yes'
moreTrans = 'yes'
moreData = 'yes'
DO ReadMast
IF moreMast = 'no'
    WRITE 'ERROR -- Master file is empty'
    moreData = 'no'
ENDIF
DO ReadTrans
IF moreTrans = 'no'
    WRITE 'ERROR -- Transaction file is empty'
    moreData = 'no'
ENDIF


MatchRecords
IF mastID = transID
    DO Match
ELSE
    IF mastID < transID
        DO ReadMast
    ELSE
        DO TransWithoutMast
    ENDIF
ENDIF


ReadMast
IF there are data (Master file)
    READ mastID, mastName, mastAddr
ELSE
    moreMast = 'no'
    mastID = 999999999
    IF moreTrans = 'no'
        moreData = 'no'
    ENDIF
ENDIF


ReadTrans
IF there are data (transaction file)
READ transID, totCredits, termCredits, totGPA, majorGPA
ELSE
    moreTrans = 'no'
    transID = 999999999
    IF moreMast = 'no'
        moreData = 'no'
    ENDIF
ENDIF
```

<u>Match</u>
EJECT page
WRITE mastName, mastAddr, totGPA, majorGPA (in letter format)
DO ReadTrans
DO ReadMast

<u>TransWithoutMast</u>
EJECT page
WRITE transID, 'Trans record does not have matching master'
DO ReadTrans

<u>Finish</u>
CLOSE files

There are some processing gaps here, but they should not interfere with your understanding of the design. To avoid a long series of WRITEs that distract from an understanding of the important steps in the design, the Match module simply calls for a write "in letter format." (The letter would be the GPA update letter.) Furthermore, any error messages are written one per page. (We hope there won't be too many.)

The design uses a third flag to control the mainline loop. MoreData is set to 'no' only when both input files are completely processed or if one or both files are determined to be empty in the Start module. Look closely at the read modules. They now include an extra test. If there are no more records left to process in a file, the design immediately checks to see if the other input file is also completed. If it is, the moreData flag is changed to 'no' to end the loop processing. Use of the moreData flag simplifies the checks in Start (it no longer needs the extra IF to avoid the loop), but makes the read modules slightly more complex.

If the mastID is less than the transID, we know that the master record will never have a matching transaction record. If the transaction record were present, it would have to be *before* the current transaction record since they are in sequence. A master without a transaction is not an error, and we simply read the next master record.

Similarly, if the transID is less than the mastID, we know that the transaction record will never have a matching master. A transaction without a matching master, however, indicates that something is wrong with our master file, so we write an error message before reading the next transaction record.

MATCHES WITH MULTIPLE TRANSACTION RECORDS

Our first matching design assumes that we will never have more than one transaction record that matches a given master. As soon as we found a match, we processed the data and read the next record in both files. With some files, however, it is likely that we will have multiple transaction records. (Our design specifications should make that clear.) In such a case, we don't want to read a new master record as soon as we have processed a match between a transaction record and a master record. There may be another transaction record that follows which will also match the same master. So we must postpone reading from the master file until we read a different transaction record. In a similar circumstance, if we have a transaction without a master, we may have multiple transactions with the same compare value. We wouldn't want to write the same error message multiple times.

Our example creates a summary report of all inventory parts ordered during the past month. It assumes that we have a transaction file containing one record for each order and including a code identifying the supplier, the part number ordered, the quantity ordered, and the date. The file is in order by supplier code. It also assumes that we have a master file containing the name and address and supplier code of all our suppliers, also in order by supplier code. The report should list all orders giving the supplier name, address, and code, the part number, quantity, and date. If a part supplier has not received any orders for the month, a message should be written identifying the supplier and stating that no orders were sent. If an order identifies a supplier code which is not included in the master file of suppliers, an error message should be written. Multiple error messages should not be written if an invalid supplier code is repeated.

```
Mainline
DO Start
WHILE moreData = 'yes'
    DO MatchRecords
ENDWHILE
DO Finish
```

```
Start
OPEN files
firstPage = 'yes'
moreMast = 'yes'
moreTrans = 'yes'
moreData = 'yes'
lineCnt = 60
DO ReadMast
IF moreMast = 'no'
    WRITE 'ERROR -- Master file is empty'
    moreData = 'no'
ENDIF
DO ReadTrans
IF moreTrans = 'no'
    WRITE 'ERROR -- Transaction file is empty'
    moreData = 'no'
ENDIF


MatchRecords
IF mastCode = transCode
    DO Match
ELSE
    IF mastCode < transCode
        DO MastWithoutTrans
    ELSE
        DO TransWithoutMast
    ENDIF
ENDIF


Finish
CLOSE files


ReadMast
IF there are data (Master file)
    READ mastCode, mastName, mastAddr
ELSE
    moreMast = 'no'
    mastCode = 999999
    IF moreTrans = 'no'
        moreData = 'no'
    ENDIF
ENDIF
```

<u>ReadTrans</u>
IF there are data (Transaction file)
    READ transCode, transPart, transQuant, transDate
ELSE
    moreTrans = 'no'
    transCode = 999999
    IF moreMast = 'no'
        moreData = 'no'
    ENDIF
ENDIF

<u>Match</u>
REPEAT
    DO WriteMatch
    DO ReadTrans
UNTIL mastCode < > transCode
DO ReadMast

<u>MastWithoutTrans</u>
IF lineCnt > = 60
    DO Heads
ENDIF
WRITE mastName, mastAddr, mastCode, 'No orders made this month'
ADD 1 to lineCnt
DO ReadMast

<u>TransWithoutMast</u>
IF lineCnt > = 60
    DO Heads
ENDIF
WRITE transCode, 'Transaction record/s without matching Master'
ADD 1 to lineCnt
oldTrans = transCode
REPEAT
    DO ReadTrans
UNTIL transCode < > oldTrans

<u>WriteMatch</u>
IF lineCnt > = 60
    DO Heads
ENDIF
WRITE mastName, mastAddr, mastCode, transPart, transQuant, transDate
ADD 1 to lineCnt

```
Heads
EJECT page
SKIP 6 lines
IF firstPage = 'yes'
    WRITE Report Headings
    SKIP 1 line
    lineCnt = 8
    firstPage = 'no'
ELSE
    lineCnt = 6
ENDIF
WRITE Page Headings
WRITE Column Headings (dbl spc)
SKIP 1 line
ADD 4 to lineCnt
```

Both the Match processing module and the TransWithoutMast processing module include UNTIL loops based on a change in the transCode. When we have a match, we write out the order information using data from both the master record and the transaction record. After the write, we have processed the transaction record, so we read the next record from the transaction file. Since there is the possibility of multiple orders (transaction records) from the same supplier (master record), we have not finished processing the master record until we know that all orders from that supplier have been completed, that is, until the transCode differs from the current mastCode indicating a new supplier. The UNTIL loop in the Match module continues to process the transaction records UNTIL mastCode < > transCode. Only when we have finished all orders from that supplier (when the transaction and master codes are no longer equal) do we read a new master record for the next supplier.

The TransWithoutMast module includes a similar concept. The module writes an error message when we have an order from an invalid supplier (a supplier not included in the master file). If additional transaction records have the same invalid transCode, we do not want to write more error messages. The solution is to read the succeeding transaction records in a loop until a record is read with a different transCode. In this loop we are comparing the transCode of the current record with the transCode of the previous record, so a compare field (oldTrans) is used to hold the code from the previous record.

EXERCISES

1. Quick 'N Spicy Pizza has just bought out Fat 'N Happy Pizza. Design a program that will merge the two employee lists. Both files include Social Security Number, name, and address, and both are sorted on SSN in ascending order. If anyone was employed by both companies, include the name only once on the new list. Write out a count of the new employee list.

2. In a new era of equality, the YMCA and the YWCA have merged. Both associations have membership lists that include the member's name, address, and membership expiration year (all memberships end as of 12/31 on the named year) in order by name. Design a program that will merge the two lists. Since both associations have accepted members of either sex for some time, it is possible that there will be matches. If anyone is a member of both associations, the membership expiration date should be extended to reflect the time left on both memberships.

3. The example in the chapter (pp. 297–300) that matches the order with the file of suppliers may look like a control break program to you. If you picture a large file of orders with a small file of suppliers, the program will seem less like a match (where we are reading through two files simultaneously) and more like a control break (where we would process the next supplier record as part of the special processing when the TransCode changes in the order file). Either design could be equally correct. Rewrite the example from a control break perspective.

4. Design a program that will help with reconciling a checking account. You will have two input files. The first is a file of checks that have been written, in order by check number, holding check number, date, payee, and check amount. The second is a file of checks that have been returned with the bank statement, also in order by check number, containing only check numbers and amounts. Your program should create a report listing checks by check number and giving a message as follows:
For checks that have been returned: "Check has been processed."
For checks that were written but not yet returned: "Check has not yet been processed."
For checks that have been returned but were not recorded as written: "Check was not recorded. Please correct."

5. Assume we have a file of all NFL players in order by their team and within the team in order by player number. For each player, the file has the following fields: team, player number, name, and address. We also have a second file giving the team and player number for all players whose annual salary is over 1 million dollars. This file is also in order by team and within team by player number. Using these two files, design a program to create a

report giving the name, team, and address of all players with salaries over 1 million. For players who are included in the NFL list but do not make over a million, do nothing. For players that somehow got into the one million list but are not included in the NFL list, write an error message.

6. Surely you noticed that the files mentioned in design # 5 are in order by team. That means that we can modify our design so that we have a count for each team of the number of players making over a million. Write the count out at the end of each team listing. If a team has no players in that salary range, write 0.

Chapter 17
File Updates

Objectives

After completing this chapter, you should be able to:

1. Define and describe the sequential update process.
2. List the three possible modifications (i.e., Add, Change, Delete) and the circumstances under which each is valid (e.g., Add is valid only when a matching master is not found).
3. Describe the usual input and output files involved in an update program.
4. Design an update program assuming only one transaction record for any one master record.
5. Design an update program including counters for each update possibility (Add, Change, Delete) as well as for the new master file.
6. Design an update program that allows multiple transaction records for any one master record.

INTRODUCTION

In the last chapter we looked at programs that "match" a master file with a transaction file that holds transient data. Many operations will require matching a relatively static master file with a second file that reflects the current data (e.g., hours worked this week, total sales this sales period, credits registered this term). We know, however, that no file is completely static. Our file of employees may not change on a daily or weekly basis, but it will change. In this chapter, we will look at the means to make the necessary modifications to the "master" file. We are "updating" the master. It is possible that we have hired a new employee (an Add to the master), that an employee has left our company (a Delete from the master), or that an employee has a new address or a new phone number (a Change in the master). The update program allows us to make these modifications to the master file.

We will have two input files: the master that is to be modified and the transaction that holds the modifications to be made. The master file will be the same form of master file that we used in the matching program and will be sorted on a unique key field found in each record (name, Social Security Number, ID, etc.). The transaction file must be sorted on the same field because that is the field by which we will match a transaction record to the master record. The update program differs from the matching program in that we now have three different processes to perform. A transaction record may call for an Add, for a Delete, or for a Change. Obviously, there must be some code included in the transaction record which indicates what transaction process is to be performed.

Usually, we also have two output files: a new master file (reflecting all the transaction modifications) and an error report. The new master file will typically utilize the same storage medium as the input master file (disk, tape, etc.) since it will replace the input master as the new, updated master file. The new master file will maintain the sorted order of the original master but will reflect any additions, deletions, and changes from the transaction file. The error report is typically a printed document. The error report identifies transaction processes that could not be performed: You cannot change or delete a record that is not in the master, and you cannot add a record which is already in the master. Some update programs will also generate a printed "audit" report listing all actions taken on the master file. As we will see in the next chapter, an audit report is more important with a non-sequential update.

What follows (on the next page) is a system flowchart for a sequential update program. (See Appendix B for more information about system flowcharts.) Naturally, we would want the transaction file to be as error-free as possible prior to an update so this chart includes an input editing check of the transaction file prior to the update. The input editing can only check for *field* errors (e.g., whether the transaction code is one of the valid codes). We still have the possibility of *record* errors when we perform the update (e.g., the code is a valid code, but is not valid in the current circumstances). Those errors would be noted in the Update Error Report.

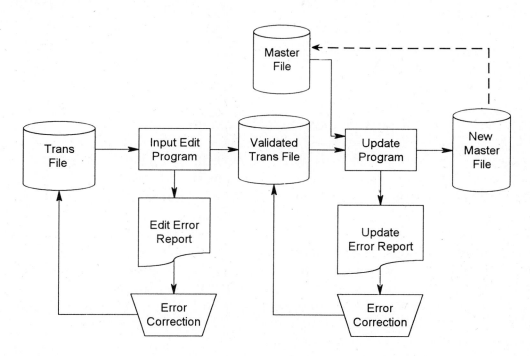

Notice that there is a broken line going back from the New Master File to the Master File. This line is to indicate that the New Master "becomes" the working master and the next time the update program is run, we will be updating what used to be the "new" master. This process is known as a generational backup. The "old" master along with the transaction file serve as a backup for the "new" master. If we somehow lost or damaged the new master file, we could always recreate it by running the update program again. If we update our master on a weekly basis, we would also then have a weekly backup. Let's say that in week one, we do our first update. The old master becomes the backup for the new master. The old master is sometimes called the "parent" (generational backup, remember). In week two, we do our second update. The current master becomes the old master and we create a new master. We now have three generations: grandparent (the original master), parent, and the current master (child?). Depending on how valuable our data are and how frequent the changes are, we might keep up to five or more generational backups.

ORGANIZING THE UPDATE POSSIBILITIES

We know that there are three ways in which a given master record and a given transaction record can "match":

Master = Transaction
Master > Transaction
Master < Transaction

We also know that there are three possible update actions:

Add a record (copying a record from the transaction file to the new master).
Delete a record (*not* copying a record from the old master file to the new master).
Change a record (making changes before copying a record from the old master file to the new master).

But not all possible actions are valid with each match possibility. If the master field is equal to the transaction field, we could change the master record or we could delete the master record, but we cannot add the transaction record. We cannot add a record that already exists in the master file.

If the master field is greater than the transaction field, we know that we will never find a master record to match the current transaction record. Therefore, the transaction cannot be a Change or a Delete because those operations require a match. But the transaction could be an Add since an Add must not have a matching master.

If the master field is less than the transaction field, the transaction record is not relevant at all. We know that the current transaction record is not related to the current master record, and that we will not find a subsequent transaction record to match the current master record. Therefore, there is no transaction record related to this master record that needs to be processed. Do we just ignore the current master? No, it is still a part of the master file, so we copy it from the old master to the new master.

Two additional questions remain. When do we write an error message in the error report? Any time we have an invalid transaction code (an Add code with a transaction record that matches a master or a Change or Delete code with a transaction record that does not match a master), we must identify that error on the error report. If our transaction file has been through an input-editing program first, we should be able to assume that the code itself is valid (e.g., if our codes are A, C, and D, we have only those three letters). Next, when do we read from an input file? In our matching and merging programs we read a record from a file when we had "processed" the previous record from that file. We will use the same rule in our update program.

The following chart summarizes the operations. Remember, we are comparing the equivalent fields from two files, such as an ID field from both files or a name field.

Condition	Code	Action	Read from
Master = Trans	A	Invalid Code, Write Error	Trans file
	C	Make changes to Master Write Master to New Master	Trans & Master Files
	D	no action	Trans & Master Files
Master > Trans	A	Write Trans to New Master	Trans file
	C	Invalid Code, Write Error	Trans file
	D	Invalid Code, Write Error	Trans file
Master < Trans	N/A	Write Master to New Master	Master file

A SAMPLE DESIGN

The following program updates an employee master file including ID, name, address, and telephone. The file is in order by ID. Each field will be identified in the design by preceding it with om (old master) as in omID or omName. The updates are found in the transaction file which includes an ID, transaction code, and possibly a name, address, and telephone. The file is sorted on ID. If the transaction code is D (Delete), only the code and ID will be present. If the transaction code is C (Change), the code, ID, and any field which is to be changed will be present. If the transaction code is A (Add), all fields will be included. Transaction fields will be identified in the design by preceding the name with a t as in tID, tname, and so on.

```
Mainline
DO Start
WHILE moreData = 'yes'
    DO ProcessUpdate
ENDWHILE
DO Finish
```

```
Start
OPEN files
moreData = 'yes'
moreTrans = 'yes'
moreMast = 'yes'
lineCnt = 60
pageCnt = 0
DO ReadTrans
IF moreTrans = 'no'
    moreData = 'no'
    WRITE 'ERROR -- Transaction file is empty'
ENDIF
DO ReadMast
IF moreMast = 'no'
    moreData = 'no'
    WRITE 'ERROR -- Master file is empty'
ENDIF

ProcessUpdate
IF omID < tID
    DO CopyMaster
ELSE
    IF omID = tID
        IF tCode = 'C'
            DO Change
        ELSE IF tCode = 'D'
            DO Delete
        ELSE IF tCode = 'A'
            DO BadAdd
        ENDIF
    ELSE
        IF tCode = 'A'
            DO Add
        ELSE IF tCode = 'C'
            DO BadChange
        ELSE IF tCode = 'D'
            DO BadDelete
        ENDIF
    ENDIF
ENDIF

Finish
CLOSE files
```

<u>Change</u>
```
IF tName not = spaces
    omName = tName
ENDIF
IF tAddr not = spaces
    omAddr = tAddr
ENDIF
IF tPhone not = spaces
    omPhone = tPhone
ENDIF
WRITE omID, omName, omAddr, omPhone (to new master file)
DO ReadTrans
DO ReadMast
```

<u>Delete</u>
```
DO ReadTrans
DO ReadMast
```

<u>Add</u>
```
WRITE tID, tName, tAddr, tPhone (to new master file)
DO ReadTrans
```

<u>CopyMaster</u>
```
WRITE omID, omName, omAddr, omPhone (to new master file)
DO ReadMast
```

<u>BadAdd</u>
```
msg = 'Add code with matching record in master'
DO WriteErrorLine
DO ReadTrans
```

<u>BadChange</u>
```
msg = 'Change code with no matching record in master'
DO WriteErrorLine
DO ReadTrans
```

<u>BadDelete</u>
```
msg = 'Delete code with no matching record in master'
DO WriteErrorLine
DO ReadTrans
```

<u>ReadTrans</u>
IF there are data
    READ tCode, tID, tName, tAddr, tPhone
ELSE
    moreTrans = 'no'
    tID = 99999
    IF moreMast = 'no'
        moreData = 'no'
    ENDIF
ENDIF

<u>ReadMast</u>
IF there are data
    READ omID, omName, omAddr, omPhone
ELSE
    moreMast = 'no'
    omID = 99999
    IF moreTrans = 'no'
        moreData = 'no'
    ENDIF
ENDIF

<u>WriteErrorLine</u>
IF lineCnt > = 60
    DO Heads
ENDIF
WRITE tCode, tID, tName, tAddr, tPhone, msg
ADD 1 to lineCnt

<u>Heads</u>
EJECT page
SKIP 6 lines
IF pageCnt = 0
    WRITE Report Heading
    SKIP 1 line
    lineCnt = 8
ELSE
    lineCnt = 6
ENDIF
ADD 1 to pageCnt
WRITE Page Heading, pageCnt
WRITE Column Headings (dbl spc)
SKIP 1 line
ADD 4 to lineCnt

Desk check the design using the following data:

Master

3	Sam	Vienna	281-4318
5	Dot	Reston	437-9117
7	Jim	Herndon	450-9494
9	Sue	Sterling	820-3326
11	Joe	Leesburg	777-1770

Transaction

3	D			
5	C		Herndon	
6	A	Tom	Vienna	281-9143
7	A	Jim	Herndon	450-9494
8	C	Carol		

Loop Iteration #1

Master: Transaction:

 3   Sam   Vienna   281-4318   3   D

Tests and Actions:

omID = tID   →   Check tCode

tCode = 'D'   →   Read next transaction record

                                 Read next master record

Loop Iteration #2

Master: Transaction:

 5   Dot   Reston   437-9117   5   C   Herndon

Tests and Actions:

omID = tID   →.   Check tCode

tCode = 'C'   →   Do Change Module

Check all fields   →   Change omAddr

                                 Write master to new master

                                 Read next transaction record

                                 Read next master record

Loop Iteration #3

Master: Transaction:

 7   Jim   Herndon   450-9494   6 A Tom   Vienna   281-9143

Tests and Actions:

omID > tID   →   Check tCode

tCode = 'A'   →   Write transaction record to new master

                                 Read next transaction record

Loop Iteration #4

Master: Transaction:
7   Jim   Herndon   450-9494   7   A   Jim   Herndon   450-9494
Tests and Actions:
omID = tID   →   Check tCode
tCode = 'A'   →   Write error message (bad add) to report
                                       Read next transaction record

---

Loop Iteration #5

Master: Transaction:
7   Jim   Herndon   450-9494   8   C   Carol
Tests and Actions:
omID < tID   →   Copy master to new master
                                       Read next master record

---

Loop Iteration #6

Master: Transaction:
9   Sue   Sterling   820-3326   8   C   Carol
Tests and Actions:
omID > tID   →   Check tCode
tCode = 'C'   →   Write error message (bad change) to report
                                       Read next transaction record (no more records, so tID set
                                          to 99999)

Loop Iteration #7

Master: Transaction:
9   Sue   Sterling   820-3326   99999
Tests and Actions:
om-ID < t-ID   →   Copy master to new master
                                       Read next master record

Loop Iteration #8

Master: Transaction:

11   Joe   Leesburg   777-1770   99999

Tests and Actions:

omID < tID   →   Copy master to new master
                                          Read next master record (no more records, so OM-ID set to
                                             99999)

MULTIPLE TRANSACTION RECORDS

We have made a major assumption in this design. After processing matching transaction and master records, we read the next record from both files. We assumed that we would not have another transaction record for that master record. But in reality, we might have several transactions. If an employee moved, we would get a notice of change of address, and we would include a change transaction in the file. Several days later (but before we ran the update program) that employee might get a new phone number and we would receive another change, which we would include as an additional change transaction record. When the update program was run, the master record for that employee should match with two transaction records. With our current design, the second one would not be processed as a match, however, because we would have read a new master after processing the first change. A similar possibility occurs when we add a new employee. We would, of course, include an add transaction record in the transaction file. But if that employee came in the next day with a change of telephone number, we would then include a change transaction. When we ran the update program, the change would be seen as invalid because it would not match a master. (It matched the previous transaction record which was already written to the new master.)

To modify the design to account for multiple transaction records, we have to make some adjustments when we write to the new master and when we read the next old master. In the chapter on file match programs, we allowed for multiple transaction matches to the same master by waiting until we read a non-matching transaction record to read from the master file. We will follow the same logic here. With an update program we must consider when do we write the updated record to the new master file. We now cannot write to the new master as soon as we have processed a change or add, because there may be another related transaction. As with the read from the old master file, we will wait to write to the new master file until we read a non-matching transaction record.

Allowing for additional transaction updates to an Add is a bit more complex. We can't simply hold the record in its current location in memory because when we read the next transaction record we will lose the "added" record. One solution is to set up a new location in memory to "hold" the record prior to writing it. The design that follows calls this holding area the newID, newName, and so forth. We could make the following, fairly simple, change to the Change and Add modules:

<u>Change</u>
```
REPEAT
    IF tName not = spaces
        omName = tName
    ENDIF
    IF tAddr not = spaces
        omAddr = tAddr
    ENDIF
    IF tPhone not = spaces
        omPhone = tPhone
    ENDIF
    DO ReadTrans
UNTIL tID < > omID
WRITE omID, omName, omAddr, omPhone (to new master file)
DO ReadMast
```

WARNING: this is not the final version

<u>Add</u>
```
newID = tID
newName = tName
newAddr = tAddr
newPhone = tPhone
DO ReadTrans
WHILE newID = tID
    IF tName not = spaces
        newName = tName
    ENDIF
    IF tAddr not = spaces
        newAddr = tAddr
    ENDIF
    IF tPhone not = spaces
        newPhone = tPhone
    ENDIF
    DO ReadTrans
ENDWHILE
WRITE newID, newName, newAddr, newPhone (to new master file)
```

This design is consistent with the modifications we made in our match program to account for multiple transaction records—i.e., nested loops within the processing module. The problem is that even this design change is making an assumption. It assumes that any additional transaction records will be Changes—it never checks the tCode! In reality, though, we could have a change and then have a delete for the same master record or an add and then a delete. We must try a different tactic. In the following version, the Change module looks almost the same as the original version; we have just removed the DO ReadMast.

The Add module is quite different. Instead of immediately writing the added transaction record to the new master, we save it in the memory location where the master record is stored. First, of course, we must save the master record in a different location (holdRecord). The advantage of this logic is that the other modules were all written so that they compared fields to the master record. Now the "added record" will be where the master record would have been, and the same comparisons can take place. We also set a flag, recInHold, to 'yes,' indicating that we have a master record already in memory waiting to be processed. When the ReadMast module is called, it first checks to see if a master record is still held in memory. If a master record is held, the design pulls that record from the holdRecord location to the memory location where the master is stored (and changes recInHold back to 'no'). The Change and Add modules no longer write a record to the new master. In both cases, the record is stored in the old master location and would be written when the old master is less than the transaction record (in CopyMaster). Two other modules need minor changes. In Start, we need to initialize recInHold to 'no' before the first call to ReadMast. In ReadTrans, we need to check to be sure recInHold is 'no' before we change Moredata to 'no'—the changed module is shown on the next page. The other modules are not changed from our original design.

```
Change
IF tName not = spaces
    omName = tName
ENDIF
IF tAddr not = spaces
    omAddr = tAddr
ENDIF
IF tPhone not = spaces
    omPhone = tPhone
ENDIF
DO ReadTrans


Add
COPY omRecord to holdRecord          [copies all fields from one memory location to another]
omID = tID
omName = tName
omAddr = tAddr
omPhone = tPhone
recInHold = 'yes'
DO ReadTrans
```

```
ReadMast
IF recInHold = 'yes'
    COPY holdRecord to omRecord
    recInHold = 'no'
    IF moreTrans = 'no' AND moreMast = 'no'
        moreData = 'no'
    ENDIF
ELSE
    IF there are data (Master file)
        READ omID, omName, omAddr, omPhone
    ELSE
        moreMast = 'no'
        omID = 99999
        IF moreTrans = 'no'
            moreData = 'no'
        ENDIF
    ENDIF
ENDIF


ReadTrans
IF there are data (Transaction file)
    READ  tCode, tID, tName, tAddr, tPhone
ELSE
    moreTrans = 'no'
    tID = 99999
    IF moreMast = 'no' AND recInHold = 'no'
        moreData = 'no'
    ENDIF
ENDIF
```

We often use flags in a program to help clarify the processing. The above design uses the moreData, moreMast, and moreTrans flags to make the program "readable." Unfortunately, the flags actually add more confusion than clarity. The moreData flag that controls the main processing loop does give the Mainline module a simplified look. But the flags can lead to confusion when we move an added transaction record into the master record memory location. If the last record in the transaction file is an Add and the master file has already been completed (moreMast = 'no'), we cannot change moreData to 'no' when we try to do the next read since we haven't finished processing the added record. That's why we have the extra check on recInHold in the ReadTrans module and the extra check on both flags in the ReadMast module when we retrieve a record from the hold area. The final example simplifies the problem by not using the flags. The loop is controlled by the actual values in tID and omID.

Try creating a data file that includes multiple transaction records for a given master and additional transaction records after an Add and desk check this design.

Another variation, much simpler this time, I promise, is to add counters to the design. In some update situations, it is helpful to know how many records were added to the master, or how many were deleted. We can easily add counters for each operation. All counters would be initialized to 0 in the Start module and written in the Finish module. Where would they be incremented? The counter keeping track of the number of deletes would be incremented in the Delete module, the counter for adds would be incremented in the Add module, and so on. It is less likely to need a count of the number of changes, but you should remember that if you increment a counter in the Change module, you are counting the number of change transaction records, not the number of records that received changes (since we could have multiple changes for one record). We could also count the number of records read from the old master file and the number of records written to the new master file. We then have a way to double-check our numbers since the records read from the old master plus the adds minus the deletions should equal the number of records written to the new master.

One final variation: We have included two output files in our sample design, the new master and the printed error report. Some update programs also include an "audit report" that records every action taken on the master file. Any change to a record, any deletion, and any addition would be recorded in the audit report. The audit report is then used as a written (human readable) record of the actions taken and would be used only if a problem or question occurs. It is not the kind of report that gets circulated. It is filed away until it is needed. But if it is needed, it may be much easier to refer to a printed document than trying to reconstruct what was done by referring to the transaction and master file (which are not in a human-readable format).

A FINAL EXAMPLE

The final example is a revision of our completed update, adding counters for the number of records written to the new master, the number of adds, and the number of deletes, and adding a printed audit report. Notice that the audit report is not a fancy report with headings.

```
Mainline
DO Start
WHILE tID < > 99999 OR omID < > 99999
    DO ProcessUpdate
ENDWHILE
DO Finish
```

<u>Start</u>
OPEN files
recInHold = 'no'
lineCnt = 60
pageCnt = 0
deleteCount = 0
addCount = 0
newMasterCount = 0
DO ReadTrans
DO ReadMast
IF tID = 99999 OR omID = 99999
   tID = 99999
   omID = 99999
   WRITE 'ERROR -- Master file and/or Transaction file empty'   (to screen)
ENDIF

<u>ProcessUpdate</u>
IF omID < tID
   DO CopyMaster
ELSE
   IF omID = tID
      IF tCode = 'C'
         DO Change
      ELSE IF tCode = 'D'
         DO Delete
      ELSE IF tCode = 'A'
         DO BadAdd
      ENDIF
   ELSE
      IF tCode = 'A'
         DO Add
      ELSE IF tCode = 'C'
         DO BadChange
      ELSE IF tCode = 'D'
         DO BadDelete
      ENDIF
   ENDIF
ENDIF

<u>Finish</u>
WRITE 'Count of records added to new master file = ', addCount (dbl spc)   (to ErrorRpt)
WRITE 'Count of records deleted from master file = ', deleteCount   (to ErrorRpt)
WRITE 'Count of records written to new master file = ', newMasterCount   (to ErrorRpt)
CLOSE files

<u>Change</u>
IF tName not = spaces
    omName = tName
ENDIF
IF tAddr not = spaces
    omAddr = tAddr
ENDIF
IF tPhone not = spaces
    omPhone = tPhone
ENDIF
WRITE 'CHANGE: ', transaction record   (to AuditRpt)
DO ReadTrans

<u>Add</u>
COPY omRecord to holdRecord   [copies all fields from one memory location to another]
omID = tID
omName = tName
omAddr = tAddr
omPhone = tPhone
recInHold = 'yes'
ADD 1 to addCount
WRITE 'ADD: ', transaction record   (to AuditRpt)
DO ReadTrans

<u>Delete</u>
WRITE 'DELETE: ', transaction record   (to AuditRpt)
DO ReadTrans
DO ReadMast
ADD 1 to deleteCount

<u>CopyMaster</u>
WRITE omID, omName, omAddr, omPhone   (to new master file)
WRITE 'MASTER WRITTEN: ', master record   (to AuditRpt)
DO ReadMast
ADD 1 to newMasterCount

<u>BadAdd</u>
msg = 'Add code with matching record in master'
DO WriteErrorLine
DO ReadTrans

<u>BadChange</u>
msg = 'Change code with no matching record in master'
DO WriteErrorLine
DO ReadTrans

BadDelete
msg = 'Delete code with no matching record in master'
DO WriteErrorLine
DO ReadTrans

ReadMast
IF recInHold = 'yes'
    COPY holdRecord to omRecord
    recInHold = 'no'
ELSE
    IF there are data (Master file)
        READ omID, omName, omAddr, omPhone
    ELSE
        omID = 99999
    ENDIF
ENDIF

ReadTrans
IF there are data (Transaction file)
    READ tCode, tID, tName, tAddr, tPhone
ELSE
    tID = 99999
ENDIF

WriteErrorLine
IF lineCnt > = 57
    DO Heads
ENDIF
WRITE tCode, tID, tName, tAddr, tPhone, msg   (to ErrorRpt)
ADD 1 to lineCnt

Heads
EJECT page
SKIP 6 lines
IF pageCnt = 0
    WRITE Report Heading   (to ErrorRpt)
    SKIP 1 line
    lineCnt = 8
ELSE
    lineCnt = 6
ENDIF
ADD 1 to pageCnt
WRITE Page Heading, pageCnt   (to ErrorRpt)
WRITE Column Headings (dbl spc)   (to ErrorRpt)
SKIP 1 line
ADD 4 to lineCnt

EXERCISES

1. Modify the sample shown on pp. 317-20 to include a count of the old master reads and changes. At the end of the program, write out all the counters plus a message indicating if the counters "balance out" (old master reads + additions – deletions should equal new master writes).

2. Design a program to update the YWCA/YMCA master file created in design # 2 at the end of Chapter 16 (page 301). The *unedited* transaction file includes the following fields:
   Action Code: A (Add), C (Change), D (Delete) [always present]
   Name: [always present]
   Addr: [present if add record or change record and the addr is being changed]
   NumYears: Gives the number of years (1 through 5) by which the membership should be extended. [present if add record or if change record and the expiration year is being changed]

3. Design a program to update our store's inventory file based on the past week's activities as reflected in a transaction file. The inventory file (in order by part number) includes the following fields:
   Part number
   Part description
   Part supplier's name
   Part cost

An *edited* transaction file (in order by part number) includes a transaction part number and a transaction code (A, C, or D) for each record. In addition, if needed for an add or change, a record can also include:
   Transaction part description
   Transaction supplier code
   Transaction part cost

A separate (third) file includes the 150 supplier codes and their names in order by code.

Chapter 18

Non-Sequential Files

Objectives

After completing this chapter, you should be able to:

1. Differentiate between sequential and non-sequential processing.
2. Describe the design adjustments needed with non-sequential processing.
3. Describe two types of non-sequential access.
4. Define hashing as it relates to direct access files.
5. Design a two-input file match program using a non-sequential master file.
6. Design an update program using a non-sequential master file.

SEQUENTIAL VERSUS NON-SEQUENTIAL FILES

All of the input files that we have used up to now have been sequential files. When we read from the files, we started reading at the first record and read *sequentially* through the file to the end-of-file marker after the last record. We could read a particular record only by first reading all the records that preceded it in the file. With our merging, matching, and update programs, we needed to be sure that both input files were sorted on the same field since we would be processing both files sequentially.

A non-sequential file sounds like it might be a file that is out of order. But it really means a file that we can *process* out of order. Instead of needing to read the first 10 records to access the 11th record, we can start with the 11th record if we want. The ability to access any record at any time changes the way we think about the two-input file programs we have been designing. Instead of having to process the master and transaction files in parallel, we can let the transaction file determine the processing order even if the transaction file has not been sorted. If the first record in the transaction file indicates that the 99th record in the master file needs to be changed, we access that 99th record and make the necessary changes. If the second transaction record indicates that we have changes for the 47th master record, we can next access the 47th record. And all without ever reading the first 46 master records!

Naturally, this kind of advantage comes at a cost. First, we can only have non-sequential files on hardware devices that provide non-sequential access. Some storage devices are limited to sequential access (tape drives, for example). Some devices can provide either sequential or non-sequential access (disk drives, for example). Second, just having the file on a non-sequential device does not assure non-sequential access. The file must have been created and maintained for non-sequential access. In other words, we can't decide later that we want to make a file a non-sequential file without completely rewriting the file.

There are other costs as well built into non-sequential access designs. Remember that with our sequential access update program we had an automatic backup system. The very process of performing the update also created a backup of the master file. With a non-sequential update, we will be making the changes directly in the original master, so no backup is created automatically. We can certainly live with this change, but we must be aware of the need to create a backup.

Non-sequential access sounds efficient and easy. But in reality, if we are updating very many of our records (say 25 percent or more), it is more efficient if we can do the update sequentially. Imagine the post office mail carrier delivering the daily mail. It would be possible to take the mail in whatever order it happened to arrive and deliver it. But of course, the mail carrier would be zig-zagging back and forth around the delivery area, and the time saved by not having to sort the mail wouldn't make up for the time lost zig-zagging. Obviously, it is much more efficient for the carrier to sort the mail first and then deliver it sequentially, even if only 25 percent of the houses actually received mail.

Some applications require non-sequential updating even though sequential would be more efficient. The problem with sequential updating is that it assumes we have all the data available at one time. We gather all the transaction records, sort them, then perform the update program. If we *must* process the transaction immediately instead of "saving" it for the daily or weekly update, we must use a non-sequential file and a non-sequential update. Imagine calling an airline to change your reservation and being told that they would process your change the following Friday when they did the weekly update!

TYPES OF NON-SEQUENTIAL ACCESS

There are a variety of ways to implement non-sequential access to a file. We will look in very general terms at two of the broad categories—each of which has multiple variations.

Direct Access

The simplest form of direct access to a record in a file is analogous to accessing data in a positional array. With a positional array, we know the exact location of an element in the array because there is a natural link between the element and the position. We could have an inventory numbering system in which our parts are numbered from one to the maximum number of parts. Part names could then be stored in a positional array by part number. Part number 10 would be in the 10th position in the array. Part number 158 would be in the 158th position. If someone asked for the name of part number 432, we would not need to do a search; the name is directly accessible by using the part number as the subscript.

Direct access to files could be done in the same way if we have a field within each file entry (record) that can be used as the address of the record. Address here refers to the actual location for that record on the storage medium, the address on the disk itself. If we have a file of students enrolled at the college and each student has a suitable student ID number, we could use the ID number as the address of the record. If a student got a new telephone number and his record was to be updated, the student would give his ID number to access the record, then the new telephone number for the update (as we shall see, the changed record would then be rewritten back to the same location in the file). Of course, if the student came in but couldn't remember his ID number, we would have trouble accessing his record.

This form of direct access, however, usually doesn't work very well. We usually don't have a field in the record that can be used directly as an address. So we do the next best thing—we manipulate a field to create a suitable address from it. A Social Security Number would not be a good number to use for positional, direct access. The range of Social Security Numbers is far too large for most operations. But we can modify the Social Security Number so that we create a suitable number. We perform a mathematical operation on the field within the record to create the address. As long as we always perform the same operation we will always be able to find the stored records. The process of creating the address based on a field in the record is called *hashing*.

Assume we have a hashing algorithm to convert an ID number to the storage address. To add a record to the file, we apply the algorithm to the new employee's ID number to "create" the address for that record. The record is then stored at that address. If we later need to access the record, we again apply the algorithm to the ID number. We will get the same address, so we can directly access the needed record. There is one problem. When we convert the ID number to an address, we might derive an address that is already used. All direct access programs have some means for handling these "collisions," and, again, as long as they are handled consistently, we will have no problem finding the record.

Fortunately for us, as designers, the hard work in performing direct access operations is done for us. When we first create the file, we must identify it as direct access, identify the field to use as the key access field, and identify the maximum number of expected records. The direct access system will build the file for us. A hashing algorithm will be applied and the address determined without any work on our part.

But direct access files are not the perfect solution to all file needs. Remember that some operations are best handled sequentially. We might want to do some operations through direct access but other operations, on the same file, sequentially. Can we access a direct access file sequentially; that is, can we read that file from the first record through to the last record? The answer is yes, but you may not want to. The order of the records in the file is determined by the hashing algorithm and will probably not have any meaning for the user.

Indexed Sequential Access

A compromise between the pure sequential file and the direct access file is an indexed sequential file. Indexed files are still stored sequentially based on some key field in the record and can still be accessed, when desired, in that sequential order. In addition, a separate area in storage holds an *index* to the file providing the value of the key field for the last record in each area of the file. Disks are divided into tracks, so an index could show the last record for each track. To access a needed record, we would enter the value of the key field. The system will check the index to determine the correct track and then will sequentially read that track looking for the needed record. Obviously, this will be slower than a direct access since the system must first read the index and then read the identified track sequentially, but it allows us to access any record we need non-sequentially while retaining the advantages of sequential processing.

If you were going to visit a friend for the afternoon, you could look for the house *sequentially* by driving systematically up one street and down the next until you got to your friend's house. If you started at the west end of town and your friend lived on the east end, it might be a long time before you got to the right house. Sequentially processing a file when we really want to process just one record wastes a lot of time.

If you knew exactly where your friend lived, you could hire a plane to fly over and you could parachute directly to your friend's house. While that's not the approach most of us would use to "drop in" for an afternoon, it gives us a reasonable comparison to direct access. A more down to earth view might be driving directly to the friend's house.

If, on the other hand, you knew which street your friend lived on but didn't know the exact address, you could go directly to the street and then drive slowly down the street looking for the correct house. This process is rather like an indexed sequential access. It is slower than driving directly to the house (although if the record is at the beginning of the identified track or the house is at the first corner it isn't much slower), but much faster than sequentially checking each house in the town or each record in the file.

Again, fortunately for us, most of the work for indexed sequential files is done for us. When we create the file, we must declare it as an indexed sequential file, and we must provide the records in sequential order. The index is automatically built and maintained for us. There are a few design "oddities" that we must account for, but the index creation and use are not our problem. For the user, the file will look and act just like a direct access file.

One of the oddities is that we don't actually delete records from an indexed sequential file, we *mark* them for deletion. That is, we're doing a "logical" deletion rather than a "physical" deletion. Each record has a delete flag stored with it, and the flag will be set if the record is a "deleted" record. The record remains in the file, however. Therefore, when we retrieve a record, we must be sure that we aren't retrieving a logically deleted record.

Non-sequential files usually assume that we will be able to read from and write to a file in the same program. Therefore, we can read a record, make the necessary changes to the record while it is in memory, and then write the record back to the file. To distinguish between an operation in which we are adding a record to a file and one in which we are replacing an existing record, we will use two different commands. WRITE will be used to indicate a new record being written to the file. REWRITE will be used to indicate the replacement of an existing record.

Finally, all accesses to an indexed sequential file are completely dependent on the validity of the key field. For that reason, some languages require a check on the key field as a part of any file access operation and require that the designer/programmer identify what steps should be taken if the key field is not valid. In these languages, any file access operation, like a READ or a WRITE, will have two steps: the file access itself and the description of what to do if the key is invalid.

AN UPDATE PROGRAM USING AN INDEXED SEQUENTIAL FILE

In the last chapter, we designed a sequential update of a master employee file which included ID, name, address, and telephone. Now we'll assume that the master file is an indexed sequential file which uses the ID as the key field. We will update the master using a transaction file containing additions (code A), deletions (code D), and changes (code C). The transaction file need not be in any particular order since we will access only the needed records in the master file. We will assume that logically deleted records have an '*' in the delete flag area and non-deleted records have a space.

```
Mainline
DO Start
WHILE there are transaction data
    DO ProcessUpdate
ENDWHILE
CLOSE Files

Start
OPEN Master file (Indexed I/O), Trans file (Seq, Input), Report (printer)
lineCnt = 60
pageCnt = 0
```

ProcessUpdate
READ transCode, transID, transName, transAddr, transPhone (from trans file)
transError = 'no'
IF transCode = 'C'
    DO ChangeRec
ELSE
    IF transCode = 'D'
        DO DeleteRec
    ELSE
        IF transCode = 'A'
            DO AddRec
        ENDIF
    ENDIF
ENDIF

DeleteRec
DO ReadMaster
IF masterRecOK = 'yes'
    IF deleteFlag = space
        deleteFlag = '*'
        REWRITE master record to file
        msg = 'Record deleted'
        DO WriteReportLine
    ELSE
        transError = 'yes'
        msg = 'Record already marked for deletion'
        DO WriteReportLine
    ENDIF
ENDIF

```
ChangeRec
DO ReadMaster
IF masterRecOK = 'yes'
    IF deleteFlag = space
        IF transName not = spaces
            mastName = transName
        ENDIF
        IF transAddr not = spaces
            mastAddr = transAddr
        ENDIF
        IF transPhone not = spaces
            mastPhone = transPhone
        ENDIF
        REWRITE master record to file
        msg = 'Master record changed'
        DO WriteReportLine
    ELSE
        transError = 'yes'
        msg = 'Cannot change deleted record'
        DO WriteReportLine
    ENDIF
ENDIF


AddRec
READ record in master file to match transID
IF master record not found
    mastID = transID
    mastName = transName
    mastAddr = transAddr
    mastPhone = transPhone
    deleteFlag = space
    WRITE master record to file
    msg = 'Record added to master'
    DO WriteReportLine
ELSE
    IF deleteFlag = '*'
        deleteFlag = space
        mastName = transName
        mastAddr = transAddr
        mastPhone = transPhone
        REWRITE master record to file
        msg = 'Record added to master'
        DO WriteReportLine
    ELSE
        transError = 'yes'
        msg = 'Record already included in file'
        DO WriteReportLine
    ENDIF
ENDIF
```

330

```
ReadMaster
READ record in master file to match transID
    (mastName, mastID, mastAddr, mastPhone)
IF master record not found
    masterRecOK = 'no'
    transError = 'yes'
    msg = 'Master record not found in employee file'
    DO WriteReportLine
ELSE
    masterRecOK = 'yes'
ENDIF


WriteReportLine
IF lineCnt > = 60
    EJECT page
    ADD 1 to pageCnt
    SKIP 6 lines
    WRITE headings, pageCnt
    lineCnt = 8
ENDIF
IF transError = 'yes'
    WRITE 'ERROR', msg, transaction record (dbl spc)
ELSE
    WRITE 'UPDATE', msg, transaction record (dbl spc)
ENDIF
ADD 2 to lineCnt
```

Let's look at these modules to see how they work together. The Mainline module shows us that the loop is controlled by the transaction file. As long as there are data to be processed in the file, we continue in the loop. The ProcessUpdate module is very straightforward. We read the next transaction record, initialize the flag transError, then call the appropriate update module (AddRec, DeleteRec, or ChangeRec) depending on the transCode value. As we shall see, this program creates a printed report that includes error messages for invalid transaction update records and audit trail messages of each update operation performed. The transError flag helps to identify whether the line being added to the report is an error message or just a record of a performed operation.

The ReadMaster module is called by both the DeleteRec and the ChangeRec modules. It attempts to read the master record that matches the current transID value. If the read is successful, the flag masterRecOK is set to 'yes' (so the calling module knows the read operation worked). If a matching master is not found, the flag is set to 'no' and an error message is written in the report. Notice that before calling the module to write the report line, the message description is assigned to the msg field and the flag transError is changed to 'yes.'

The WriteReportLine module is called every time an update error is found or an update operation is successfully performed. If the transError flag is 'yes,' the printed line begins with 'ERROR.' Otherwise, the line begins with 'UPDATE,' so the user can distinguish the two kinds of messages in the report. In reality, it would be better to have two separate reports since the audit report is retained for reference as needed if something happens to the file and the error report must be used immediately to correct any errors. Presumably, different people need the two different sets of information.

The ChangeRec module calls the ReadMaster module to read the matching master record. Assuming a matching master is found (masterRecOK = 'yes'), the module checks to be sure the matching master has not been logically deleted. If the delete flag is a space, the record is not logically deleted. The appropriate fields are then changed to match the transaction record, the record is rewritten to the master file, and an audit line is included in the report. If the record is logically deleted (the delete flag is an '*'), an error message is written.

The DeleteRec module also calls ReadMaster to read the matching master record. If a matching master is found, it then checks to see if the record already has been deleted (deleteFlag would be equal to '*'). If the record was not deleted already, it is flagged as a deleted record and rewritten. If the record already was deleted, an error message is written in the report.

The AddRec module also attempts to read a matching record from the master, but it does not call the ReadMaster module. ReadMaster writes an error message if it does not find a matching record. With the AddRec module we do not expect or want to find a matching record. If a matching record is found, we must check to see if the record is flagged as logically deleted. If it is a deleted record, it is not an error and we can simply change deleteFlag back to a space, make sure that all the fields are updated, and rewrite the record to the master file. If the matching record was found and was not logically deleted, it means we are attempting to add a record which already exists in the master file; therefore, an error message is written on the report.

In our sequential update program in Chapter 17, we needed to revise the design to allow for multiple transaction records for a single master record. When we do a non-sequential update, we process each transaction record separately. We still may have multiple changes for a given master or even a change and then a delete and then an add, but they are processed separately. They probably wouldn't even be together in the transaction file.

EXERCISES

1. Rewrite design # 4 from page 301. Assume that the file of checks written is an indexed sequential file and the file of checks returned is an unsorted sequential file. For checks that have been returned, write the check number, check amount, and the message "Check has been processed." For returned checks that aren't in the master file, write the check number and an error message. For checks that haven't been returned, don't do anything. NOTE: This is not an update program.

2. Rewrite design # 2 from page 321. Assume that the master file is an indexed sequential file.

3. Rewrite design # 3 from page 321. Assume that the master file is an indexed sequential file.

4. In Chapter 9 (. 155–57), we looked at an example program that loaded flight information (city, fare, and flight time) into parallel arrays. We needed the arrays so that we could access the information about flights in any order. (We searched the arrays to find the desired row to match the input city.) With an indexed sequential file we could access the flight information directly in the file. Rewrite the example program so that it uses an indexed sequential file accessed by city. Notice that this program uses both sequential and indexed sequential access to the file.

5. Chances are that registration at your school uses some form of direct or indexed sequential access. Based on your registration experience, try to outline the processing steps (essentially an ordered task list) for the registration process as it currently exists. Now, how would it be changed if registration were done sequentially? What would it be like for you as a student, and what would the processing steps be?

REVIEW E: Review Exercises for Chapters 15 through 18

1. The Northwest Sterling Regional Bank is considering offering Visa credit cards to their account holders. The bank wants you to design several different programs so that the management can decide how to set up operations (if the bank does indeed decide to go ahead and offer the cards).

    A. Assume an indexed sequential file of all credit card holders in order and accessed by account number and including the account number, name, current balance, and credit limit. A sequential file, in no particular order, would hold all the transactions made that day and would include account number, action code (P = purchase, C = payment, F = finance charge applied), and amount (all amounts are positive). The program should update the existing master so that all balances are current. If a purchase put someone over a credit limit, a warning should be written on an error report. Any other "irregularities" should also be noted on an error report.

    B. Sort the transaction file from A above using an insertion sort. You may assume the file has a maximum of 1000 elements. (Once you have the file stored in memory in a sorted array, write it back to the file so that you have a sorted file.)

    C. Since you now have a sorted transaction file, you can process the master file from A above sequentially. Redo 1A with sequential processing.

    D. Modify 1C above to allow for three additional transactions: A to add a new account, D to delete an existing account, and G to increase or decrease a credit limit (given as a positive or negative number). An add transaction will require additional fields. You should assume that any add transaction record includes the name, balance, and credit limit in addition to the account number and action code.

2. We have two files, one containing the name, addr, and ID of students applying for graduation from University of California, Los Angeles and the other with the same fields for students from University of California, San Diego. Both files are in ascending order by ID. We want to combine these two files into a third file still in order by ID. However, we have an additional file listing the ID of all students at any UC campus who still owe money for parking tickets. Any student whose ID is included in the parking ticket file should not be included in the new, combined graduate file.

    A. The parking ticket file is not in order, so first you need to sort it—use a bubble sort. (You may assume there are no more than 100 IDs.)

    B. Design your merge without considering the parking ticket problem.

C. Now modify the design from 2B, to be sure those with outstanding tickets are not written to the new file.

APPENDIX A: Alternative EOF Testing

We know that when the computer system creates a file, it automatically adds an end-of-file marker at the end of the file. With many programming languages, it is possible to check at any time during a program to see if the end-of-file marker is about to be read. The system, in other words, is peeking into the data file to see if the next thing that would be read is the end-of-file marker.   That's the capability we have been assuming in our programs. We have said in our WHILE statement "WHILE there are data," meaning while the system hasn't gotten to the end-of-file marker yet.

A few programming languages take a very different approach to testing for the end of the data file. Instead of "peeking" ahead into the file, they make you read the next value in the file and then test to see if the value read was a data value or the end-of-file marker. For these languages, we must make some modifications to our designs. We must check to see what we have read immediately after the read (because we don't want to try to process the end-of-file marker as a value), and we need to change the loop control around a bit. If you think of the end-of-file marker as a form of sentinel value, you will understand the processing. We are essentially saying that we will read until we see the sentinel value of the end-of-file marker. Since we're using a sentinel value, we will use a priming read. Since the check on the end-of-file marker is associated with the read, we will also use a flag for the test associated with the loop control.

We'll look at a fairly simple example first, then move on to variations of some of the designs included in the chapters.

Let's assume we are designing a program that will read a record, write the record, and finally write out a counter giving the total number of records. Our traditional design would look something like this:

```
Mainline
counter = 0
WHILE there are data
    READ record
    WRITE record
    ADD 1 to counter
ENDWHILE
WRITE counter
```

When we rewrite this design to use the EOF test in the read, looking for the EOF marker as though it were a sentinel value, we get the following design (notice the use of the flag moreData to control the loop):

```
Mainline
counter = 0
moreData = 'yes'
READ a record
IF end-of-file marker was read
    moreData = 'no'
ENDIF
WHILE moreData = 'yes'
    ADD 1 to counter
    WRITE a record
    READ a record
    IF end-of-file marker was read
        moreData = 'no'
    ENDIF
ENDWHILE
WRITE counter
```

We can simplify our design a bit by pulling the read out into a separate module that can be called when needed.

```
Mainline
counter = 0
moreData = 'yes'
DO ReadRec
WHILE moreData = 'yes'
    ADD 1 to counter
    WRITE a record
    DO ReadRec
ENDWHILE
WRITE counter

ReadRec
READ a record
IF end-of-file marker was read
    moreData = 'no'
ENDIF
```

Remember we're doing this type of check only for those programming languages that cannot check for the end of a file without performing the READ itself.

The following pages include examples of this direct end-of-file testing by rewriting design samples included in some of the chapters. You should notice that if the previous design included a priming read, the design requires only minor changes: usually simply a rewrite of the Read module. If the previous design did not use a priming read, then the rewrite requires a change to a priming read design.

Chapter 8, p. 141—Loading Positional, Parallel Arrays (then using the arrays to find the price for a part when given the part number which is also the position in the array).

```
Mainline
DECLARE names(100), prices(100)
DO StartUp
WHILE moreData = 'yes'
    DO Process
ENDWHILE
CLOSE files

StartUp
OPEN files
moreToLoad = 'yes'
ptr = 0
DO ReadArrayData
WHILE moreToLoad = 'yes'AND ptr < 100
    ADD 1 to ptr
    names(ptr) = nameIn
    prices(ptr) = priceIn
    DO ReadArrayData
ENDWHILE
IF moreToLoad = 'yes'
    WRITE 'ERROR -- more than 100 items in input file'
ENDIF
numItems = ptr
moreData = 'yes'
DO ReadData

Process
WRITE names(partNum), prices(partNum)
DO ReadData

ReadArrayData
READ nameIn, priceIn
IF end-of-file marker was read
    moreToLoad = 'no'
ENDIF

ReadData
READ partNum
IF end-of-file marker was read
    moreData = 'no'
ENDIF
```

Chapter 12, pp. 215–17 —Single Level Control Break with Subtotals and Final Total

Mainline
DO StartUp
WHILE moreData = 'yes'
    DO ProcessRecord
ENDWHILE
DO Finish

StartUp
OPEN files
moreData = 'yes'
DO Read
lastDept = department
lineCnt = 40
pageCnt = 0
deptTot = 0
compTot = 0

ProcessRecord
DO WriteDetailLine
ADD salary to deptTot
DO Read
IF department < > lastDept
    DO DeptBreak
ENDIF

Finish
WRITE compTot
CLOSE files

Read
READ name, department, salary
IF end-of-file marker was just read
    moreData = 'no'
    department = 'ZZZZZ'
ENDIF

WriteDetailLine
IF lineCnt > = 40
    DO Heads
ENDIF
WRITE name, salary
ADD 1 to lineCnt

DeptBreak
WRITE deptTot
ADD deptTot to compTot
deptTot = 0
pageCnt = 0
lineCnt = 40
lastDept = department

Heads
EJECT page
ADD 1 to pageCnt
SKIP 6 lines
WRITE report heading, department, pageCnt
WRITE column heading (dbl spc)
lineCnt = 0

Chapter 13, pp. 231–33—Three Level Control Break

<u>Mainline</u>
```
DO StartUp
WHILE moreData = 'yes'
    DO ProcessRecord
ENDWHILE
DO Finish
```

<u>StartUp</u>
```
OPEN files
moreData = 'yes'
DO ReadRecord
lastDept = department
lastComp = company
lastRegion = region
deptTot = 0
compTot = 0
regionTot = 0
finalTot = 0
lineCnt = 40
```

<u>ProcessRecord</u>
```
DO WriteDetailLine
ADD salary to deptTot
DO ReadRecord
IF region < > lastRegion
    DO RegionBreak
ELSE
    IF company < > lastComp
        DO CompanyBreak
    ELSE
        IF department < > lastDept
            DO DeptBreak
        ENDIF
    ENDIF
ENDIF
```

<u>Finish</u>
```
WRITE finalTot (dbl spc)
CLOSE files
```

<u>ReadRecord</u>
```
READ name, region, company, department, salary
IF end-of-file was read
    moreData = 'no'
    region = 'ZZZZZ'
ENDIF
```

```
RegionBreak
DO CompanyBreak
WRITE regionTot (dbl spc)
ADD regionTot to finalTot
regionTot = 0
lastRegion = region

CompanyBreak
DO DeptBreak
WRITE compTot (dbl spc)
ADD compTot to regionTot
compTot = 0
lastComp = company
lineCnt = 40

DeptBreak
WRITE deptTot (dbl spc)
ADD 2 to lineCnt
ADD deptTot to compTot
deptTot = 0
lastDept = department

WriteDetailLine
IF lineCnt > = 40
    DO Heads
ENDIF
WRITE region, company, department, name, salary
ADD 1 to lineCnt

Heads
EJECT page
SKIP 6 lines
WRITE page headings
WRITE column headings (dbl spc)
lineCnt = 0
```

Chapter 17, pp. 294–96—Matching two input files to write grade report letters.

```
Mainline
DO Start
WHILE moreData = 'yes'
    DO MatchRecords
ENDWHILE
DO Finish

Start
OPEN files
moreMast = 'yes'
moreTrans = 'yes'
moreData = 'yes'
DO ReadMaster
IF moreMast = 'no'
    WRITE 'ERROR -- Master file is empty'
    moreData = 'no'
ENDIF
DO ReadTransaction
IF moreTrans = 'no'
    WRITE 'ERROR -- Transaction file is empty'
    moreData = 'no'
ENDIF

MatchRecords
IF mastID = transID
    DO Match
ELSE
    IF mastID < transID
        DO MastWithoutTrans
    ELSE
        DO TransWithoutMast
    ENDIF
ENDIF

ReadMaster
READ mastID, mastName, mastAddr
IF end-of-file marker was read
    moreMast = 'no'
    mastID = 999999999
    IF moreTrans = 'no'
        moreData = 'no'
    ENDIF
ENDIF
```

<u>ReadTransaction</u>
READ transID, totCredits, totPoints, termCredits, termPoints
IF end-of-file marker was read
    moreTrans = 'no'
    transID = 999999999
    IF moreMast = 'no'
        moreData = 'no'
    ENDIF
ENDIF

<u>Match</u>
ADD termCredits to totCredits
ADD termPoints to totPoints
totGPA = totPoints / totCredits
termGPA = termPoints / termCredits
EJECT page
WRITE mastName, mastAddr, totGPA, termGPA (in letter format)
DO ReadTransaction
DO ReadMaster

<u>MastWithoutTrans</u>
DO ReadMaster

<u>TransWithoutMast</u>
EJECT page
WRITE transID, 'Trans record does not have matching master'
DO ReadTransaction

<u>Finish</u>
CLOSE files

APPENDIX B: Other Design Tools

INTRODUCTION

In this text, we have looked at only two design tools: flowcharts and pseudocode. There are many tools in use, however, and a program designer should have familiarity with a cross-section of what's available. As a designer, you may have the luxury of choosing the tools with which you are most comfortable. But it is likely that you will find that your employer will specify the design tools that must be used. Since program designers may come and go but the designs (and programs) will stay behind, it is important for the company to standardize the tools to be used and how they are applied. In addition, not all tools have the same capabilities. A carpenter probably has several different hammers because straight-claw, curved-claw, and ball-peen hammers all have different uses. And a carpenter would never use a wrench to drive a nail, even if the wrench happens to be the tool closest at hand. You should learn the strengths of different tools for program design also and always use the tool that is most appropriate for the task at hand.

There are a variety of tools that are designed to perform the same tasks that pseudocode and flowcharts will accomplish: Nassi-Schneiderman charts and Warrnier-Orr diagrams, to name just two. We will not cover other program design tools here. You have learned the design process and putting the design in a different format is a reasonably simple matter of learning a new set of symbols. If you can ride a bike that has 21 gears, it won't take you long to learn how to shift the gears on a new bike even if the gear shifts are slightly different. The concepts and purposes are the same.

We will look here at tools that serve other purposes such as zooming in on one small section of a module to show even greater detail or backing away to show in a broader view with less detail how one program fits into a system of related programs. And we will look at some of the tools that might be used by the systems analyst to design that broad system of programs and provide us with the program specifications. Keep in mind that this is just an introduction to these tools. If you want to learn more about them, you will need to continue your study with additional resources.

DECISION TABLES

A decision table can be a great help in designing a specific segment of a design. It provides another way to look at a complex, nested selection to help clarify the conditions to be tested and how those conditions should be nested to arrive at the proper actions.

The decision table is really just a table with four parts, divided by a horizontal and a vertical line. In the upper left quarter, we write the conditions to be tested. Usually we write the conditions so that they will have yes or no answers, but on occasion the conditions are more clearly stated with other possible responses. For example, if the condition concerns how a student commutes to school, the responses might be car, bus, bicycle, or walk. If we were to limit ourselves to yes or no conditions, we would have to ask four questions (Do you commute by car? Do you commute by bus? etc.) In the lower left quarter, we list the possible actions to be taken. The right side of the table is a collection of "rules," combinations of true conditions and the action or actions to be taken for each rule, one column for each rule. An "exhaustive table" lists all the possible combinations of conditions, and in truth, can be very exhausting. If a table has five yes/no conditions, there will be 32 different combinations of those conditions, so an exhaustive table would have 32 rules or columns to be completed. If you have n (yes/no) conditions, then you will have 2^n combinations. A table with 6 conditions will have 2^6 or 64 combinations. The upper right quarter will have a check mark or x for each true condition in a given rule. The lower right quarter will have a check mark or x for each action to be taken given that rule's combination of true conditions. Since the number of combinations will grow very quickly as we add additional conditions, we frequently do a limited table and leave out the "impossible" combinations.

Assume we are trying to write a selection statement to create a listing of the students at the college. We want to identify all honors students by including the appropriate classification by their names in the listing. To qualify for "With Honors" the student must have a cumulative GPA of 3.1. To qualify for "Dean's Honor Roll" the student must have completed 50 credits, have a cumulative GPA of 3.4, and a major GPA of 3.7. To qualify for "President's Select" the student must have completed 50 credits, have a cumulative GPA of 3.4, a major GPA of 3.8, and have recommendations from three faculty. Only the highest qualified honor will be written for each student.

A listing of the conditions and actions would like something like this:

```
Major GPA > = 3.8          ‖
Major GPA > = 3.7          ‖
Cum GPA > = 3.4            ‖
Cum GPA > = 3.1            ‖
Credits > = 50             ‖
Recomm > = 3               ‖
═══════════════════════════╬═══════════════════════
Write "With Honors"        ‖
Write "Dean's Honor Roll"  ‖
Write "President's Select"  ‖
```

An exhaustive list of the combinations would include 64 rules since we have six different conditions. However, we know that some of the combinations are impossible. IF "Major GPA > = 3.7" is false, then we know that the major GPA could not be > = 3.8. What follows is a partial listing of combinations with the action-taken entries also completed. An x indicates a yes or true and a space indicates no or false. This listing includes all the "possible" combinations. The digits along the top number the rules from 1 to 35 for identification in the discussion that follows.

	1	2	3	4	5	6	7	8	9	10	11	12	13	14	15	16	17	18	19	20	21	22	23	24	25	26	27	28	29	30	31	32	33	34	35
Major GPA > = 3.8	x	x	x							x	x	x								x	x	x								x	x	x			
Major GPA > = 3.7	x	x	x	x	x	x				x	x	x	x	x	x					x	x	x	x	x	x					x	x	x	x	x	x
Cum GPA > = 3.4	x			x			x			x			x			x				x			x			x				x			x		
Cum GPA > = 3.1	x	x		x	x		x	x		x	x		x	x		x	x			x	x		x	x		x	x			x	x		x	x	
Credits > = 50	x	x	x	x	x	x	x	x	x											x	x	x	x	x	x	x	x	x							
Recomm > = 3	x	x	x	x	x	x	x	x	x	x	x	x	x	x	x	x	x	x																	
Write "With Honors"		x		x	x		x	x			x		x	x		x	x				x		x	x		x	x				x		x	x	
Write "Dean's Honor Roll"										x										x										x					
Write "President's Select"	x																																		

The next step is to try to simplify the decision table. We look for pairs of rules in which one of the conditions is meaningless because we have the same action whether the condition is true or false. For example, if the Cum GPA is less than 3.1, it doesn't make any difference what the Major GPA is or how many credits the student has. Rule #3 and rule #12 have the same conditions except for Credits > = 50, but they both have the same action (no honor written) so the Credits > = 50 condition does not affect the test. We could then combine those two rules into one rule with a "-" as the entry for Credits > = 50 to indicate that the entry doesn't make any difference. In the same manner, we can condense rules # 6, 9, 15, 18, 21, 24, 27, 30, and 34 all into one rule along with rules 3 and 12 indicating a false (marked with 0) for Cum GPA > = 3.1. The table on the following page shows those rules combined into one rule.

347

	1	2	3	4	5	6	7	8	9	10	11	12	13	14	15	16	17	18	19	20	21	22	23	24	25
Major GPA > = 3.8	x	x	-				x	x			x	x								x	x	x			
Major GPA > = 3.7	x	x	-	x	x			x	x	x	x					x	x	x	x	x	x	x	x		
Cum GPA > = 3.4	x		-	x		x		x		x		x		x		x		x		x		x		x	
Cum GPA > = 3.1	x	x	0	x	x	x	x	x	x	x	x	x	x	x	x	x	x	x	x	x	x	x	x	x	x
Credits > = 50	x	x	-	x	x	x	x							x	x	x	x	x	x						
Recomm > = 3	x	x	-	x	x	x	x	x	x	x	x	x	x												
Write "With Honors"				x	x	x	x	x	x	x	x	x	x			x		x	x	x	x	x	x	x	x
Write "Dean's Honor Roll"		x													x		x								
Write "President's Select"	x																								

We can condense the decision table even further. If the major GPA is not > = 3.8, the test on the number of recommendations is irrelevant, so we can collapse rule 4 with rule 16, rule 5 with rule 17, rule 6 with rule 18, rule 7 with rule 19, rule 11 with rule 23, rule 12 with rule 24, and rule 13 with rule 25. We can just keep studying the table to collapse any pairs of rules (columns) in which all the conditions but one are either the same or already determined as nonapplicable and the resulting actions are the same. Our final, much simplified, decision table has only four rules and will help write a clear, consise nested IF statement.

	1	2	3	4
Major GPA > = 3.8	x	-	-	-
Major GPA > = 3.7	-	-	x	-
Cum GPA > = 3.4	x	-	x	-
Cum GPA > = 3.1	-	0	-	x
Credits > = 50	x	-	x	-
Recomm > = 3	x	-	-	-
Write "With Honors"			x	
Write "Dean's Honor Roll"		x		
Write "President's Select"	x			

HIERARCHY AND STRUCTURE CHARTS

We know that good designs are modular in construction with a given module focusing on a specific, well-defined task. There are many advantages to modular construction, but one of the few disadvantages is that the number of modules can increase rapidly and overwhelm the designer or programmer. A hierarchy chart can help the designer or programmer maintain sanity. It shows in a graphic form the modules (identified by module name) and how each module relates to the other modules in the program. None of the details of any module is shown. You can easily see which module may call any other module, but you will not see when a module is called, how often it is called, if it is called conditionally or every time the calling module is executed, or even what happens in the module.

What follows is a hierarchy chart for a typical report generating program like many that you have done.

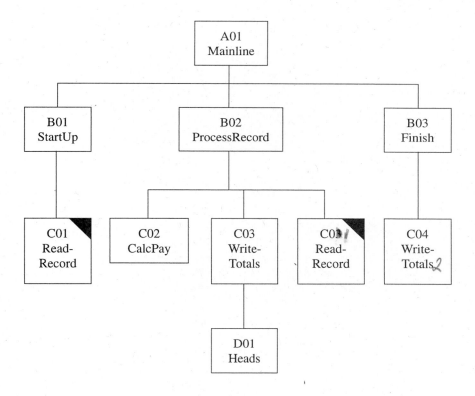

Each module of the program is shown in a process-type box. By following the line entering the box from above you can identify the module which can call it. By following the line exiting below the box, you can identify which module(s) it may call. Notice that the ReadRecord module is called from more than one location. We do not draw multiple lines to one box to represent multiple calls. The box itself is repeated, but the upper right corner is filled in to show that it is a repeated box.

It is common to have some form of numbering system to further highlight the relationship between modules although we have not used such a numbering system in this text. The hierarchy chart shows one common system that uses a letter to identify the level of the module within the hierarchy and a number to identify the modules within a given level. Some designers use a separate letter to identify any module that is called from more than one location, so the ReadRecord module might be labeled U01 (U for utility).

A **structure chart** is really a hierarchy chart with a bit more information added. The structure chart shows the flow of data between modules. An arrow with an open circle as its tail indicates that data are passed from one module to the other in the direction of the arrow. An arrow with a filled in circle as its tail indicates that a flag or switch value is passed from one module to the other. In each case, the name of the variable(s) is included along with the arrow. The following example is a structure chart for a simple input editing program.

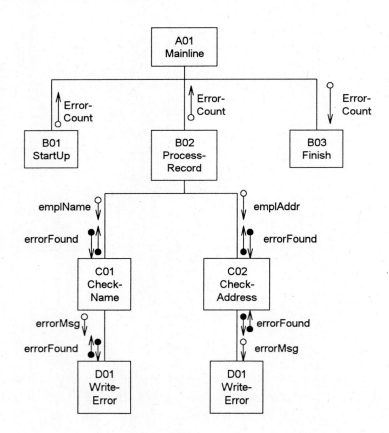

Obviously a structure chart can quickly get very cluttered with variable names, but it can also be a useful tool to help you clarify how your modules relate and how closely tied the modules are. (If you are passing an excessive number of variables between modules the modules may be better redesigned as one module.)

SYSTEM FLOWCHARTS

In this text, most of our designs have dealt with isolated programs, but in reality most programs are designed and used as part of a broad, interrelated system of programs in which the output from one program may be the input to another program. As designers, we must consider not just the specifications for the particular program segment on which we are working but also the specifications for the entire system in order to be sure that our segment fits into the system as needed. A system flowchart shows how the programs fit together.

The system flowchart looks, at first, very much like a program flowchart, but there are two major differences. First, the program flowchart shows the detail steps in a program, and the system flowchart shows that same program as one process box without showing any details. Second, the program flowchart uses the same symbol for all types of input and output. With a system flowchart, we need to show more information. The particular input/output hardware device must be shown to insure compatibility within the system. So the system flowchart utilizes a wide variety of input/output symbols to identify the medium (disk, tape, keyboard, etc.) used.

The main symbols used in a system flowchart are shown below.

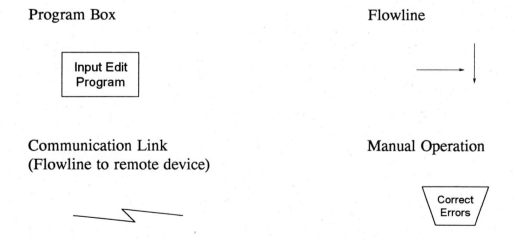

Program Box

Input Edit
Program

Flowline

Communication Link
(Flowline to remote device)

Manual Operation

Correct
Errors

351

Magnetic Tape (I/O)

Employee
File

Magnetic Disk (I/O)

Employee
File

Document (Output)

Error
Report

Video Display (Output)

Menu
Display

Keyboard (Input)

User Input

Most of us are accustomed to the grocery check-out scan systems that read the UPC from the product packaging and display the price on the cash register. That system is checking some form of on-line storage for the price and at the same time modifying the inventory count to indicate that one item has been sold. The inventory file can also be used as input for a product ordering program that will produce printed Reorder Forms. A typical system flowchart might look something like the one on the next page.

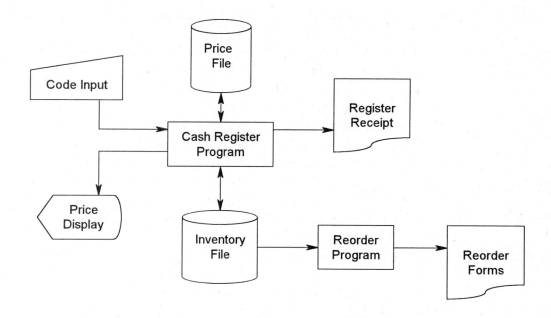

Notice that we have shown the particular hardware used for the input and output. This system is a simplification of a true point-of-sale inventory system, but you can see how the system flowchart clarifies the relation between programs. You can see in the above chart, for example, that both the cash register program and the reorder program use the inventory disk file. The system flowchart does not replace a program design. It is a supplement that shows another view which is not available from a program flowchart or pseudocode. To see the details happening within one of the programs, we would need to have a *program* design.

DATA FLOW DIAGRAMS

As the name implies, a data flow diagram shows how the data progress through the program system. Remember that the program flowcharts that you have done show the flow of *control* through the program. Data flow diagrams can be either a *physical* design of an existing or a proposed system referencing actual forms and devices or a *logical* design that references the data elements (e.g., name, address, phone) without indicating the form or the device on which the data may be used.

There are only four symbols used in a data flow diagram (DFD). An "external entity" is the origin (also called a source) or a recipient (also called a sink) of data but is not a part of the process. For example, a customer may place an order, a supplier may provide the product, and the state may receive data about the sale in a tax report. All three of these are external entities. An external entity is shown as a square with a description included in the square.

A "process" is an action performed on data and is shown in a rectangle with rounded corners. The process will usually be identified with an action-oriented description (e.g., Write Order Form or Calculate Pay), a number that shows the process's position in a hierarchy of processes, and (if it is a physical diagram) the person or program that performs the process. A "data store" is a collection of data. The collection could be a file on a computer disk or a paper file in a file cabinet. It is shown using a rectangle with one open-side with a description of the store written inside. Each store should also be identified with a unique ID code. Finally, a "data flow" is an arrow that shows the movement of data among stores, external entities, and processes. The data must be identified above or below the line.

Data flow diagrams are shown in levels much like the layers in a hierarchy chart. The first level will show just one overall process along with the sources and sinks that provide or receive the data. The next level down expands the major (first level) process to subtasks. Each process in this level will then be broken down (expanded) into the lower level processes. This strategy of expansion (decomposition) continues until the processes have been broken down to their lowest level.

The DFD below is a physical diagram of the purchase portion of the same point of sale system shown in the previous system flowchart.

Level 0

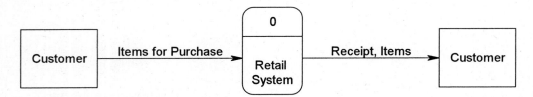

Level 1

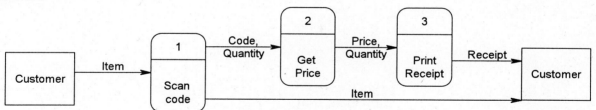

Level 2 (Expansion of Process #1)

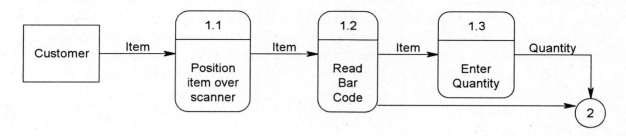

Level 2 (Expansion of Process #2)

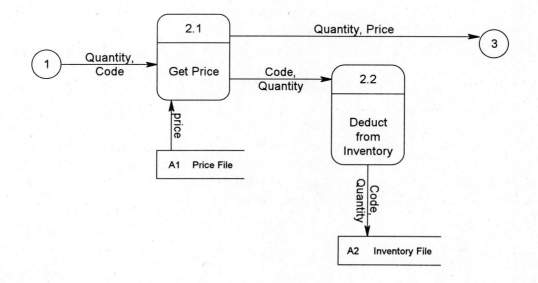

Level 2 (Expansion of Process 3)

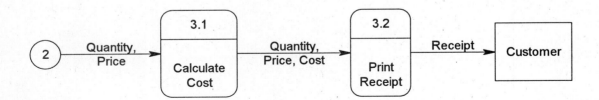

A systems analyst will often use DFDs to help in designing a new system or redesigning an existing system. The analyst can create a set of physical DFDs to represent an existing system, then convert the physical DFDs to logical DFDs. Logical DFDs are more suitable for design or redesign since they free the analyst from physical constraints and highlight the logical processes being completed. Once the analyst has completed the logical design or redesign, it can be converted to a physical DFD for use as a guide to developing the system.

CASE TOOLS

In recent years the computer has become a more helpful tool in program and system design. You may well have been using word processing software to create your pseudocode and perhaps even a graphics package to create your flowcharts, but you have still had to do all the analysis yourself. There is a bit of irony in realizing that we are working so hard at designing and analyzing logical processes for the greatest analytical, logical tool of all times: the computer. Tools are now being developed that help use the computer's analytical ability to assist in designing computer programs and systems. Computer-Aided Systems (or Software) Engineering (CASE) provides a means to involve the computer in system/software development.

A CASE tool will not do all the work for you, but it will help you organize, analyze, and critique the work you do. For example, a CASE tool can make sure you are consistent with variable names, and it can link the various levels of a DFD. Because a CASE tool can organize and maintain all the various design documents you may be using (hierarchy charts, DFDs, decision tables, system flowchart, pseudocode, data dictionary, etc.) in a standard and accessible format, use of a CASE tool is particularly beneficial when a team of designers is working together on a project.

A CASE tool may include a variety of capabilities such as the following:

- Prompted data dictionary development: A data dictionary is a complete reference of all data records and elements defining the source and use of the data, where and how the data may be modified, and a description of the data element. Prompted data dictionary development will automatically add a new entry in the dictionary when you reference a new variable and prompt you for the complete data description.

- Form and screen reference point and/or development aid: Most systems will utilize a variety of paper forms and screen displays for input and output. Keeping them accessible is one important task. Some CASE tools will also assist with developing format prototypes.

- Reverse engineering: A CASE tool may be able to generate design documentation (hierarchy chart, pseudocode, etc.) from existing program code. If an existing, undocumented program is being modified, reverse engineering can be an important first step.

- Forward engineering: A CASE tool may be able to generate program code when given the design documentation.

- Data flow diagram creation: Most CASE tools will include the graphical capability to create DFDs as well as a variety of other graphical design tools according to your detailed input and specifications. These CASE tools will also be able to provide some level of checking for consistency and completeness.

- Screen, format, and report generation: A CASE tool may be able to translate a screen or form design into the code necessary to create the format.

- Developing prototype systems: A prototype is a model that allows the user to see what the final system will look and act like, but is generally not capable of completing all the background processing.

The above list is incomplete, but it should give you a sense of the type of support you can gain from a CASE tool. Keep in mind, however, that the tool is not replacing you as an analyst/designer. It is simply removing much of the tedious, repetitive paperwork from your task and providing a means for you to check your work for completeness and consistency.

APPENDIX C: Answers to Chapter Exercises
Chapter 1

2. **Task List:**
   Read record
   Process record
   Process average

   Process Record Subtasks
   Calculate age (1994 – year)
   Add age to total
   Add 1 to counter

   Process Average Subtasks
   Calculate average (total divided by counter)
   Write average

Ordered Tasks:

While there are data
   Read record
   Process record
      Calculate age
      Add age to total
      Add 1 to counter
   Process average
      Calculage average
      Write average

4. **Task List:**
   Read record
   Test & Process record
   Process average

   Test & Process Subtasks
   If major = COMPUTER
      Add GPA to total
      Add 1 to count

   Process Average Subtasks
   Calculate average (total divided by count)
   Write average

Ordered Tasks:

While there are data
   Read record
   Test if major = COMPUTER
      If yes: Add GPA to total
               Add 1 to counter
   Process average
      Calculage average
      Write average

6. **Task List:**
   Read record
   Test & Process record

   Test & Process Subtasks
   If Subscription = Sunday
      Write record

Ordered Tasks:

While there are data
   Read record
   Test if Subscription = Sunday
      If yes: Write record

Chapter 2
2. Selection within a WHILE loop

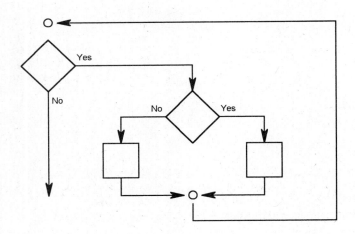

Selection within an UNTIL loop

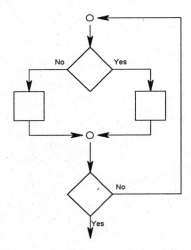

WHILE loop within a selection

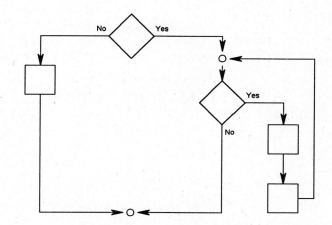

WHILE loop within a WHILE loop

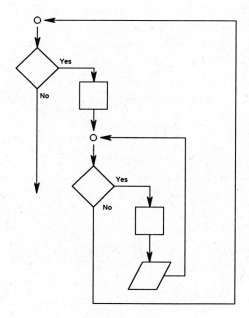

Selection within a selection

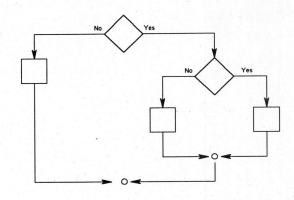

4. **Major tasks:**

Before loop: Initialize variables

In loop: Read record
              Write record
              Add values

After loop: Calculate average
              Write average

Add Values subtasks
    Add 1 to counter
    Add GPA to total

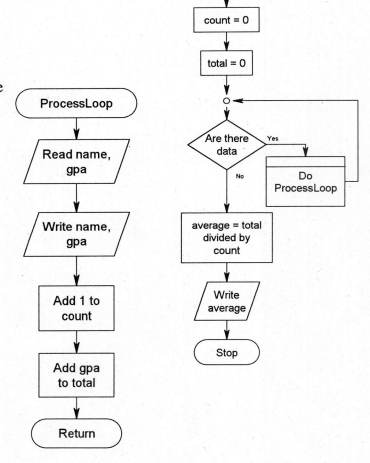

6. **Major tasks:**

Before loop: nothing

In loop: Read record
              Calculate values
              Test and write

After loop: nothing

Calculate values subtasks
   lenSqFt = length * 8 * 2
   widSqFt = width * 8 * 2
   Total = SqFtLen + SqFtWid
   Gallons = total / 500

Test and Write subtasks
   IF gallons >= 5
      Write values & msg
   IF gallons < 5
      Write values

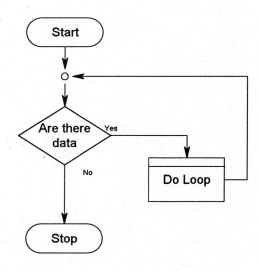

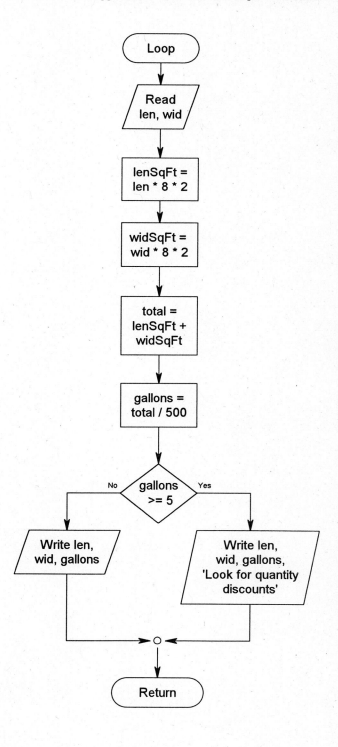

Chapter 3
2. Flowchart:

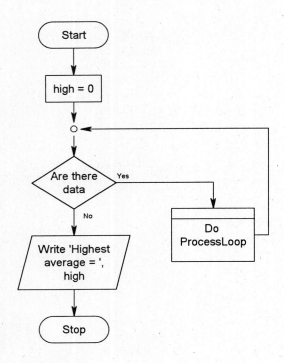

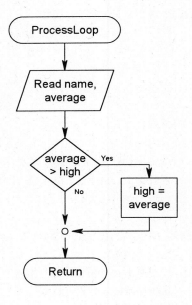

Pseudocode:

Mainline
high = 0
WHILE there are data
    DO ProcessLoop
ENDWHILE
WRITE 'Highest Average = ', high

ProcessLoop
READ name, average
IF average > high
    high = average
ENDIF

4. Pseudocode:

<u>**Mainline**</u>
OPEN files
WHILE there are data
    DO ProcessRecord
ENDWHILE
CLOSE files

<u>**ProcessRecord**</u>
READ name, classCode, gpa
IF classCode = 1
    class = 'Freshman'
ELSE
    class = 'Sophomore'
ENDIF
WRITE name, class, gpa

Note that the test in ProcessRecord assumes that the classCode must be either a 1 or a 2. If that is not a safe assumption, the test must be changed to:

OR, if an error message is desired, change the test to:

IF classCode = 1
    class = 'Freshman'
ELSE
    IF classCode = 2
        class = 'Sophomore'
    ENDIF
ENDIF

IF classCode = 1
    class = 'Freshman'
ELSE
    IF classCode = 2
        class = 'Sophomore'
    ELSE
        class = 'Invalid'
    ENDIF
ENDIF

Flowchart:

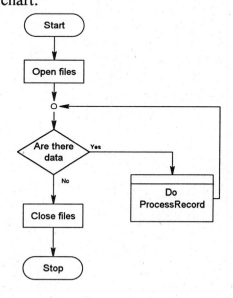

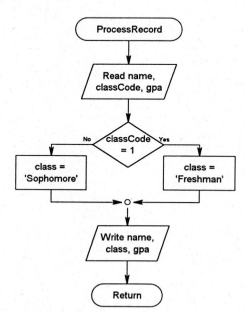

6. Pseudocode:

Mainline
OPEN files
WHILE there are data
    DO ProcessStudent
ENDWHILE
CLOSE files

ProcessStudent
READ name, major, gpa
IF gpa < 1.0
    WRITE name, major, gpa,
        "Unsatisfactory Progress"
ELSE
    WRITE name, major, gpa
ENDIF

Flowchart:

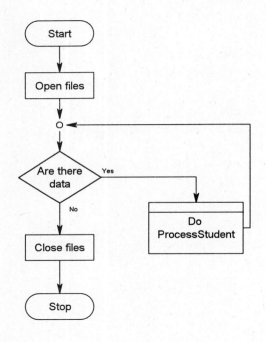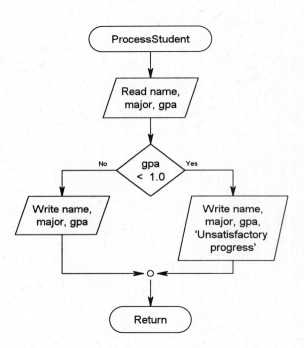

Chapter 4

2. **Task List:**

Initialize Flag
Initialize counter
Read record

Test Checknumber
Write record
Write final message

Ordered Tasks:

InOrder = 'yes'
TestNum = 200
Read record
Test: CheckNumber = TestNum
    If not: InOrder = 'no'
Write record
Increment TestNum
Write final message based on InOrder value

While there are data

Mainline
DO StartUp
WHILE there are data *check # >= 0*
    DO ProcessCheck
ENDWHILE
DO Finish

StartUp
OPEN files
inOrder = 'yes'
testNum = 200

ProcessCheck
READ checkNum, amt
IF checkNum < > testNum
    inOrder = 'no'
ENDIF
WRITE checkNum, amt
ADD 1 to testNum

Finish
IF inOrder = 'no'
    WRITE 'At least one check number was skipped'
ELSE
    WRITE 'No check number was skipped'
ENDIF
Close Files

4. **Task List:**

While
there
are
data

Initialize flag
Initialize highSales
Read record
Test sales for 0
Compare sales with highSales
Write record
Write final zero-sales message
Write final high-sales message

Pseudocode:

Mainline
Do StartUp
WHILE there are data ~~IO <> '007'~~
    DO ProcessSalesperson
ENDWHILE
DO Finish

StartUp
OPEN files
highSales = 0
~~hadZero~~ = 'no'
  ZeroSales =
  Do Read

Read
READ id, name, sales

ProcessSalesperson
~~READ id, name, sales~~
IF sales = 0
    ZeroSales ~~hadZero~~ = 'yes'
ELSE
    IF sales > highSales
        highSales = sales
    ENDIF
ENDIF
WRITE id, name, sales

Finish
WRITE 'The highest sales total is ', highSales
IF hadZero = 'yes'
    WRITE 'At least one salesperson had a sales total of zero.'
ELSE
    WRITE 'No one had a sales total of zero.'
ENDIF
CLOSE files

6. **Task List:**

```
                        Initialize kGross
           While      / Read record
           there     (  Calculate gross pay, deductions, net pay
           are       (  Test gross pay
           data       \ Write record
                        Write final kGross message
```

Pseudocode:
Mainline
DO StartUp
WHILE there are data
    DO ProcessPayroll
ENDWHILE
DO Finish

StartUp
OPEN files
kGross = 'no'

ProcessPayroll
READ id, hours, payRate, dedPerct
gross = hours * payRate
deductions = gross * dedPerct
netPay = gross - deductions
WRITE id, gross, deductions, netPay
IF gross > 1000
    kGross = 'yes'
ENDIF

Finish
IF kGross = 'yes'
    WRITE 'At least one person had a gross pay over $1000.'
ELSE
    WRITE 'No one had a gross pay over $1000.'
ENDIF
CLOSE files

Chapter 5

2. **Mainline**
   DO StartUp
   WHILE there are data
       DO ProcessRecord
   ENDWHILE
   CLOSE files

   StartUp
   OPEN files
   lineCnt = 45
   date = System date
   pageCnt = 0

   ProcessRecord
   READ record
   IF lineCnt > = 45
       DO Heads
   ENDIF
   WRITE record
   ADD 1 to lineCnt

   Heads
   EJECT page
   SKIP 6 lines
   ADD 1 to pageCnt
   WRITE page heading #1
   WRITE date, page heading #2, 'Page ', pageCnt (dbl spc)
   WRITE column headings (dbl spc)
   SKIP 1 line
   lineCnt = 0

4. **Mainline**
   DO StartUp
   WHILE there are data
       DO ProcessRecord
   ENDWHILE
   DO Finish

   StartUp
   OPEN files
   linesUsed = 65
   firstPage = 'yes'

   ProcessRecord
   READ record
   IF linesUsed > = 58
       DO Heads
   ENDIF
   WRITE record (dbl spc)
   ADD 2 to linesUsed

   Heads
   IF firstPage = 'yes'
       EJECT page
       SKIP 6 lines
       WRITE report header
       SKIP 1 line
       firstPage = 'no'
       linesUsed = 8
   ELSE
       DO Footer
       EJECT page
       SKIP 6 lines
       linesUsed = 6
   ENDIF
   WRITE column heads
   ADD 1 to linesUsed

   Finish
   DO Footer
   CLOSE files

   Footer
   SKIP (60-linesUsed) lines
   WRITE 'Designing is FUN'

6. **Mainline**
   DO StartUp
   WHILE there are data
       DO ProcessRecord
   ENDWHILE
   DO Footer
   CLOSE files

   StartUp
   OPEN files
   linesUsed = 65
   pageCnt = 0
   date = System date

   ProcessRecord
   READ record
   IF linesUsed > = 59
       DO Heads
   ENDIF
   WRITE record (dbl spc)
   ADD 2 to linesUsed

   Footer
   SKIP (62-linesUsed) lines
   WRITE pageCnt

   Heads
   IF pageCnt = 0
       EJECT page
       SKIP 3 lines
       WRITE report heading
       SKIP 1 line
       linesUsed = 5
   ELSE
       DO Footer
       EJECT page
       SKIP 3 lines
       linesUsed = 3
   ENDIF
   WRITE page heading, date
   ADD 1 to linesUsed
   ADD 1 to pageCnt

Chapter 6

2. **Mainline**
   DO StartUP
   WHILE there are data
       DO ProcessStudent
   ENDWHILE
   DO Finish

StartUp
OPEN files
READ tuitionRate (Param File)
totalTuition = 0
lineCnt = 60

ProcessStudent
READ id, credits
tuition = tuitionRate * credits
IF lineCnt > = 60
    EJECT page
    SKIP 6 lines
    WRITE page heading
    WRITE column heading (dbl spc)
    SKIP 1 line
    lineCnt = 10
ENDIF
WRITE id, credits, tuition
ADD 1 to lineCnt
ADD tuition to totalTuition

Finish
WRITE totalTuition (dbl spc)
CLOSE files

4. **Mainline**
   DO StartUp
   WHILE there are data
       DO ProcessSale
   ENDWHILE
   DO Finish

   StartUp
   OPEN files
   WRITE 'Please enter quantity discount rates as follows:' (to scr)
   WRITE 'Rate for quantities of 10 to 49' (to scr)
   READ rate10 (from keybrd)
   WRITE 'Rate for quantities of 50 to 99' (to scr)
   READ rate50 (from keybrd)
   WRITE 'Rate for quantities of 100 to 200' (to scr)
   READ rate100 (from keybrd)
   WRITE ' and finally, Rate for quantities over 200' (to scr)
   READ rate 201 (from keybrd)
   grossTot = 0
   netTot = 0
   cnt10 = 0
   cnt50 = 0
   cnt100 = 0
   cnt201 = 0
   lineCnt = 60

   ProcessSale
   READ poNum, item, qty, price
   gross = qty * price
   IF qty > = 201
       discount = gross * rate201
       ADD 1 to cnt201
   ELSE
       IF qty > = 100
           discount = gross * rate100
           ADD 1 to cnt100
       ELSE
           IF qty > = 50
               discount = gross * rate50
               ADD 1 to cnt50

```
        ELSE
            IF qty > = 10
                discount = gross * rate10
                ADD 1 to cnt10
            ELSE
                discount = 0
            ENDIF
        ENDIF
    ENDIF
ENDIF
net = gross - discount
ADD net to netTot
ADD gross to grossTot
DO WriteDetailLine
```

(handwritten margin note: Put after you establish where gross)

Finish
```
EJECT page
SKIP 6 lines
WRITE Headings for total page
WRITE 'Total of gross price = ', grossTot
WRITE 'Total of net price = ', netTot
SKIP 1 line
WRITE 'Count of orders with quantity 10 to 49 = ', cnt10
WRITE 'Count of orders with quantity 50 to 99 = ', cnt50
WRITE 'Count of orders with quantity 100 to 200 = ', cnt100
WRITE 'Count of orders with quantity over 200 = ', cnt201
CLOSE files
```

WriteDetailLine
```
IF lineCnt > = 60
    EJECT page
    SKIP 6 lines
    WRITE page heading
    WRITE column heading (dbl spc)
    SKIP 1 line
    lineCnt = 10
ENDIF
WRITE poNum, item, gross, discount, net
ADD 1 to lineCnt
```

6. **Mainline**
   DO StartUp
   WHILE there are data
      DO ProcessSale
   ENDWHILE
   DO Finish

StartUp
OPEN files
READ hogPrice, lambPrice,
   steerPrice, cowPrice
hogCnt = 0
hogTotal = 0
lambCnt = 0
lambTotal = 0
steerCnt = 0
steerTotal = 0
cowCnt = 0
cowTotal = 0
lineCnt = 60
WRITE 'Please enter date for prices'
   (to scr)
READ priceDate (from keybrd)

ProcessSale
READ categ, wgt
IF categ = 'Hog'
   price = wgt * hogPrice
   ADD price to hogTotal
   ADD 1 to hogCnt
ELSE
   IF categ = 'Lamb'
      price = wgt * lambPrice
      ADD price to lambTotal
      ADD 1 to lambCnt
   ELSE
      IF categ = 'Cow'
         price = wgt * cowPrice
         ADD price to cowTotal
         ADD 1 to cowCnt

   ELSE
      IF categ = 'Steer'
         price = wgt * steerPrice
         ADD price to steerTotal
         ADD 1 to steerCnt
      ELSE
         price = 0
      ENDIF
   ENDIF
ENDIF
ENDIF
IF lineCnt > = 58
   EJECT page
   SKIP 6 lines
   WRITE page heading, priceDate
   WRITE Column heading (dbl spc)
   SKIP 1 line
   lineCnt = 10
ENDIF
WRITE categ, wgt, price
ADD 1 to lineCnt

Finish
hogAvg = hogTotal / hogCnt,
lambAvg = lambTotal / lambCnt
cowAvg = cowTotal / cowCnt
steerAvg = steerTotal / steerCnt
SKIP 1 line
WRITE 'Average Weights: Hog-',
   hogAvg, ' Lamb-', lambAvg,
   ' Cow-', cowAvg,
   ' Steer-', steerAvg
CLOSE files

Chapter 7

2. NOTE: All output is to speech synthesizer.
                    All input is from keyboard.

<u>Mainline</u>
OPEN files
DO GetNumTickets
WHILE numTickets > 0
    DO GetTicketType
    DO ProcessOrder
    DO GetNumTickets
ENDWHILE
CLOSE files

<u>GetTicketType</u>
WRITE 'Thank you. Now, how many of those tickets are for children under 12?'
REPEAT
    WRITE 'Please enter the number on the key pad and press ENTER.'
    READ numKids
    WRITE 'You have entered ', numkids, ' is that correct? Enter Y or N.'
    READ resp
UNTIL resp = 'Y'
numAdult = numTickets – numKids
WRITE 'Which theater do you wish to attend: A, B, C, or D?'
REPEAT
    WRITE 'Please enter the letter on the key pad and press ENTER.'
    READ theater
    WRITE 'You have entered ', theater, ' Is that correct? Enter Y or N.'
    READ resp
UNTIL resp = 'Y'

<u>GetNumTickets</u>
WRITE 'Welcome. How many tickets would you like?'
REPEAT
    WRITE 'Please enter number on key pad and press ENTER key.'
    READ numTickets
    WRITE 'You have entered ', numtickets, ' is that correct? Enter Y or N.'
    READ resp
UNTIL resp = 'Y'

ProcessOrder

```
IF theatre = 'A' or 'B'
    adultPrice = 6
    kidPrice = 4
ELSE
    adultPrice = 5
    kidPrice = 2.5
ENDIF
cost = numAdult * adultPrice + numKids * kidPrice
WRITE 'Your cost for tickets is ', cost, 'Please put money through slot.'
REPEAT
    WRITE 'Please enter amount paid on key pad and press ENTER.'
    READ amtPaid
    WRITE 'You have entered ', amtPaid, ' is that correct?  Y or N'
    READ resp
UNTIL resp = 'Y'
change = amtPaid - cost
WRITE 'Your change is ', change
WRITE 'Enjoy the movie!'
```

4. Pseudocode Version

Mainline

```
DO Start
WHILE continue = 'yes'
    DO ProcessPayroll
ENDWHILE
DO Finish
```

Start

```
OPEN files
totGross = 0
continue = 'yes'
DO Read
```

ProcessPayroll
```
gross = hrs * rate
WHILE gross > 1500 AND continue = 'yes'
    WRITE 'Invalid Hours or Rate for ', name (to scr)
    WRITE 'Re-enter hours and rate -- Enter 0 to quit' (to scr)
    READ hrs, rate (from keybrd)
    IF hrs = 0
        continue = 'no'
    ELSE
        gross = hrs * rate
    ENDIF
ENDWHILE
IF continue = 'yes'
    WRITE name, gross
    ADD gross to totGross
    DO Read
ENDIF
```

Finish
```
IF totGross < > 0
    WRITE totGross
ENDIF
CLOSE files
```

Read
```
IF there are data
    READ name, hrs, rate
ELSE
    continue = 'no'
ENDIF
```

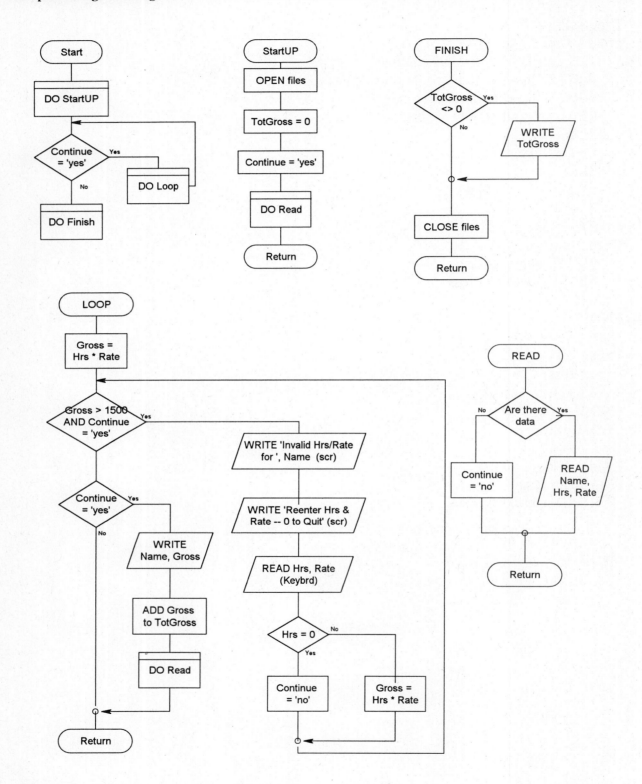

Chapter 8

2. **Mainline**
   DECLARE maxDays(12)
   DO StartUp
   WHILE there are data
       DO CheckDate
   ENDWHILE
   CLOSE files

   StartUp
   OPEN files
   maxDays(1) = 31
   maxDays(2) = 29
   maxDays(3) = 31
   maxDays(4) = 30
   maxDays(5) = 31
   maxDays(6) = 30
   maxDays(7) = 31
   maxDays(8) = 31
   maxDays(9) = 30
   maxDays(10) = 31
   maxDays(11) = 30
   maxDays(12) = 31

   CheckDate
   READ month, day, year
   IF day > maxDays(month)
       WRITE 'The date is invalid.'
   ELSE
       WRITE 'The date appears valid.'
   ENDIF

4. DECLARE students(3000)

StartUp
```
OPEN files
ptr = 0
READ nameIn
WHILE nameIn < > 'NotAName'
    ADD 1 to ptr
    students(ptr) = nameIn
    READ nameIn
ENDWHILE
numStudents = ptr
```

6. **Mainline**
```
DECLARE students(3000), allGpa(3000), allPhone(3000)
DO StartUp
WHILE there are data
    DO ProcessStudent
ENDWHILE
CLOSE files
```

StartUp
```
OPEN files
ptr = 0
WHILE there are data
    ADD 1 to ptr
    READ students(ptr), allGpa(ptr), allPhone(ptr)
ENDWHILE
numStudents = ptr
```

ProcessStudent
```
READ idNum
IF (idNum > = 1) AND (idNum < = numStudents)
    WRITE students(idNum), allGpa(idNum), allPhone(idNum)
ELSE
    WRITE 'ID Number is out of valid range.'
ENDIF
```

Chapter 9

2. There are no changes needed to the Finish, LoadArray, or RaiseFare modules. The Mainline module changes only in the length of the declared array (from 500 to 40.) StartUp changes the loop control for the Load module so that it checks for a maximum of **40** elements. The Process module changes because we would not use a binary search for 40 or fewer flights. Since the cities are still sequentially ordered, we would use a sequential search with early exit.

<u>**Process**</u>
```
READ cityIn
ptr = 0
search = 'yes'
WHILE ptr < flightCnt AND search = 'yes'
    ADD 1 to ptr
    IF cityIn = city(ptr)
        search = 'found'
    ELSE
        IF cityIn < city(ptr)
            search = 'stop'
        ENDIF
    ENDIF
ENDWHILE
IF search = 'found'
    WRITE cityIn, fare(ptr), time(ptr)
ELSE
    WRITE "Sorry, We Fly 'Em does not fly to that city."
ENDIF
```

4A. **Mainline**
DECLARE rooms(35), max(35), av(35), food(35)
DO StartUp
DO WriteReport
CLOSE files

StartUp
OPEN files
ptr = 0
WHILE there are data
    ADD 1 to ptr
    READ rooms(ptr), max(ptr), av(ptr), food(ptr)
ENDWHILE
numRooms = ptr

WriteReport
EJECT page
SKIP 6 lines
WRITE 'Conference Room Attributes'
SKIP 1 line
WRITE 'Room Number   Maximum Seats   AV Available?   Food Available?'
SKIP 1 line
ptr = 0
WHILE ptr < numRooms
    ADD 1 to ptr
    WRITE rooms(ptr), max(ptr), av(ptr), food(ptr)
ENDWHILE

[NOTE: Assumption is that the report will fit on only one page since there are only 35 rooms.]

4B. **Mainline**
DECLARE rooms(35), max(35), av(35), food(35)
DO StartUp
REPEAT
    DO CheckRoom
UNTIL continue = 'no'
CLOSE files

StartUp
OPEN files
ptr = 0
WHILE there are data
    ADD 1 to ptr
    READ rooms(ptr), max(ptr), av(ptr), food(ptr)
ENDWHILE
numRooms = ptr

CheckRoom
DO GetRoomNum
DO FindPosition
IF search = 'found'
    WRITE 'For room number ', roomIn (to scr)
    WRITE '   the maximum occupancy is ', max(ptr) (to scr)
    WRITE '   Is AV hookup available?', av(ptr) (to scr)
ELSE
    WRITE 'There is no room numbered ', roomIn (to scr)
ENDIF
WRITE 'Would you like to check another room? Y or N' (to scr)
READ answer (from keybrd)
IF answer = 'N' or 'n'
    continue = 'no'
ELSE
    continue = 'yes'
ENDIF

GetRoomNum

WRITE 'Please enter the number for the room you would like to check.' (to scr)
REPEAT
    READ roomIn (from keybrd)
    WRITE 'Do you want to edit or change the entered number? Y or N' (to scr)
    READ answer (from keybrd)
    IF answer = 'Y' or 'y'
        WRITE 'Please re-enter the number.' (to scr)
    ENDIF
UNTIL answer = 'N' or 'n'

FindPosition

search = 'yes'
ptr = 0
WHILE ptr < numRooms AND search = 'yes'
    ADD 1 to ptr
    IF roomIn = rooms(ptr)
        search = 'found'
    ELSE
        IF roomIn < rooms(ptr)
            search = 'stop'
        ENDIF
    ENDIF
ENDWHILE

4C.   ### Mainline

DECLARE rooms(35), max(35), av(35), food(35)
DO StartUp
REPEAT
    DO MakeRoomList
UNTIL continue = 'no'
CLOSE files

StartUp
```
OPEN files
ptr = 0
WHILE there are data
    ADD 1 to ptr
    READ rooms(ptr), max(ptr), av(ptr), food(ptr)
ENDWHILE
numRooms = ptr
```

MakeRoomList
```
DO GetRequirements
WRITE 'For your requirements: ' (to scr)
DO CheckList
IF check = 'nomatch'
        WRITE 'There is no room available.' (to scr)
ENDIF
WRITE 'Would you like to make another check?  Y or N' (to scr)
READ answer  (from keybrd)
IF answer = 'N' or 'n'
    continue = 'no'
ELSE
    continue = 'yes'
ENDIF
```

CheckList
```
ptr = 0
check = 'nomatch'
WHILE ptr < numRooms
    ADD 1 to ptr
    IF max(ptr) >= numSeats AND needFood = food(ptr)
        check = 'match'
        WRITE 'You could use room number ', rooms(ptr) (to scr)
    ENDIF
ENDWHILE
```

GetRequirements

```
WRITE 'Please enter the number seats you need.' (to scr)
REPEAT
    READ numSeats (from keybrd)
    WRITE 'Do you want to edit or change the entered number?  Y or N' (to scr)
    READ answer (from keybrd)
    IF answer = 'Y' or 'y'
        WRITE 'Please re-enter the number.' (to scr)
    ENDIF
UNTIL answer = 'N' or 'n'
WRITE 'Please enter whether you need kitchen access—enter yes or no.' (to scr)
REPEAT
    READ needFood (from keybrd)
    IF needFood = 'Yes' or 'yes' or 'YES'
        needFood = 'yes'
        testAns = 'OK'
    ELSE
        IF needFood = 'No' or 'no' or 'NO'
            needFood = 'no'
            testAns = 'OK'
        ELSE
            WRITE 'Your answer must be a yes or a no.  Please re-enter.' (to scr)
            testAns = 'BAD'
        ENDIF
    ENDIF
UNTIL testAns = 'OK'
```

4D.   With 100 conference rooms, a binary search would be a more efficient search. In step 4B, you are searching the room number array which is in sequential order, so a binary search would be used. In step 4C, you must check the number of seats and the food access for each room, so it still requires a sequential process.

Chapter 10

2. **Mainline**
   DO StartUP
   WHILE there are data
       DO ExtractHouses
   ENDWHILE
   CLOSE files

   StartUp
   OPEN files
   linesUsed = 60

   ExtractHouses
   READ record
   IF lot = .5
       IF firePl = 'Y'
           IF zip = '22090'
               DO WriteDetailLine
           ELSE
               IF zip = '22091'
                   DO WriteDetailLine
               ENDIF
           ENDIF
       ENDIF
   ENDIF

WriteDetailLine
IF linesUsed > = 60
    EJECT page
    SKIP 6 lines
    WRITE Page Heading
    WRITE Column Heading (dbl spc)
    SKIP 1 line
    linesUsed = 10
ENDIF
WRITE name, price, addr, city, zip
ADD 1 to linesUsed

NOTE: Record includes the following:

Name	Price	Addr
City	Zip	Bath
Bedrm	Lot	Firepl
Deck	Pool	Tennis

4. **Mainline**
DO StartUp
WHILE there are data
   DO ExtractHouses
ENDWHILE
CLOSE files

StartUp
OPEN files
linesUsed = 60

ExtractHouses
READ record
IF lot = 2
   IF firePl = 'Y'
      IF price >= 250000
         IF price <= 300000
            DO WriteDetailLine
         ENDIF
      ENDIF
   ENDIF
ENDIF

WriteDetailLine
IF linesUsed >= 60
   EJECT page
   SKIP 6 lines
   WRITE Page Heading
   WRITE Column Heading (dbl spc)
   SKIP 1 line
   linesUsed = 10
ENDIF
WRITE name, price, addr, city, zip
ADD 1 to linesUsed

NOTE: Record includes the following:

Name	Price	Addr
City	Zip	Bath
Bedrm	Lot	Firepl
Deck	Pool	Tennis

6. **Mainline**
   DO StartUp
   WHILE there are data
      DO ExtractHouses
   ENDWHILE
   CLOSE files

NOTE: Record includes the following:

Name	Price	Addr
City	Zip	Bath
Bedrm	Lot	Firepl
Deck	Pool	Tennis

StartUp
OPEN files
linesUsed = 60

ExtractHouses
READ record
IF lot > = 5
   IF lot < = 10
      IF firePl = 'Y'
         IF bedRm > = 3
            IF deck = 'no'
               DO WriteDetailLine
            ENDIF
         ENDIF
      ENDIF
   ENDIF
ENDIF

WriteDetailLine
IF linesUsed > = 60
   EJECT page
   SKIP 6 lines
   WRITE 'Lot 5 - 10 acres, with Fireplace, without Deck, with 3 or more Bedrooms'
   WRITE Column Heading (dbl spc)
   SKIP 1 line
   linesUsed = 10
ENDIF
WRITE name, price, addr, city, zip
ADD 1 to linesUsed

Chapter 11

2. **Mainline**
DO StartUp
WHILE there are data
   DO CheckInputRecord
ENDWHILE
DO Finish

StartUp
OPEN files
validCnt = 0
invalidCnt = 0
testID = -99
lineCnt = 60

CheckInputRecord
errorFnd = 'no'
READ name, price, code, id, qty, dept
DO CheckID
DO CheckQty
DO CheckCode
DO CheckDept
IF errorFnd = 'no'
   WRITE record to valid file
   ADD 1 to validCnt
ELSE
   ADD 1 to invalidCnt
ENDIF

CheckID
IF id < = testID
   msg = 'ID is out of order'
   DO ErrorRtn
ENDIF
testID = id

CheckQty
IF qty not numeric
   msg = 'Quantity is not numeric'
   DO ErrorRtn
ENDIF

CheckCode
IF code < 1
   msg = 'Minimum code is 1'
   DO ErrorRtn
ELSE
   IF code > 10
      msg = 'Maximum code is 10'
      DO ErrorRtn
   ENDIF
ENDIF

CheckDept
IF dept < > 'A'
   IF dept < > 'B'
      IF dept < > 'C'
         msg = 'Dept code must be
            A, B, or C'
         DO ErrorRtn
      ENDIF
   ENDIF
ENDIF

ErrorRtn
IF errorFnd = 'no'
   errorFnd = 'yes'
   IF lineCnt > = 57
      DO Heads
   ENDIF
   WRITE (input record), msg
ELSE
   WRITE (spaces), msg
ENDIF
ADD 1 to lineCnt

Finish

WRITE 'Number of Invalid Records', invalidCnt
WRITE 'Number of Valid Records', validCnt
CLOSE files

Heads

EJECT page
SKIP 6 lines
WRITE page heading
WRITE column heading (dbl spc)
SKIP 1 line
lineCnt = 10

Chapter 12

2. **Mainline**
DO StartUp
WHILE there are data
    DO ProcessRecord
ENDWHILE
DO Finish

StartUp
OPEN files
lastClass = 'start'
pageNum = 0
linesUsed = 60
firstRecord = 'yes'

ProcessRecord
READ owner, dog, class, number,
    score
IF class < > lastClass
    IF firstRecord = 'yes'
        lastClass = class
        firstRecord = 'no'
    ELSE
        DO ClassBreak
    ENDIF
ENDIF
IF linesUsed > = 57
    DO Heads
ENDIF
WRITE owner, dog, class, number,
    score
ADD 1 to linesUsed

Finish
CLOSE files

ClassBreak
lastClass = class
linesUsed = 60
pageNum = 0

Heads
EJECT page
SKIP 6 lines
ADD 1 to pageNum
WRITE page heading, class, pageNum
WRITE column heading (dbl spc)
SKIP 1 line
linesUsed = 10

4. **Mainline**
   DO StartUp
   WHILE continue = 'yes'
       DO ProcessRecord
   ENDWHILE
   CLOSE files

   StartUp
   OPEN files
   DO ReadRecord
   lastClass = class
   newClass = 'yes'
   highScore = 0
   linesUsed = 60

   ReadRecord
   IF there are data
       READ owner, dog, class, number,
           score
   ELSE
       continue = 'no'
       class = 'stop'
   ENDIF

   ProcessRecord
   IF score > highScore
       highScore = score
       highName = owner
   ENDIF
   IF linesUsed > = 56
       DO Heads
   ENDIF
   IF newClass = 'yes'
       WRITE 'Listing for Class ', class
       newClass = 'no'
       ADD 1 to linesUsed
   ENDIF
   WRITE owner, dog, number, score
   ADD 1 to linesUsed
   DO ReadRecord

   IF class < > lastClass
       DO ClassBreak
   ENDIF

   ClassBreak
   WRITE 'CLASS = ', lastClass (dbl-
       spc)
   WRITE 'Highest score in class = ',
       highScore
   WRITE 'Owner of dog = ',
       highName
   SKIP 5 lines
   ADD 9 to linesUsed
   highScore = 0
   lastClass = class
   newClass = 'yes'

6. **Mainline**
   DECLARE classList(4),
      avgScoreList(4)
   DO StartUp
   WHILE continue = 'yes'
      DO ProcessRecord
   ENDWHILE
   DO Finish

StartUp
OPEN files
continue = 'yes'
DO ReadRecord
lastClass = class
pageNum = 0
linesUsed = 60
ptr = 0
scoreTotal = 0
scoreCount = 0

ProcessRecord
IF linesUsed > = 60
   DO Heads
ENDIF
WRITE owner, dog, class, number,
   score
ADD 1 to linesUsed
ADD score to scoreTotal
ADD 1 to scoreCount
DO ReadRecord
IF class < > lastClass
   DO ClassBreak
ENDIF

Finish
EJECT page
SKIP 6 lines
WRITE 'Average scores by class'
SKIP 1 line
ptr = 0

WHILE ptr < 4
   ADD 1 to ptr
   WRITE classList(ptr),
      avgScoreList(ptr)
ENDWHILE
CLOSE files

ReadRecord
IF there are data
   READ owner, dog, class, number,
      score
ELSE
   continue = 'no'
   class = 'stop'
ENDIF

ClassBreak
lastClass = class
linesUsed = 60
avg = scoreTotal / scoreCount
ADD 1 to ptr
classList(ptr) = class
avgScoreList(ptr) = avg
scoreTotal = 0
scoreCount = 0

Heads
EJECT page
SKIP 6 lines
ADD 1 to pageNum
WRITE Page heading, pageNum
WRITE Column heading (dbl spc)
SKIP 1 line
linesUsed = 10

Chapter 13

2. **Mainline**
   DO StartUp
   WHILE continue = 'yes'
       DO Process
   ENDWHILE
   DO Finish

   ProcessRecord
   ADD 1 to compCnt
   ADD numSold to compSold
   IF linesUsed > = 56
       DO Heads
   ENDIF
   IF newClass = 'yes'
       WRITE classif, company, number,
           performer, numSold
       newClass = 'no'
       newComp = 'no'
   ELSE
       IF newComp = 'yes'
           WRITE spaces, company,
               number, performer,
               numSold
           newComp = 'no'
       ENDIF
   ENDIF
   ADD 1 to linesUsed
   DO ReadRecord
   IF classif < > lastClassif
       DO CompanyBreak
       DO ClassifBreak
   ELSE
       IF company < > lastCompany
           DO CompanyBreak
           SKIP 3 lines
           ADD 3 to linesUsed
       ENDIF
   ENDIF

   StartUp
   OPEN files
   continue = 'yes'
   DO ReadRecord
   lastClassif = classif
   lastComp = company
   classCnt = 0
   classSold = 0
   compCnt = 0
   compSold = 0
   totalCnt = 0
   totalSold = 0
   linesUsed = 60
   newClass = 'yes'
   newComp = 'yes'

   Finish
   avg = totalSold / totalCnt
   WRITE 'Average recordings sold = ',
       avg
   CLOSE files

   ReadRecord
   IF there are data
       READ classif, company, number,
           performer, numSold
   ELSE
       continue = 'no'
       classif = 'stop'
   ENDIF

   ClassifBreak
   avg = classSold / classCnt
   WRITE 'Average sales for
       classification ', lastClassif, ' are ',
       avg
   linesUsed = 60
   ADD classSold to totalSold
   ADD classCnt to totalCnt
   classSold = 0

```
classCnt = 0
lastClass = classif
newClass = 'yes'
```

CompanyBreak
```
avg = compSold / compCnt
WRITE 'Average sales for company ',
    lastComp, ' are ', avg (dbl spc)
ADD 2 to linesUsed
ADD compSold to classSold
ADD compCnt to classCnt
compSold = 0
compCnt = 0
lastComp = company
newComp = 'yes'
```

Heads
```
EJECT page
SKIP 6 lines
WRITE page heading
WRITE column heading (dbl spc)
SKIP 1 line
newClass = 'yes'
linesUsed = 10
```

4. ## Mainline
```
DO StartUp
WHILE continue = 'yes'
    DO ProcessRecord
ENDWHILE
CLOSE files
```

StartUp
```
OPEN files
continue = 'yes'
DO ReadRecord
lastClassif = classif
lastCompany = company
lastPerformer = performer
performerCount = 0
companyCount = 0
classifCount = 0
linesUsed = 60
```

ProcessRecord
```
IF linesUsed > = 57
    DO Heads
ENDIF
WRITE classif, company, label,
    performer, numSold
ADD 1 to linesUsed
DO ReadRecord
IF classif < > lastClassif
    DO NewPerformer
    DO NewCompany
    DO NewClassif
ELSE
    IF company < > lastCompany
        DO NewPerformer
        DO NewCompany
    ELSE
        IF performer < >
            lastPerformer
            DO NewPerformer
        ENDIF
    ENDIF
ENDIF
```

ReadRecord
```
IF there are data
    READ classif, company, label,
        performer, numSold
ELSE
    continue = 'no'
    classif = 'stop'
ENDIF
```

NewClassif
```
ADD 1 to classifCount
lastClassif = classif
```

NewCompany
```
ADD 1 to companyCount
lastCompany = company
```

NewPerformer
```
ADD 1 to performerCount
lastPerformer = performer
```

Heads
```
EJECT page
SKIP 6 lines
WRITE page heading
WRITE column heading (dbl spc)
SKIP 1 line
linesUsed = 10
```

Finish
```
avgCompInClass = companyCount / classifCount
avgPerfInClass = performerCount / classifCount
WRITE 'Average number of companies in a classification is ', avgCompInClass (dbl spc)
WRITE 'Average number of performers in a classification is ', avgPerfInClass
CLOSE files
```

6. **Mainline**
   DO StartUp
   WHILE continue = 'yes'
      DO Process
   ENDWHILE
   DO Finish

StartUp
OPEN files
continue = 'yes'
DO ReadRecord
lastClassif = classif
lastComp = company
highSalesCompany = 0
highSalesClassif = 0
linesUsed = 60
newClass = 'yes'
newComp = 'yes'

ProcessRecord
IF numSold > highSalesCompany
   highSalesCompany = numSold
   highPerfComp = performer
   highlabelComp = label
ENDIF
IF linesUsed > = 52
   DO Heads
ENDIF
IF newClass = 'yes'
   WRITE classif, company, number, performer, numSold
   newClass = 'no'
   newComp = 'no'
ELSE
   IF newComp = 'yes'
      WRITE spaces, company, number, performer, numSold
      newComp = 'no'
   ENDIF
ENDIF
ADD 1 to linesUsed
DO ReadRecord
IF classif < > lastClassif
   DO CompanyBreak
   DO ClassifBreak
ELSE
   IF company < > lastCompany
      DO CompanyBreak
      SKIP 5 lines

```
            ADD 5 to linesUsed
        ENDIF
    ENDIF
```

Finish
```
CLOSE files
```

ReadRecord
```
IF there are data
    READ classif, company, label, performer, numSold
ELSE
    continue = 'no'
    classif = 'stop'
ENDIF
```

ClassifBreak
```
WRITE "Highest selling recording for classification: ", lastClassif
WRITE "Performer:  ", highPerfClassif
WRITE "Label number:  ", highLabelClassif
WRITE "Number sold:  ", highSalesClassif
highSalesClassif = 0
lastClassif = classif
linesUsed = 60
newClass = 'yes'
```

CompanyBreak
```
WRITE "Highest selling recording for company: ", lastCompany
WRITE "Performer:  ", highPerfComp
WRITE "Label number:  ", highLabelComp
WRITE "Number sold:  ", highSalesComp
IF highSalesComp > highSalesClassif
    highSalesClassif = highSalesComp
    highPerfClassif = highPerfComp
    highLabelClassif =
        highLabelComp
ENDIF
highSalesComp = 0
lastCompany = company
ADD 4 to linesUsed
newComp = 'yes'
```

Heads
```
EJECT page
SKIP 6 lines
WRITE page heading
WRITE column heading (dbl spc)
SKIP 1 line
newClass = 'yes'
linesUsed = 10
```

Chapter 14

2. Mainline
```
DECLARE nameList(30),
    gradeList(30,10)
DO StartUp
```

StartUp
```
OPEN files
row = 0
WHILE there are data AND row < 30
    ADD 1 to row
    READ nameList(row)
    col = 0
    WHILE col < 10
        ADD 1 to col
        READ gradeList(row,col)
    ENDWHILE
ENDWHILE
numStudents = row
```

4. Mainline
```
DECLARE nameList(30), gradeList(30,10)
DO StartUp
WHILE assignNum < 10
    DO CalcAverageGrade
ENDWHILE
CLOSE files
```

StartUp
```
as above in #2 with addition of
assignNum = 0
```

CalcAverageGrade
```
gradeTotal = 0
student = 0
ADD 1 to assignNum
WHILE student < numStudents
    ADD 1 to student
    ADD gradeList(student,assignNum) to gradeTotal
ENDWHILE
avg = gradeTotal / numStudents
WRITE 'Average grade for assignment number ', assignNum, 'is ', avg
```

6. **Mainline**
   DECLARE nameList(30), gradeList(30,10)
   DO StartUp
   REPEAT
       Do GetName
       DO ListGrades
       DO TestforMore
   UNTIL more = 'no'

   StartUp
   [as above in #2]

   GetName
   REPEAT
       WRITE 'Please enter the name of student whose grades you want listed.' (scr)
       READ nameIn (keybrd)
       WRITE 'Do you wish to modify the entry? Y / N' (scr)
       READ resp (keybrd)
   UNTIL resp = 'n' or resp = 'N'

   ListGrades
   search = 'yes'
   row = 0
   WHILE row < 30 AND search = 'yes'
       ADD 1 to row
       IF nameIn = nameList(row)
           search = 'found'
       ENDIF
   ENDWHILE
   IF search = 'found'
       col = 0
       WRITE 'The grades are: ' (scr)
       WHILE col < 10
           ADD 1 to col
           WRITE gradeList(row,col) (scr)
       ENDWHILE
   ELSE
       WRITE 'Sorry, that name is not in the class list. Please try again.' (scr)
   ENDIF

TestforMore
WRITE 'Do you have another name to be checked? Y / N' (scr)
READ resp   (keybrd)
IF resp = 'n' or resp = 'N'
   More = 'no'
ELSE
   More = 'yes'
ENDIF

8. **Mainline**
DECLARE minTemps(9), seasons(4), adjectives(4,9)
DO StartUp
WHILE there are data
   DO GetAdjective
ENDWHILE
CLOSE files

StartUp
OPEN files
ptr = 0
WHILE ptr < 9
   ADD 1 to ptr
   READ minTemps(ptr)   [array data file]
ENDWHILE
row = 0
WHILE row < 4
   ADD 1 to row
   READ seasons(row)   [array data file]
   col = 0
   WHILE col < 9
      ADD 1 to col
      READ adjectives(row,col)   [array data file]
   ENDWHILE
ENDWHILE

GetAdjective

```
READ currentSeason, currentTemp
row = 0
search = 'yes'
WHILE search = 'yes' AND row < 4
    ADD 1 to row
    IF currentSeason = seasons(row)
        search = 'match'
    ENDIF
ENDWHILE
IF search = 'match'
    col = 10
    search = 'again'
    WHILE search = 'again' AND col > 1
        SUBTRACT 1 from col
        IF currentTemp > = minTemp(col)
            search = 'found'
        ENDIF
    ENDWHILE
    IF search = 'found'
        WRITE 'For a temperature of ', currentTemp, 'in ', currentSeason, 'use the
            adjective ', adjectives(row,col)
    ELSE
        WRITE 'The temperature ', currentTemp, ' is too low for this program!'
    ENDIF
ELSE
    WRITE 'The entry contains an invalid season: ', currentSeason
ENDIF
```

Chapter 15

2. **Mainline**
   DO StartUp
   WHILE there are data
      DO ProcessRunner
   ENDWHILE
   DO Finish

StartUp
OPEN files
SORT input file on state (ascending order)
lastState = 'AK'
linesUsed = 60
numRunners = 0

Note: this assumes that there will
be a runner from Alaska

ProcessRunner
READ name, number, state, phone, time
IF state < > lastState
   WRITE 'Number of runners from ', lastState, ' is ', numRunners (dbl spc)
   SKIP 3 lines
   ADD 5 to linesUsed
   numRunners = 0
   lastState = state
ENDIF
ADD 1 to numRunners
IF linesUsed > = 58
   EJECT page
   SKIP 6 lines
   WRITE page heading
   WRITE column heading (dbl spc)
   SKIP 1 line
   linesUsed = 10
ENDIF
WRITE name, number, state, phone, time
ADD 1 to linesUsed

Finish
WRITE 'Number of runners from ', lastState, ' is ', numRunners (dbl spc)
CLOSE files

4. **SortList**
```
length = 100
lastCheck = 100
hadSwitch = 'yes'
numPass = 1
WHILE numPass < length AND hadSwitch = 'yes'
    hadSwitch = 'no'
    ptr = 0
    WHILE ptr < lastCheck
        IF list(ptr) < list(ptr+1)
            DO Switch
        ENDIF
        ADD 1 to ptr
    ENDWHILE
    SUBTRACT 1 from lastCheck
    ADD 1 to numPass
ENDWHILE
```

Switch
```
hold = list(ptr)
list(ptr) = list(ptr + 1)
list(ptr+1) = hold
hadSwitch = 'yes'
```

6. **Mainline**
```
DECLARE nameList(5000)
DO StartUp
WHILE len < 5000
    DO AddRunner
ENDWHILE
CLOSE files
```

StartUp
```
OPEN data file  (as input file)
len = 1
READ nameList(1), age, state, time
WHILE there are data
    READ name, age, state, time
    DO Insert
ENDWHILE
CLOSE data file as input file
OPEN data file for append
```

AddRunner
DO GetData
DO Insert
APPEND name, age, state, time (to existing data file)

Insert
ptr = len
WHILE nameList(ptr) > name AND ptr > 0
   nameList(ptr+1) = nameList(ptr)
   SUBTRACT 1 from ptr
ENDWHILE
nameList(ptr+1) = name
ADD 1 to len

GetData
WRITE 'Please enter data for next applicant'   (to scr)
REPEAT
   WRITE 'Name?'   (to scr)
   READ name   (from keybrd)
   WRITE 'Age?'   (to scr)
   READ age   (from keybrd)
   WRITE 'State?'   (to scr)
   READ state   (from keybrd)
   WRITE 'Expected finishing time?'   (to scr)
   READ time   (from keybrd)
   WRITE 'Are all entries correct? Y or N' (to scr)
   READ resp   (from keybrd)
UNTIL resp = 'Y' or 'y'

Chapter 16

2. **Mainline**
DO StartUp
WHILE ymName < > 'zzzz' OR ywName < > 'zzzz'
    DO MergeRecords
ENDWHILE
CLOSE files

StartUp
OPEN files
DO ReadYMRecord
DO ReadYWRecord
IF ymName = 'zzzz' OR ywName = 'zzzz'
    ymName = 'zzzz'
    ywName = 'zzzz'
    WRITE 'WARNING: one or both file empty -- merge not completed'
ENDIF
currentYear = year of system date

MergeRecords
IF ymName < ywName
    WRITE ymName, ymAddr, ymExpirYear (disk file)
    DO ReadYMRecord
ELSE
    IF ywName < ymName
        WRITE ywName, ywAddr, ywExpirYear (disk file)
        DO ReadYWRecord
    ELSE
        moreYears = ymExpirYear – currentYear
        ADD moreYears to ywExpirYear
        WRITE ywName, ywAddr, ywExpirYear (disk file)
        DO ReadYWRecord
        DO ReadYMRecord
    ENDIF
ENDIF

ReadYMRecord
IF there are data (YMCA file)
    READ ymName, ymAddr, ymExpirYear (YMCA file)
ELSE
    ymName = 'zzzz'
ENDIF

ReadYWRecord
IF there are data (YWCA file)
    READ ywName, ywAddr, ywPhone, ywExpirYear (YWCA file)
ELSE
    ywName = 'zzzz'
ENDIF

4. ### Mainline
DO StartUp
WHILE retCheckNum < > 99999 OR writtenCheckNum < > 999999
    DO ProcessChecks
ENDWHILE
CLOSE files

StartUp
OPEN files
DO ReadReturnedCheck
DO ReadWrittenCheck
IF retCheckNum = 999999 OR writtenCheckNum = 999999
    WRITE 'WARNING -- one file is empty -- match not completed'
    retCheckNum = 999999
    writtenCheckNum = 999999
ENDIF
linesUsed = 60

ProcessChecks
IF linesUsed > = 60
    DO Heads
ENDIF
IF retCheckNum = writtenCheckNum
    WRITE retCheckNum, 'Check has been processed'

        DO ReadReturnedCheck
        DO ReadWrittenCheck
ELSE
    IF retCheckNum > writtenCheckNum
        WRITE writtenCheckNum, 'Check has not yet been processed'
        DO ReadWrittenCheck
    ELSE
        WRITE retCheckNum, 'Check was not recorded. Please correct.'
        DO ReadReturnedCheck
    ENDIF
ENDIF
ADD 1 to linesUsed

ReadReturnedCheck

IF there are data
    READ retCheckNum, amt
ELSE
    retCheckNum = 999999
ENDIF

ReadWrittenCheck

IF there are data
    READ writtenCheckNum, date, payee, writtenAmt
ELSE
    writtenCheckNum = 999999
ENDIF

Heads

EJECT page
SKIP 6 lines
WRITE page heading
WRITE column heading (dbl spc)
SKIP 1 line
linesUsed = 10

6. **Mainline**
DO StartUp
WHILE rosterTeam < > 'ZZZ' OR millionTeam < > 'ZZZ'
   DO MatchTeams
ENDWHILE
WRITE 'Number of million dollar players from ', lastTeam, 'is ', playerCnt (dbl spc)
CLOSE files

StartUp
OPEN files
DO ReadRosterRecord
DO ReadMillionRecord
IF rosterTeam = 'ZZZ' OR millionTeam = 'ZZZ'
   WRITE 'WARNING: One or more files empty -- processing not completed.'
   rosterTeam = 'ZZZ'
   millionTeam = 'ZZZ'
ENDIF
linesUsed = 60
playerCnt = 0
lastTeam = rosterTeam

MatchTeams
IF lastTeam < > rosterTeam
   WRITE 'Number of million dollar players from ', lastTeam, 'is ', playerCnt (dbl
     spc)
   playerCnt = 0
   lastTeam = rosterTeam
   SKIP 3 lines
   ADD 5 to linesUsed
ENDIF
IF rosterTeam = millionTeam
   IF rosterNumber = millionNumber
     ADD 1 to playerCnt
     IF linesUsed > = 58
       DO Heads
     ENDIF
     WRITE rosterTeam, rosterName, rosterNumber, rosterAddress
     ADD 1 to linesUsed
     DO ReadRosterRecord
     DO ReadMillionRecord

```
        ELSE
            IF rosterNumber < millionNumber
                DO ReadRosterRecord
            ELSE
                IF linesUsed > = 58
                    DO Heads
                ENDIF
                WRITE 'WARNING: player in million dollar file but not on roster: ',
                    millionTeam, millionNumber
                ADD 1 to linesUsed
                DO ReadMillionRecord
            ENDIF
        ENDIF
    ELSE
        IF rosterTeam < millionTeam
            REPEAT
                DO ReadRosterRecord
            UNTIL rosterTeam > = millionTeam
        ELSE
            REPEAT
                WRITE 'WARNING: player in million dollar file but not on roster. ',
                    millionTeam, millionNumber
                ADD 1 to linesUsed
                DO ReadMillionRecord
            UNTIL millionTeam > = rosterTeam
        ENDIF
    ENDIF
ENDIF
```

<u>ReadRosterRecord</u>
```
IF there are data
    READ rosterTeam, rosterNumber, rosterName, rosterAddress
ELSE
    rosterTeam = 'ZZZ'
ENDIF
```

<u>ReadMillionRecord</u>
```
IF there are data
    READ millionTeam,
        millionNumber
ELSE
    millionTeam = 'ZZZ'
ENDIF
```

Chapter 17

2. **Mainline**
   DO StartUp
   WHILE masterName < > 'ZZZ' OR transName < > 'ZZZ'
       DO ProcessUpdate
   ENDWHILE
   CLOSE files

   StartUp
   OPEN files
   recInHold = 'no'
   linesUsed = 60
   pageCnt = 0
   currentYear = year of system date
   DO ReadTrans
   DO ReadMast
   IF masterName = 'ZZZ' OR transName = 'ZZZ'
       transName = 'ZZZ'
       masterName = 'ZZZ'
       WRITE 'ERROR -- Master file and/or Transaction file empty, update not done.'
   ENDIF

   ProcessUpdate
   IF masterName < transName
       DO CopyMaster
   ELSE
       IF masterName = transName
           IF transCode = 'C'
               DO Change
           ELSE IF transCode = 'D'
               DO Delete
           ELSE IF transCode = 'A'
               DO BadAdd
           ELSE
               DO InvalidCode
           ENDIF
       ELSE
           IF transCode = 'A'
               DO Add

```
        ELSE IF transCode = 'C'
            DO BadChange
        ELSE IF transCode = 'D'
            DO BadDelete
        ELSE
            DO InvalidCode
        ENDIF
    ENDIF
ENDIF
```

Change

```
IF transAddr not = spaces
    masterAddr = transAddr
ENDIF
IF transYears not = spaces
    ADD transYears to masterYear
ENDIF
WRITE 'CHANGE: ', transaction record          (to AuditRpt)
DO ReadTrans
```

Add

```
COPY holdRecord to masterRecord          [copies all fields from one memory
masterName = transName                            location to another]
masterAddr = transAddr
masterYear = currentYear + transYears
recInHold = 'yes'
WRITE 'ADD:  ', transaction record          (to AuditRpt)
DO ReadTrans
```

Delete

```
WRITE 'DELETE:  ', transaction record          (to AuditRpt)
DO ReadTrans
DO ReadMast
```

CopyMaster

```
WRITE masterName, masterAddr, masterYear          (to new master file)
WRITE 'MASTER WRITTEN:  ', master record          (to AuditRpt)
DO ReadMast
```

415

BadAdd

msg = 'Add code with matching record in master'
DO WriteErrorLine
DO ReadTrans

Bad Change

msg = 'Change code with no matching record in master'
DO WriteErrorLine
DO ReadTrans

BadDelete

msg = 'Delete code with no matching record in master'
DO WriteErrorLine
DO ReadTrans

InvalidCode

msg = 'Invalid transaction code'
DO WriteErrorLine
DO ReadTrans

ReadMast

```
IF recInHold = 'yes'
    COPY holdRecord to masterRecord
    recInHold = 'no'
ELSE
    IF there are data (Master file)
        READ masterName, masterAddr, masterYear
    ELSE
        masterName = 'ZZZ'
    ENDIF
ENDIF
```

ReadTrans

```
IF there are data (Transaction file)
    READ  transCode, transName, transAddr, transYears
ELSE
    transName = 'ZZZ'
ENDIF
```

<u>WriteErrorLine</u>
IF linesUsed > = 60
   DO Heads
ENDIF
WRITE transCode, transName, transAddr, transYears, msg   (to ErrorRpt)
ADD 1 to linesUsed

<u>Heads</u>
EJECT page
SKIP 6 lines
IF pageCnt = 0
   WRITE Report Heading   (to ErrorRpt)
   SKIP 1 line
   linesUsed = 8
ELSE
   linesUsed = 6
ENDIF
ADD 1 to pageCnt
WRITE Page Heading, pageCnt   (to ErrorRpt)
WRITE Column Headings (dbl spc)   (to ErrorRpt)
SKIP 1 line
ADD 4 to linesUsed

Chapter 18

2. **Mainline**
   DO StartUp
   WHILE there are transaction data
       DO ProcessUpdate
   ENDWHILE
   CLOSE Files

StartUp
OPEN master file (Indexed I/O), trans file (Seq, Input), report (printer)
linesUsed = 60
pageCnt = 0
currentYear = year of system date

ProcessUpdate
READ transCode, transName, transAddr, transYears (from trans file)
transError = 'no'
IF transCode = 'C'
    DO ChangeRec
ELSE
    IF transCode = 'D'
        DO DeleteRec
    ELSE
        IF transCode = 'A'
            DO AddRec
        ELSE
            DO InvalidCode
        ENDIF
    ENDIF
ENDIF

InvalidCode
transError = 'yes'
msg = 'Invalid transaction code'
DO WriteReportLine

DeleteRec
```
DO ReadMaster
IF masterRecOK = 'yes'
    IF deleteFlag = space
        deleteFlag = '*'
        REWRITE master record to file
        msg = 'Record deleted'
        DO WriteReportLine
    ELSE
        transError = 'yes'
        msg = 'Record already marked for deletion'
        DO WriteReportLine
    ENDIF
ENDIF
```

ChangeRec
```
DO ReadMaster
IF masterRecOK = 'yes'
    IF deleteFlag = space
        IF transAddr not = spaces
            mastAddr = transAddr
        ENDIF
        IF transYears not = spaces
            ADD transYears to mastYear
        ENDIF
        REWRITE master record to file
        msg = 'Master record changed'
        DO WriteReportLine
    ELSE
        transError = 'yes'
        msg = 'Cannot change deleted record'
        DO WriteReportLine
    ENDIF
ENDIF
```

AddRec
```
READ record in master file to match transName
IF master record not found
    mastName = transName
    mastAddr = transAddr
```

```
            mastYear = currentYear + transYears
            deleteFlag = space
            WRITE master record to file
            msg = 'Record added to master'
            DO WriteReportLine
        ELSE
            IF deleteFlag = '*'
                deleteFlag = space
                mastName = transName
                mastAddr = transAddr
                mastYear = currentYear + transYears
                REWRITE master record to file
                msg = 'Record added to master'
                DO WriteReportLine
            ELSE
                transError = 'yes'
                msg = 'Record already included in file'
                DO WriteReportLine
            ENDIF
        ENDIF
```

ReadMaster
```
READ record in master file to match transName
    (mastName, mastAddr, mastYear)
IF master record not found
    masterRecOK = 'no'
    transError = 'yes'
    msg = 'Master record not found in club roster file'
    DO WriteReportLine
ELSE
    masterRecOK = 'yes'
ENDIF
```

WriteReportLine
```
IF linesUsed > = 60
    EJECT page
    ADD 1 to pageCnt
    SKIP 6 lines
    WRITE headings, pageCnt
    linesUsed = 8
```

```
    ENDIF
    IF transError = 'yes'
        WRITE 'ERROR', msg, transaction record (dbl spc)
    ELSE
        WRITE 'UPDATE', msg, transaction record (dbl spc)
    ENDIF
    ADD 2 to linesUsed
```

4. **Mainline**
```
    DO StartUp
    WHILE there are data
        DO ProcessFlightSchedule
    ENDWHILE
    DO Finish
```

StartUp
```
    linesUsed = 60
    REPEAT
        WRITE 'Please enter new minimum fare level'                 (to screen)
        READ fareMin  (from keybrd)
        WRITE 'You have entered ', fareMin, '.  Is that correct?  Y or N?'   (to screen)
        READ resp
    UNTIL resp = 'Y' or 'y'
    DO RaiseFare
    OPEN master file (indexed seq., Input/Output), transaction file (Sequential, Input)
```

ProcessFlightSchedule
```
    READ cityIn                                                     (trans  file)
    IF linesUsed > = 60
        EJECT page
        SKIP 6 lines
        WRITE page heading
        WRITE column heading (dbl spc)
        SKIP 1 line
        linesUsed = 10
    ENDIF
    READ master record to match cityIn              (mastCity, mastFare, mastTime)
    IF master record not found
        WRITE 'Sorry.  We Fly 'Em does not fly to ', cityIn
```

```
        ELSE
            WRITE cityIn, mastFare, mastTime
        ENDIF
```

<u>Finish</u>
```
CLOSE transaction file, master file
OPEN master file  (sequential, input)
linesUsed = 60
WHILE there are data                                              (master file)
    READ mastCity, mastFare, mastTine
    IF linesUsed > = 60
        EJECT Page
        SKIP 6 lines
        WRITE report heading
        WRITE column heading (dbl spc)
        SKIP 1 line
        linesUsed = 0
    ENDIF
    WRITE mastCity, mastFare, mastTime
    ADD 1 to linesUsed
ENDWHILE
CLOSE master file
```

<u>RaiseFare</u>
```
OPEN master file  (sequential, input/output)
WHILE there are data                                              (master file)
    READ mastCity, mastFare, mastTime
    IF mastFare < fareMin
        mastFare = fareMin
        REWRITE mastCity, mastFare, mastTime               (to master file)
    ENDIF
ENDWHILE
CLOSE master file
```

INDEX